Night Hurdling

- to Sam Droden
from
James Dickey

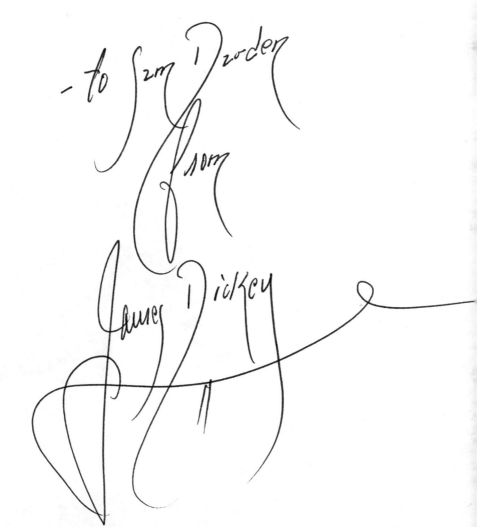

James Dickey

Night Hurdling

Poems,
Essays, Conversations,
Commencements, and
Afterwords

BC

Bruccoli Clark
Columbia and Bloomfield Hills, 1983

"The Enemy from Eden" first appeared in *Esquire*. "Purgation" first appeared in *Head-Deep in Strange Sounds: Free Flight Improvisations from the Unenglish*, Paleamon Press, Ltd. "Craters" and "Farmers" first appeared in the *American Poetry Review*. "The Starry Place Between the Antlers" first appeared in *Esquire* under the title "Why I Live in South Carolina." "Excellently Bright" first appeared in *Harper's Bazaar*. "Imagination and Pain" first appeared in *Mademoiselle*. "The Weathered Hand and Silent Space" aka "Robert Penn Warren's Courage" first appeared in the *Saturday Review*. "The Geek of Poetry" first appeared in the *New York Times Book Review*. "The Unreflecting Shield" is reprinted from *F. Scott Fitzgerald: Poems 1911-1940*, copyright © James Dickey, 1981. Afterword to *Through the Wheat* by James Boyd reprinted by permission of Southern Illinois University Press. "Bare Bones" first appeared in *Deliverance*, a screenplay, Southern Illinois University Press. "Preface to *The Early Motion*" and "Preface to *Falling, May Day Sermon, and Other Poems*" is used by permission of Wesleyan University Press. Acknowledgment is made to the Ecco Press for permission to include the "Afterword" from their edition of *Babel to Byzantium*. The "Afterword" was first published in *Antaeus*.

"Delights of the Edge" was first published in *Mademoiselle*. "Night Hurdling" aka "James Dickey's Glory" first appeared in *Esquire*. "Body, Backstretch, and the Outside Man" aka "Why Men Drive" first appeared in *Playboy*. "Complicity" aka "Female Sexuality" first appeared in *Mademoiselle*. "In Texas" aka "Ritual Magic" was first published in the *Lone Star Review*; interview by Paul Christensen. "In North Carolina" aka "Getting to the Gold" first appeared in the *Arts Journal*; interview by Terry

Roberts. "In Virginia" first appeared in *Shenandoah Review*; interview by C. Kizer and J. Boatwright. "In *Mademoiselle*" aka "The Poet Tries to Make a Kind of Order" was first published in *Mademoiselle*. "In New York" is reprinted by permission of *New York Quarterly*; craft interview by William Packard.

"At Home" first appeared in *Writers Yearbook 1981*, Writers Digest; interview by Bruce Joel Hillman.

Lines from Robert Penn Warren's "Tell Me a Story" from *Selected Poems 1923-1975* reprinted by permission; copyright Random House, Inc. Lines from Robert Lowell's "Waking Early Sunday Morning" from *Selected Poems* reprinted by permission; copyright Farrar, Straus & Giroux. Lines from Theodore Roethke's "The Far Field" from *Collected Poems* reprinted by permission; copyright Doubleday.

Library of Congress Cataloging in Publication Data

Dickey, James.
Night hurdling.

"A Bruccoli Clark book."
I. Title.
PS3554.I32N5 1983 811'.54 83-7096
ISBN 0-89723-038-8
ISBN 0-89723-040-X (lim. ed.)

To Bronwen

and to Matt—

for her coming

his continuing

Contents

Introduction

> Perilous, terrible art! This thread I spin out of my body
> And at the same time the thread serves as my path through
> the air.

I have reflected on this, and been—and am—indebted to Hofmannsthal for it, without knowing exactly what it means. I feel its implications, though, and it does seem appropriate for *Night Hurdling*, for there are a good many threads here, all out of the same body. I don't have much of an idea as to where they lead, or if they weave themselves into a fabric, but they are the threads that have come, and the air of the book is the air through which I have followed them.

Any collection of writings is an assertion of identity; Wallace Stevens, when he says that the impress of a personality is the important quality in poetry, is right, and Eliot is wrong. I needn't argue this, really, though, but merely wish to use it to preface this particular collection, beginning with the bafflement I feel in following out my own line of reasoning just announced.

Though I do firmly believe that personality has the importance that Stevens says it has, I am not quite sure in what ways it is evidenced amongst these pieces. When getting them together I kept asking myself "Where *is* the identity? Whose and why?" There are some poems here, some translations of poems with which I have taken extreme liberties, some book reviews and introductions to the books of others, one of them a photographer, several interviews conducted by various periodicals and other agencies, and graduation addresses given at widely scattered times and places. It was while going through the addresses that I was astonished to find a quotation I thought I had forgotten for years, but which turned up as part of a poem I wrote for and presented at the Inauguration of President Jimmy Carter. The phrase had been in my mind for a long time, but not until I unearthed the Pitzer address, which was made—must have been made—just after I read the short story by Alun Lewis in which it appears, "They Came," that I realized where it had originated. If, belatedly now, I were to say that I wish to make my use of Lewis's phrase as the last line of the Inaugural poem a kind of homage to Lewis, killed in Burma in 1945, it would be exactly what I intend. The fact that his words were floating around in my mind for years until they seemed to be part of it is tribute enough, but I also like to think that if "The Strength of Fields" has any longevity, Alun Lewis will share in it, brave spirit that he must have been.

The question of identity, though, continued to preoccupy me with the topics and forms of this book. I have decided, after making whatever "tests" I could on the material, that such identity as these pieces have comes at odd, instinctive moments, in flickers of meaning, metaphors, chains of words, assumptions, assertions—some of them contradictory—and in places that not everyone would think likely. To compound things, some readers may find such passages where I would not. I have not hesitated to include any selection in which there may be any possible hint of such a flicker for any reader, even though such possibilities may occur at times when the flicker may be neither strong nor bright, but may for someone be authentic, the realization being present that it could not exist at all except for the context in which it appears.

I ask the reader's indulgence in matters of topicality—such as the discussion with William Buckley on Vietnam—because it seems to me that such subjects carry with them on-going philosophical and ethical considerations as yet unresolved.

I have done some editing on several of the interviews, because these were transcribed a little too faithfully from tapes, and included, as is inevitable, a certain amount of parenthesizing, back-tracking, repetition and just noise-making, all of which are detrimental to the line of thought or the development of an argument. I have tempered a few of the remarks I made, particularly those pertaining to my immediate family, but I have not changed anything that my interlocutors have said, or taken out anything unless I also excised what I said in response. I assumed that the purchaser or reader of this book would be interested primarily in what I have expressed at certain times, and I have tried to keep the emphasis on that without detracting from the questioner. My identity, such as it is, is the subject for emphasis here, and as such is seen to be in some sense definable, and as making an attempt at the memorable, if not the permanent, whereas the identities of my interlocutors are here relatively unimportant and passing; they exist as the origin of their questions.

Perhaps in the end the whole possibility of words being able to contain one's identity is illusory; opinions, yes; identity, maybe. Perhaps the whole question of identity itself is illusory. But one must work with such misconceptions for whatever hint of insight—the making of a truth—they may contain: that fragment of existence which could not be seen in any other way and may with great good luck, as in the best poetry, be better than the truth.

James Dickey

The Enemy from Eden

THE GUN

It comes out of Provo, Utah—The House of Weapons—through the mails, where the baggage handlers think it is some kind of fishing pole or something. It is an awkward thing to send through U.P.S., as it will be so, later in the woods, amongst the Perplexing Thorn. It is called a Survival Blowgun, and is six feet long with a rubber handgrip about where you would want it for such work, and a hard-rubber mouthpiece. A length of aluminum pipe. But there is something that will do the same job that you can get at your friendly local hardware store. The blowgun out of Provo is shorter than some you can buy in a hardware store, though why the store-bought pipe exists—what it is used for, other than blowgunning—is unknown to me. But let us not say Me. From this sentence on, the Blowgunner is the One.

In the hardware store, the One buys an eight-foot aluminum pipe he intends to use as a weapon against the most deadly. It is not quite plumb-line true, in deference to gravity, but it is true enough. He wants a long gun, because there is more value of death-breath in more length, more lung-fury is involved. The One stands in the store, shucking a few dollars out of his suburban pants. Anybody could do exactly the same thing; though, like the One, you will never know why you choose to do it. But you *can* do it. I can, the One can, and so can you. There are plenty of snakes. They hate you and the human race instinctively hates them. All the naturalists in the world, pleading for better treatment of serpents, are not going to change that feeling. The One takes his length of pipe, wrapped in brown paper. He goes home to the suburbs, getting ready for the coat hanger.

THE MISSILE

Around every house there are pliers. There are also coat hangers. Usually there is a driveway, or at least a paved street. There is paper, and the strange ubiquitousness of Scotch tape. The rest is up to the One and the snake. The One takes the pliers, and about six or eight of the most ordinary of coat hangers. He walks out of the house onto his driveway and sits down on it. He has the Gun with him, Scotch tape, and a sheet of typing paper.

He is thinking of where to go; he is thinking like a snake, as though his head were full of low-lying poison. He is thinking of Means, and no longer of why he is doing this. If the One thought questions of that sort, he would not do what he is about to do.

Using the pliers, he twists off the necks—the hanging-fundamentals—of all the hangers. He holds the mutilated coat-holders in his left hand and chooses about eight-inch lengths of metal—they need not be uniform—and twists the metal back and forth until it comes apart. This is done with a certain savagery. He puts the cut-off pieces on the neighborly pavement beside him until he has all he wants: twelve pieces of soft, black-painted steel, dim and haunted with civilized closet-dark. All this, in bright sun.

Then sharpening. He sweeps each piece over his gritty driveway in long strokes, turning the shaft. The operation leaves, on the man-made, personal, impersonal little road for cars, a dirty, moon-like ellipse. But he has mighty sharp points. He goes into the house and gets some scissors, which he'd forgotten to bring with him.

These are for the paper. Typing paper is going to be the Guiding Spirit of the Snake-Death. It is to function, in the Gun, like the feathered vanes of arrows in archery. But each must be right. Life and breath depend on this being so. Rattlesnakes do not fool around. He cuts strips of paper and makes cones of them. They are too large for the Gun, but that is part of the plan. He sticks each cone into place on each shaft, the Gun lying beside him, getting hot with the rising sun. The One himself, outfitting in this strange way, feels his enthusiasm for the project getting hot, with some strange hotness of the soul that seems augmented by the lifting of the sun; it takes hold of him more and more as his equipment advances, there in the split-level driveway. He is going to do this thing. One more time. He is going up against Universal Evil, with his breath.

He fits the sharpened coat-hanger lengths—now darts—into the Gun, and trims them down with his wife's sewing scissors. The darts must hang in the pipe perfectly. They cannot slide through, and they have to be breath-exploded. He is going to be shooting *down*, and the cone-vanes must be tight. But not so tight as to hang fire. That would be bad. An ordinary dime-store rubber band, twisted shrewdly, will hold all Evil-slayers on the Gun, so that the One can carry everything in one hand, as it is best to do, amongst the Perplexing Thorn.

THE ENEMY

He is there, somewhere, lying along the rice-canals, or perhaps back from them a little. The possibility of him is a haunting thing. He may be under a palmetto, where he dearly loves to be, or in the reeds, he and the foliage merging, as they were meant by God to do. The patterning of a rattlesnake is one of the incredible facts of the first Creation. That deadly thing is far beyond the dreams of a fag couturier, and yet his skin suggests something dreamed up by one. For example, the One has been in a cinder-block motel where the wallpaper motif was of rattlesnake design. The One hankers for both the beauty and the danger of such a creature, and also the fact that he carries poison, and knows nothing of how and why he does. Somewhere he is waiting, and so are the man-made, primitive Gun and the sharpened coat hanger.

THE CANALS

There is a place. There is a canoe as well. It will never see white water, for this is very flat land. Very flat and very hot. The One arranges to be there, in the abandoned rice plantation, in his high, hot boots, his open-throated heat shirt, with his paddle, his Gun, and his death-darts.

There are no cutbanks where he is going. Thank God for that. He has a terror of being snakebit in the face, where the skin and flesh are thin. He can see himself stumbling and sobbing, trying to get to a doctor fifty miles away. He can feel his eyes going out, and he can see the vision of the end, something which includes the towers of Babylon. He can see taking a knife and carving his face up in the only possible way to save his life. He can see his face in New York bars, and hear himself explaining to strangers how it all was.

No; there are no cutbanks. Thank God, he will be underfoot. Snakes strike off red clay cutbanks awfully quickly. A big rattlesnake hits with the power of George Foreman, or harder. The One has been struck *at* from an eye-level cutbank, but the snake overestimated, and led too much on his poison. For once, he struck and missed. It was the only time the One ever saw a snake fly. He hit the road and was off in the bushes. That was it.

But the birds along the canal are terrific. The living blues and golds, the greens and the stupefying plumage-white, the quick dartings, the blue jays and their mean-sounding air-voices, the herons spanning their level, gracious flight; well, these are good things to have going along with a man on a death-mission. His or Universal Evil's. One or the other, for he is bent on making this encounter. Some basic thing is involved, here in these level fields, the reeds, the insects, the birds, the parasites—down here called no-see-ums—the Edenic soarings, the silence, and the slipping-forward canoe. The sun is coming, inevitably. And again, with the sun, come the snakes. No cutbanks, though. Thank God. No self-inflicted knife in the only face.

THE PERPLEXING THORN

One place is as good as another. The heat is up, the snakes are out. The general plan is to walk into the brush, and listen. Evil always rattles. That is what the books say, but it is not always true. The snake can strike from a position that you could not tell from its sleep. The heat-sensitive pits in the fist-head register, and he fires out.

But the One moves through the Perplexing Thorn, that engages as he disengages, moving delicately, with all five senses sweating. It is great to be here, doing this, the Gun glancing and dodging leaf-spotted sunlight off its eight feet of breath.

THE SOUND

Out of the canebrake no-sound and all-sound of insect-silence, it comes. Comes.

There is no mistaking it. The human water of the bladder has a tendency to run, and the One has to use all his body-force to hold it back. There is a snake, somewhere. The sound is nervous, and has a vitality that the One—or you or me—could never encounter in any other place than the wilderness. You may never see that canoe again, old buddy. Something is waiting for you.

The sound is inescapable, and unplaceable. The One stands in the tall grass immobilized. Adrenaline is working, and the bladder is quavering. But the One knows he has put himself in the position he wished to be in, in the tense and full of existence. He would not be any other place at any other time. He is scared to death.

Where *is* the damned thing? The sound has the quality of being from all sides, coming from everywhere and nowhere, from the Bible, from God in His endless malevolence, from out of the depths of the universal abyss, from the stars, from the death of all life.

Again, *where?* If the One takes a single step in any direction, he may, by that step, be dead. If he moves in any way at all, he may be going right into the fangs, the jungle hypodermic.

He looks. He looks right and left and front and center. He turns slowly around.

The Beast is behind him, about fifteen feet away. The deep-pitted head is drawing back into the beautiful coils, and the tail is not quite visible; it is making a strange blur on the close, reedy air. All right. All *right*.

THE ENCOUNTER

You can move, now. Let's go just a little to the left. You know that the King Reptile can strike only a third of his length (but don't trust the guidebooks all *that* much), and that he can't strike upward more than just a fraction. So—what are those big snake boots for? Well, they're not for the object of tempting our old diamondback buddy on the ground, right there in a crisscross of twig-light. Not this time.

Let's go around back.

The puzzle-solving side of things now enters into the One. My old friend, my one Self, you can do this thing. Let the snake undo his coil, and turn to face you. If you get him out of his strike-position, you're already one up on him. By God, let him cope with *you*. Get yourself behind the heat-sensitive head-pits. You can bank on another thing, too. His attention span is short. If he can't strike you, he'll get bored with you. Then, if you can steady down just a bit, the Gun can black-flash with the coat hanger. If you're lucky, it'll only take one.

THE BREATH

Position those human lungs. You are trying to kill, with the breath of life: that is, of *your* life. The Gun is very hot in your hand, and the enemy very still, lying with his head on a strong leaf. The Gun comes down, flashing with woods-sun. You are close; you are very close.

Explode your lungs.

You do.

The needle is in the brain. Universal Evil does not know what to do with it. He writhes, he turns over and over, he thrashes, he shows his obscene white belly, a terribly inadequate contrast to his beautiful back, he rattles hopelessly, he strikes at phantoms. The One stands watching, thinking of the Universe, and how it was put together, and why it is like it is.

The snake is dead, and the One pulls out the coat-hanger dart.

THE SKIN

He can feel the inertness of all death, in this long, lovely body. He puts the Garden of Eden around his neck, checks his wrist-compass, and sets out for the canoe.

He gets there, and stretches the dead snake out in a life-position—though not in a coil—on the Grumann-metal floor. This skin is going to be on the wall, and he knows just where. It is something to have a drink with, at all times of day or night. It is something to have good lamps and candles arranged to show. My God, would you look at just the sheer *design* of the thing!

The One is tired and exalted. The paddle is taking him home, and the magnificent birds are just as they were before he hit the reed beds. For some reason, the One is well, full of himself and out of himself.

Determined, dared and done.

Poems

AGE

Purgation

—Homage, Po Chu-yi—

Before and after the eye, grasses go over the long fields.
Every Season they walk on
by us, as though I —no; I and you,
Dear friend—decreed it. One time or another

They are here. Grass season . . . yet we are no longer the best
Of us.
Lie stiller, closer; in the April I love

For its juices, there is too much green for your grave.
I feel that the Spring should ignite with what is
Unnatural as we; ours, but God-suspected. It should come in one
furious step, and leave
Some—a little—green for us; never quite get every one of the hummocks
tremoring vaguely
Tall in the passed-through air. They'd make the old road *be*
The road for old men, where you and I used to wander toward
The beetle-eaten city gate, as the year leant into us.
Oh fire, come *on*! I trust you!

My ancient human friend, you are dead, as we both know.

But I remember, and I call for something serious, uncalled-for
By anyone else, to sweep, to *use*

the dryness we've caused to become us! Like the grasshopper

I speak, nearly covered with dust, from the footprint and ask
Not for the line-squall lightning:
the cloud's faking veins—Yes! I catch myself:
No; not the ripped cloud's open touch, the fireball hay
Of August
but for flame too old to live
Or die, to travel like a wide wild contrary
Single-minded brow over the year's right growing
In April
over us *for us* as we sway stubbornly near death
From both sides age-gazing

Both sighing like grass and fire.

NATURE

The Eagle's Mile

for William Douglas

The Emmet's Inch & Eagle's Mile
—Blake

Unwarned, catch into this
With everything you have:
the trout streaming with all its quick
In the strong curve all things on all sides
In motion the soul strenuous
And still
in time-flow as in water blowing
Fresh and for a long time

Downhill something like air it is
Also and it is dawn

There in merciless look-down
As though an eagle or Adam
In lightning, or both, were watching uncontrollably
For meat, among the leaves. Douglas, with you
The soul tries it one-eyed, half your sight left hanging in a river
In England, long before you died,

And now that one, that and the new one
Struck from death's instant—
Lightning's: like mankind on impulse blind-
siding God—true-up together and ride
On silence, enraptured surveillance,

The eagle's mile. Catch into this, and broaden

Into and over

The mountain rivers, over the leaf-tunnel path:

Appalachia, where the trail lies always hidden

Like prey, through the trembling south-north of the forest
Continent, from Springer Mountain to Maine,
And you may walk

Using   not surpassing

The trout's hoisted stand-off with the channel,
Or power-hang the same in the shattered nerves
Of lightning: like Adam find yourself splintering out
Somewhere on the eagle's mile, on peerless, barbaric distance
Clairvoyant with hunger,

Or can begin   can be   begin to be
What out-gentles, and may evade:
This second of the second year
Of death, it would be best for the living
If it were your impulse to step out of grass-bed sleep

As valuably   as cautiously

As a spike-buck, head humming with the first male split
Of the brain-bone, as it tunes to the forked twigs
Of the long trail

Where Douglas you once walked in a white shirt as a man
In the early fall, fire-breathing with oak-leaves,
Your patched tunnel-gaze exactly right
For the buried track,
the England-curved water strong
Far-off with your other sight, both fresh-waters marbling together

Supporting not surpassing

What flows   what balances

In it. Douglas, power-hang in it all now, for all
The whole thing is worth: catch without warning

Somewhere in the North Georgia creek like ghost-muscle tensing

Forever, or on the high grass-bed
Yellow of dawn, catch like a man stamp-printed by God-
shock, blue as the very foot
Of fire. Catch into the hunted
Horns of the buck, and thus into the deepest hearing—
Nerveless, all bone, bone-tuned
To leaves and twigs—with the grass drying wildly
When you woke where you stood with all blades rising
Behind you, and stepped out
possessing the trail,
The racked bramble on either side shining
Like a hornet, your death drawing life
From growth
from flow, as in the gill-cleansing turn
Of the creek
or from the fountain-twist
Of flight, that rounds you
Off, and shies you downwind
Side-faced, all-seeing with hunger,

And over this, steep and straight-up
In the eagle's mile
Let Adam, far from the closed smoke of mills
And blue as the foot
Of every flame, true-up with blind-side outflash
The once-more instantly
Wild world: over Brasstown Bald

Splinter uncontrollably whole.

DOUBLE TONGUE

Craters

(with Michel Leiris)

Roots out of the ground and on-going
The way wé are, some of them—

Spokes   earth-slats   a raft made of humped planks
Slung down and that's right: wired together
By the horizon: it's what *these* roads
Are growing through: fatal roads,
No encounters, the hacked grass burning with battle-song—

Then when we get *our* voices together,
When we mix in that savage way, in the gully of throats
Where the fog piles up, and we turn our long cadences loose
Over the grooved pasture, the running fence of song

Will flap and mount straight up for miles

Very high, all staring stridulation,
Softer than beer-hops:

one of the days when the wind breathes slackly,
Making the lightest perches tremble
Like hostile stems interlacing
As in the heart a lock of blond hair knots on itself
Suicidally, insolubly
someone will plough-out a door,
A staircase will dig itself down, its haunted spiral

Will blacken and come out

Where the ashes of those who were once turned to Pompeiian lava
Will abandon their smouldering silkworks,

Their velvet slags, and take on the courtliness
Of ghosts: then, then the sky will be gone from us

Forever, we wretched ones who can love nothing
But light.
Such will the craters tell you—any crater
Will tell you, dry-heaving and crouching:
will tell us we've stumbled
Onto one:
we're ín one, dry-heaving and crouching.

Farmers

a fragment

(with André Frénaud)

There are not many meteors over the flat country

Of the old; not one metaphor between the ploughblade
And the dirt
not much for the spirit: not enough
To raise the eyes past the horizon-line
Even to the Lord, even with neck-muscles like a bull's
For the up-toss. The modest face has no fear

Of following a center-split swaying track
Through grain and straw
To the grave, or of the honor of work
With muck and animals, as a man born reconciled
With his dead kin:

When love gives him back the rough red of his face he dares

To true-up the seasons of life with the raggedness of earth,
With the underground stream as it turns its water
Into the free stand of the well: a language takes hold

And keeps on, barely making it, made

By pain: the pain that's had him ever since school,
At the same time the indivisible common good
Being shared among the family
Came clear to him: he disappears into fog

He reappears he forces out his voice

Over the field   he extends his figures

With a dead-right clumsiness,
And the blazon which changes every year
Its yellow and green squares, announces at each moment
What must be said: the justice that the power of man installs
In exhausted fresh-air coupling with the earth:
Slogger—

Figure of glory

Less and more than real, fooled always
By the unforeseeable: so nailed by your steps
Into the same steps   so marked by wisdom calamitously
come by,
And always uncertain, valiantly balancing,
So stripped, so hog-poor still, after a long day
In the immemorial, that I cannot say to you
Where you will hear me,
Farmer, there will be no end to your knowing

The pastures drawn breathless by the furrow,
The fields, heart-sick, unquenchable   arid
avid,

The forgivable slowness, the whispered prophecies of weather:
Winter   spring, the season which always comes through
For you, and never enough,

But only dies, turning out
In its fragile green, its rich greens,
To be nothing but the great stain of blankness
Changing again—

17

Double Tongue

Gravedigger

On Sunday, you come back Monday to the laying-out
In squares, of your infinite land
the furs of snow do not reach us
When they should
the moon has troubled the sown seed . . .

Low Country

THE STARRY PLACE BETWEEN THE ANTLERS

If I said that the stars in their courses had to do with my living in Columbia, South Carolina, this would not be entirely true, but there is something to it; in an odd way, it has come to *be* true. From the wartime South Pacific I have kept on remembering a few moments of twilight when I talked with bomber crews, and the navigators showed me their sextants and octants, *mana*-rich implements in which mirrors banked light back and forth between their slants in what seemed to me, even at twenty-one, certain proof of the relationship of human bodies to celestial: the complex star-angled keys to everything.

My interest in mythological mathematics followed me back into civilian life and through Vanderbilt, which gave me as much numerology as I could command; not a great deal but sufficient to encourage a gradual build-up of celestial equipment over the years: sextant—a cheap one at first and then a good one at a windfall Christmas—chronometers, sight-reduction tables, a circular slide-rule (the shape seemed righter), and even an artificial horizon, for the real skyline of the lake on which I live is unreliable with shagginess, pine-obfuscation. There is a dock in my back yard, and I sit there and calculate, for this is the place the stars in their courses tell me I most am at this moment in Time: on the west bank of Lake Katherine, in Columbia, South Carolina, 34°00.2 N 80°58.5 W, nailed down by the numbers, by post-dated Pythagorean calculations, though the Master's famous spherical space-time harmonics are not heard; the music here is bluegrass.

Before I moved down from Washington there had been California; before California, Oregon; before Oregon, Italy. It had been a long time since I had lived in the Deep South, where I was born, and I had been steadily wandering since I was seventeen. I was feeling the magnetic pull that draws from pine roots and kudzu vines for those born among them, and was being pulled South, deeper and deeper, not only by the sun-moon opposition over Lake Katherine but by a root-system something like veins, the whole of an underground as well. When my term at the Library of Congress was up I thought we would probably go back to California, since my family liked it out there—better than I did, to tell the truth—but my best friend from graduate school days was teaching in the English department at the University of South Carolina and liking it, and I came down here to see him, and out of curiosity as to what kind of offer the school might be willing to make, if any.

The president of the college was full of good sly half-naive cracker honesty. When I asked him what incentive might cause me to wish to live in South Carolina, I brought in, as though a matter of general knowledge, the opinion that the state is a depressed area economically, perennially snake-bit as to its money crop. The turpentine from the pine trees had lost its money when sail gave way to steam, I said, having looked this up in a John Gunther *Inside U.S.A.* thirty years out of date. Indigo had not done well either, killed off by the advent of aniline dyes; even the indigo *snake* is on the endangered list. And the rice they used to raise in South Carolina, which had to be cultivated under water by hand, could not compete with the highland rice of Arkansas and Texas, and furthermore, Sea Island—or long staple—cotton had been blitzed by the boll weevil during the Depression, and improvements in textile machinery had made it even less valuable, into the bad bargain. So now, as far as I knew, South Carolina was soybeans, illiteracy, and maybe even pellagra and hookworm, and my chief mental image of it was of a dilapidated outhouse and a rusty '34 Ford with a number 13 painted on it, both covered by kudzu. Why should I become part of such an environment? President Tom Jones looked at me with sincere friendliness and said, If you like two things, you would like to live in South Carolina. What two things? I asked suspiciously. Flowers and birds, he replied. Talk on, I said.

In short, I moved to Columbia, bought a house, and settled down to work on a novel I was writing. I finished it the first year I lived in Columbia while I was learning to take the noon-position sight with a plastic sextant, using the pine-shagged south as a horizon, and coming out in my calculations somewhere in eastern Somaliland, though the people there never knew it. The novel was scheduled to be made into a movie. The director was an Englishman, who knew nothing at all of the Appalachian setting of the story. However, my father's people came from an area about forty miles west of the river where we ended up making *Deliverance*; I had some relatives there and knew some other mountain people from the years when I was a child and went with my father to visit cousins and look over various farms where he walked his gamecocks. All this violence of waters and feathers was only about four hours from Columbia, so that I could both teach at the university and do whatever work on the screenplay needed to be done on the location.

When the shooting was done, I was back into a relationship with rivers, rhododendron, whitetail deer and mountain snakes, and I was also free to explore outward from Columbia in the other direction, toward the sea. The Low Country, its huge public and private gardens, the plantations and the beaches, represented another part of the South for me, though I had heard and read plenty about it. It began to be borne in on me that the conjunction of stars over Columbia was in a weird and exciting relation to the conjunction of my other interests, and I became more enthusiastic about finding out what I could of the area, chance being the main exploratory means, plus a little haphazard self-direction governed only by the largest natural Entities: the mountains of Appalachia and their hot and cold sweats, their dulcimers, rivers and thickets, and the Atlantic Ocean and its Southern version of sawgrass and sand, and all that unbroken openness. I went "down on the salt."

It was an odd thing. The first rice plantation I saw branded two words so strongly on the front of my brain that I may even have thought, at that first flat endless glimpse just down from the mountain and still wanting to roll but not able, that the words had also come to be stamped across the skin of my forehead, and were quite visible: tragic landscape. For some reason a phrase from graduate school came back to me then. The subject of my thesis was Herman Melville's poetry, which is God-awful. From all those wretched stanzas of a gifted, form-misjudging poet I retained only one line, but it too sprang across my eyebrows from the marshes: Mosby moves through the hauntedness. *Hauntedness* is one of the few good coinages that civilian Civil War buff Melville—that Pittsfield Yankee—ever came up with, but it is more than just right to describe the ruined rice-flats, the treed clouds of heavy-sensitive moss, the doom-sultry landscape of coastal South Carolina, where every plantation house is the House of Usher, and where in all that sun-core sunlight the pale, sick, huge-eyed ghost of Edgar Allan Poe in his ripped plantation death-suit and sweat-rimed Panama hat is forever likely to materialize; he owns it all; Poe and the place invented each other. The air, even a handbreadth in front of the face, is thick and hazy, and this indefiniteness extends on out to the horizon; there is the same haze, but the clarity is not reduced by distance, either: it is the same all the way out, out of sight, in any direction. Bizarre thoughts come of this. You are enveloped in a terrifying, depthless sense of guilt, a guilt that seems right for you, because there is no explanation for it, and you have come. There is nothing but you, the reed-beds around you and the trees and the swaying half-gray hang. The sensation is something like Poe's unaccountable correlation of the color yellow and electric shock, but softly done, and suffusive.

In such places there are plenty of snakes, and I fear and like that too. In the field I have never met up with another blowgunner, and I had just as soon not, for such occupation is even more solitary than bow-hunting, and should be. Whenever I can I pursue snakes with a long, dusty aluminum pipe and darts made of coat-hangers and typing paper, and whatever weapon my breath is, as I have dreamed all my life that they are pursuing me with only their sunny venom, and subtler poisons drawn from the roots of mossy trees. With my peculiar interest in hunting—deer and snakes—the rotating Pythagorean vectors that fixed me in South Carolina are very fortunate, at least up to now. There are plenty of deer and snakes in the mountains of Appalachia, and an entirely different kind of deer on the coastal islands, and even more and bigger snakes, like the fullest-blown (no pun) and most dangerous snake in the New World, or at the least in North America, the eastern diamondback. To paraphrase a line from the Nineties poet John Davidson, "Stags to bow and snakes to blow are waiting everywhere."

About halfway between the mountains and the ocean Columbia is hung up between two worlds of a distinction more than absolute, and is agreeably odd itself: a mixture of university town, southern political capital and military base. The dock from which I sight the noon and the moon is on the west bank of a dammed lake on the other side of which is Fort Jackson, a basic training installation which is among the largest in the world. With daybreak each day come the sounds of firing, of voices marching in unison, of bugles, of militaristic hymns, as though coming from a ghostly takeover army waiting for the day. After twelve years this is still vaguely disturbing to me, and even more so when I go infrequently into the city and note the astonishing number of pawn shops and Army surplus stores and the things in them: the blades, the military cutlery, the brass knucks and other implements of mass and individual assault; on a sunny day, walking down Main Street, one is blinded by the glitter of knives, also waiting for the day, or perhaps the night. Generally, though, Columbia is an easygoing place, with some fine old houses, good local theater, and the most imaginative small zoo I have seen.

But the best thing about Columbia is its meridional aspect: the way it balances Appalachia and the Atlantic. On the salt lie Charleston and Savannah, both almost equidistant from Columbia. No Hollywood dream of antebellum Southernism could be as beautiful as these heavy-aired, muffled towns, or the gardens in and around them. The softness of all things there is slowly and inexorably overwhelming: a kind of delicate blur, so that even the stones die with slow genius, bringing blurred, vivid life into sight in bewildering richness, the setting of an existence gracious, opulent, creatively out-of-focus, a heartbreaking and heartening unclearness:

a triumph of the creative nearsightedness of God on the third day of Creation, when He was still trying things out, and liking some of them.

Charleston and Savannah are full of walled gardens, which I love more than any other constructions of man. Whenever I'm in one, I feel like the character in the Harold Pinter play who comes into a room, looks around in disbelief, and exclaims, "Jesus! A guy's got a chance in a place like this." For some reason connected with my distant college astronomy, I think of Max Planck's black-box black-body experiments with heat, light and radiation, for in a walled garden I quite distinctly feel radiation—quanta—of pure Good, of uncontaminated metaphysical well-being, coming inward on me with the full force of the way things are—at least are, here: *de rerum natura* from every brick. And I like also the fact that the walled garden is surrounded by a great many other images of the soft and strange: many shadowy squares, brick walks, innumerable fences of all descriptions from slats to baronial wrought-iron palings decorated with huge creosoted acorns and griffins'-feet blunting with moss. In the air too there are soft and strange intonations, the extraordinary pronunciation of ordinary words, said this way only here; boat is "bow-ut" and date "day-ut." The food is wonderful and unique: she-crab soup, red rice, shrimp or oyster pilau, Hoppin' John, chicken bog. While there I am living proof-positive of John Peale Bishop's dictum that the true test of a civilization is an indigenous cookery. On the salt, I participate; I am rapturously civilized.

Among coastlines I have my favorites; one of them is Cannon Bay, Oregon, with its wild Wagnerian cliffs and haystack rocks. But Pawley's Island, South Carolina, is the prettiest beach I have seen anywhere in all my travels except perhaps for the eastern beach of Bull's Island in the Cape Romain Wildlife Preserve nearby, where the biggest buck and the biggest rattlesnake are taking their time growing and waiting, in a landscape out of Rimbaud.

Though I respect and revere the snakes and would crawl down a gopher-hole to get at one, I love the deer the most; I return to those, in any direction. The sea-deer I cherish above the mountain deer, even, because I have never seen them doing what I have been told they do: swimming in moonlight from island to island. I would like to see that; I am glad it happens in my state. There would not have to be any reason for them to be swimming; in fact, I had rather there were not any reason. But with the mere possibility the heart of the imagination blazes up like stump-kindling, and starts throwing moonlit shadows, which are antlered. If I maintained that one of these deer, a huge buck with at least twelve points, is said to be dead-white, or moon-white, or breaking-wave-white, or angel-white, or black-body-white, I would be accused of making it up, as I just did. But too many hunters and foresters have told me of the swimming deer for me to doubt it. There are deer, they do swim, and at night, and I plan to stay until I see them. Between the deer of the mountains and those of the sea, those down on the salt between the South Carolina islands: that is my balance, and it is right for me: the starry place between the antlers: between the bucks of the rhododendron gullies and those of the ocean, the mountain horns and the swimming.

EXCELLENTLY BRIGHT, OR SHELL ROADS

If you came, you would come with, you would be left beneath the newest total lift-off of light over the ocean, which is this sundown. It is clear, and these are the precincts of borderline flames on small waves, of mainland singing at the edge of great water, all under the passing, ruined, hypnotized unstoppable stone rising and broadening roundly. Here, all light is round, and if you come you must be here in your own moves (which are rounded), your own secret justice of rhythm, with the profound slight shifts of a grainfield, a tidal dignity, a southern calm and candor, a legendary persuasiveness. Everything around you gives and takes of a suave and classic energy: the long leaves, the curious marble spaced on dark blue, sea sand, the white roads made of shell and smelling of deep salt.

In what it newly wears on summer nights the body is important, is all-important, being closer to the air than usual, and swaying, warmly and obliquely lit, and because of this it may be that your remembering is as inclusive as this moonlight itself, and is of places the most opposite to this that memory can summon: a distant city may have come with you, may now be a part of your movement—and perhaps, also, a certain narrowing and curving and downhill of water from mountains is part, mountains penetrable as clouds, and perhaps also snows, rains, expanses of rock and sand, walled gardens, rooms weightless with aerial dust, all night-held and moon-full, wide-open with summer.

By now the shell roads have achieved the full of their drama, the sea is blazing with undivided promise, rarefied and opulent, and for you the other places, the other images—of cities, of valleys, mountains, of clouds, of things lighter than life and more permanent than death—become an enormous delicate realm of accessible mystery, through which the small sound of the unprotected sea is mixed with the fabulous, honed voice of crickets—thousands of them, perhaps imaginary—: a continuous scything murmur of yearning and fulfillment, of recognition and necessity, desire, obsessive and tender unreason. Now each wave comes in with thorned light, and breaks with modest candor, slides back into the next; one firefly shows itself far out, most purely.

If you can conceive of moonlight, and if you bring the right moves, you can conceive of marble spaced on blue air, or of baffling and rewarding new constellations, or of steel and glass, or underbrush, or bare slopes, clouds, fountains and quarries, and can bring into your summer moves everything that is, or bring only you, or you and one other. Wear something light and long, for if your body is closer to the air than usual, in the banked flame of stone going higher and making light rounder as you pass through it—perhaps with others, perhaps with one other—you can say that at least "one of the gods is being good to us," and mean it.

Writers and Beholders

THE WATER-BUG'S MITTENS
Ezra Pound: What We Can Use*

Since I have chosen to deal with those aspects of Ezra Pound's work and influence that appear to me to be profitable, to provide a continuing direction, a kind of enchanted vector for present and future poets, these remarks must of necessity deal with specific writers and demonstrable debts as well as the ideas and theories that produced certain poems. Pound's enormous, scattered, dismayingly wrong-headed and dazzlingly right-headed learning is of course very much a part of his literary attitude, which in his case is to say a life-attitude, and can plainly be seen, dismayingly and dazzlingly, in the work of the Welsh-English writer David Jones, whose mythographizing novel of World War I, *In Parenthesis*, and long poem, *The Anathémata*, have been extravagantly praised by T. S. Eliot, W. H. Auden, and others of authority.

> "I have made a heap of all that I could find." So wrote Nennius, or whoever composed the introductory matter to the *Historia Britonnum*. He speaks of an "inward wound" which was caused by the fact that certain things dear to him

*This essay was originally given as the 1979 Ezra Pound lecture, administered by the University of Idaho. During the process of organizing and writing the lecture, I found the enterprise turning into a search in which, almost without my knowing it, I sought to clarify my own feelings about Pound's work, and to ascertain and evaluate the aspects of it which might implement the poetry I would presumably write, as well as pay homage to Pound for his influence—shadowy but vast—on my earlier verse. What I feel about Pound's example is given here and I believe that my opinion has solidified to a degree that will make any further changes of attitude on my part unlikely if not impossible.—J.D.

> "should be like smoke dissipated." Further, he says, "not trusting my own learning, which is none at all, but partly from writings and monuments of the ancient inhabitants of Britain . . . I have lispingly put together this . . . about past transactions, that this material might not be trodden under foot."
>
> Part of my task [says Jones, in reference to his poem *The Anathémata*] has been to allow myself to be directed by motifs gathered together from such sources as have by accident been available to me and to make a work out of those mixed data. This, you will say, is, in a sense, the task of any artist in any material, seeing that whatever he makes must necessarily show forth what is his by this or that inheritance. True, but since, as Joyce is reported to have said, "practical life or 'art' . . . comprehends all our activities from boat-building to poetry," the degrees and kinds of complexities of this showing forth of our inheritance must vary to an almost limitless extent.[1]

And so, in the works of both Pound and David Jones, it is so: "the degrees and kinds of complexities of this showing forth of our inheritance [varies] to an almost limitless extent." The preponderance of Pound's original work has been conceived in accordance with this assumption, and all of Jones's has. Since it is beyond the intent of this occasion to attempt anything even approaching a full-scale assessment of Pound's achievement or place in literary history, I shall limit myself to a necessarily biased and fiercely personal summation of those qualities in Pound that I have found of imaginative and above all of practical value in writing the poetry that I have written and am trying to write. Pound's presence is so pervasive that a contemporary poet cannot put down a single word, cannot hear, even far off or far back in his head, a cadence, a rhythm, without the suspicion that Pound has either suggested it or is in the process of causing him to accept it or reject it. Pound's influence is both direct and insidious; I believe it on the whole to have been—no; to *be*—not only beneficial but releasing and exhilarating, and I believe also that it will continue to possess these qualities for as long as human language is capable of exciting in disparate sensibilities the joys and revelations that certain words in conjunction with other words can afford.

There are four Ezra Pounds, or at least four main ones. The first is the Pound of ideas, discoveries and rediscoveries, the Pound of preferences. Simply to make a personal, fragmentary survey, I would never have heard of Guido Cavalcanti and Arnaut Daniel, or indeed of Provençal verse, or the curious culture of woman-worship, warfare and poetry that produced it, had it not been for Pound. I have never shared Pound's *all-out* enthusiasm for those poets, that culture, or for medieval Italy, or for Roman poetry, but I am grateful to know something of them, and what I know is due to Pound. And I am grateful past the telling of it to know the poetry of Tristan Corbière, whose use of local idiom and argot—in his case the Breton—has taught me with delight what *not* to do with the Southern country-talk of my native Georgia.

But for Pound I would not have in my memory—that is to say, in my mind, my blood and nerves and the rest of me—Lionel Johnson's beautiful line: "Clear lie the fields, and fade into blue air."[2] No; I would not see fields that way, though of course I did all the time. The point is that I did not have those *words* with which to see them, though the fields—in Georgia or Idaho or China or anywhere—are the same. The line is Lionel Johnson's, but the finding of it, the perception of its beauty and the *qualities* of its beauty, the relation of word to world, and, following all this, the insistence on the validity of the perception, the wording or *voicing* of the perception, come from one's simplest and most spontaneous reaction to a fragment of what existence has momentarily made available: these Pound has made available.

Again, in a poem of one of Pound's closest followers, there is the question:

> Have you seen a falcon stoop
> accurate, unforseen
> and absolute, between
> wind-ripples over harvest?[3]

The image of the bird over harvest-ripples is in itself very strong as an image, but with the qualifying words "accurate," "unforseen," and "absolute" stooping with it, that bird becomes *necessary*; all other birds—real birds—will have to learn to fly like that. In fact, those three words of Basil Bunting's could with equal justice be applied as criteria for the kind of untrammeled and primitive observation and careful, simple wording that the best of Pound's own poetry exemplifies and encourages: "The water-bug's mittens show on the bright rock below him."[4] Ah, yes! Those mittens! *Mittens*! The *water-bug's* mittens! How curious, and how exactly, exactingly, observably and unforeseeably right! For that is what the water-bug's invisible tracks—his feet, his fingers—look like, transformed by the sun and water and rock into shadow. It is an amazing picture, an amazing image, and I for one would not want to do without it. Next winter, when I wear mittens, I shall certainly believe that I can walk on water. Why not?

"The central act of the mind, in the 'Imagist' poems Pound was writing about 1913," as Hugh Kenner points out, "is a leaping that interprets one thing clearly seen with the aid of another seen in the mind's eye."[5] This triple conjunction—of associating mind, thing observed, and thing remembered—is fundamental to Pound's practice insofar as the imagery of his poems is concerned, and the encouragement toward its widespread and idiosyncratic employment is the best tool he has put into our hands. Randall Jarrell says somewhere that Imagism failed as a school because none of the Imagists could write poetry, and, though there are a few observations still retaining a kind of half-life in F. S. Flint and H. D., Jarrell's harsh judgment is largely true. But the principles of direct unclouded observation and Occam's law of parsimony as applied to the *number* of words in a poem are still useful, and would not have come to such obvious good in the works of Basil Bunting and David Jones—to say nothing of those of T. S. Eliot—if Pound had not formulated them. The characteristic that raises Pound's images far above those of H. D., Richard Aldington, Flint, Amy Lowell and the rest of the programmatic Imagists is no more than the highly personal and imaginative distinctiveness that Pound brought to them; no more, and that is everything. Pound was more adventurous, more trusting of his senses, more verbally daring than the others, and the faculty that presented and then chose among his linguistic options was both wider and more discriminating than theirs. The French poet, Pierre Reverdy (whom, incidentally, Pound knew) says that "Plus les rapports des deux réalités rapprochées seront lointains et justes, plus l'image sera forte, plus elle aura de puissance émotive et de réalité poétique."[6] Let me run that back to you through English, very roughly: "The farther-removed the points of similarity of two realities taken in conjunction with each other are, and at the same time the more just they are, the stronger the image will be, and the more emotive power and poetic reality it will have." The principle that underlies the application of the word *justes* in this context is that of the hitherto unnoted, the hidden similarity, the farfetched comparison that may be seen to have some measure of demonstrable or *felt* reasonableness about it: some measure of the "accurate, the unforseen," which then becomes, or seems to become, "the absolute."

Pound has always insisted on this kind of distinctiveness; his watchword, his battle-banner, his national anthem is "Make It New." He has put forth daring observation, plain diction, and strong unhesitant rhythm as desirable elements in the memorable presentation of an insight, and his stressing of these factors has resulted in a poetry far more exciting, more intellectually invigorating, and above all more humanly resonant than we would have had without it. More than any other single writer, Pound has stripped poetry of unnecessary ornamentation, of linguistic fat, and given the things of the world back to people in terms they could actually see and feel, unashamed of responding to their simplicity, their existence as they were or seemed to the observer to be. Pound has destroyed the false distinction between poetic and nonpoetic subject matter (a distinction that cruelly damaged the work of John Keats, for example) and opened up the whole universe of real and imagined subjects for contemplation, communication-in-depth and "significant form." The inspired image-maker, the answer to his own Platonic dream-image of the ideal Imagist poet, is the second Pound. Without him we would probably not have the arresting disturbances (arresting, once you look at them) on the New York martini, described by John Updike: "Ringlets of vibration, fine as watch springs, oscillated on the surface of his Gibson."[7]

The impact of this second, Imagistic Pound has been variously felt, over the past seventy-five or so years, by a great many poets, and it is probably fair to say that the Imagistic practice has resulted in poems (and poets) that were better for Imagism than they would have been without it. It has been an excellent influence in the work of Eliot, and in that of Basil Bunting and David Jones. It has created the poems and reputations of writers whom I consider only moderately good, such as William Carlos Williams, Louis Zukofsky, Denise Levertov and Robert Creeley, and has been disastrously misused and even unconsciously parodied by talentless writers like Charles Olson and Robert Duncan. Pound's "keep your eye on the object" injunction is not a panacea, but a useful tool in the unearthing of talent where talent already existed. The power of eye is still individual power, and trivialization of the object is always the Longinian "pitfall" awaiting the Imagist poet without insight as well as biological sight.

This lack of a personal vision, for example, brings all the poetry of William Carlos Williams to the same dead level of commonplaceness: commonplaceness of fact and commonplaceness of apprehension of the fact. Perhaps it is idle to speculate on whether or not Williams's writing would have been better if it had been couched in the almost ludicrously "literary" diction of Pound's early poems—all "haths," "thees," "thous," "mids," "yeas," and "nays": all this Pre-Raphaelitism from the subsequent champion of plain speech, "living language"—or whether the observing-the-nailhead-and-saying-that-it-is-a-nailhead, the matter-of-fact recording of a literal part of mutually observed reality, is better. Idle speculation, almost surely. And yet one does it anyway, and if that one is myself, and is forced to choose, I would opt for the Williams that we have: the Williams of the red wheelbarrow and the rose frozen in the cake of ice in front of the plumber's shop. But the case of Pound's influence, even in one of its more salutary directions, does not really rest there, either. A universe of brute facts and *uninspired* notations about them is a very dull universe: if I had to choose between seeing the rose in the cake of ice and reading about it in Williams's "shredded prose" offered as poetry, I would choose to look at the rose, if I could find the right plumber. Or I would go back to the verbal rose on Rilke's tombstone: " . . . pure contradiction, / To be no one's sleep / Under so many lids." Yes, I would do that, and then go to a real rose with the understanding—and love—of it that only a real poet could have given me. I don't wish to berate Williams, for he was a brave, an unselfish, a dedicated and truthful man. But a real poet, in any sense in which I can understand the term, he was not. His work exhibits, as Henry James said of Whitman's, "the effort of an essentially prosaic mind to lift itself, by a prolonged muscular strain, into poetry."[8] This effort, insisted on and championed by Pound and resulting in the work of Williams, Zukofsky, Olson, Rexroth (a ludicrous example of ineptitude), Duncan, Levertov, Jonathan Williams, and almost *any*body who went to Black Mountain College in North Carolina in the fifties, can now be seen as an interesting but decidedly small factor in the imaginative literature that followed Pound's general insistence on the mind-object relationship and the word's plain-speaking of it. Even though some of the truly creative poets that came after Pound owed something to this aspect of him, Theodore Roethke, John Berryman, James Wright, Margaret Atwood, Ann Stanford, Jane Cooper, and Wendell Berry owed more to their subjective selves than they did to Pound's objective method, and that is the main reason that the future will be theirs, if I am any judge.

The third Pound, after the promotional and proselytizing Pound and the direct-observation and plain-statement Pound, is, unfortunately, the Pound that both the literate and illiterate portions of humanity have identified as the main Ezra: this might be called the culture-plundering Pound, the complex-associational Pound, the riddling Pound: the Pound that Yvor Winters refers to as "a barbarian on the loose in a museum."[9] Winters says that Mr. Pound resembles "a village loafer who sees much and understands little." When I go through Pound's major poem, his lifelong effort, *The Cantos*, I feel that I see a good deal, too, but that, despite the help of predecessors in the Pound lectureship like Hugh Kenner and Marshall McLuhan, I, too, understand very little. What hope for me from Pound, indeed? What help from Kenner and McLuhan, if Randall Jarrell is right when he says "*The Cantos* are less a 'poem containing history' than a poem containing history recollections, free associations, obsessions"?[10] Jarrell says also that:

> A great deal of *The Cantos* is interesting in the way an original soul's indiscriminate notes on books and people, countries and centuries, are interesting; all these fragmentary citations and allusions remind you that if you had read exactly the books Pound has read, known exactly the people Pound has known, and felt about them as Pound has felt, you could understand *The Cantos* pretty well. Gertrude Stein was most unjust when she called that ecumenical alluder a village explainer: he can hardly *tell* you about anything (unless you know it already), much less explain it. He makes notes on the margin of the universe; to tell you how just or unjust a note is, you must know that portion of the text itself.

This third Pound, the one that attempts to make a kind of rebirth ritual of everything Pound has ever run across or been impressed by in one way or another, is a curious and despairing darkness to me, though when light flashes through, it is exceptionally bright, pure, and clear: or—a word that recurs to me again and again in connection with these moments: *clean*.

> Maelid and bassarid among the lynxes;
>   how many? There are more under the oak trees,
> We are here waiting the sunrise
>   and the next sunrise
> for three nights amid lynxes. For three nights
>   of the oak-wood
> and the vines are thick in their branches
>   no vine lacking flower,
> no lynx lacking a flower rope
>   no Maelid minus a wine jar
>   this forest is named Melagrana
>
>   O lynx, keep the edge on my cider
>   Keep it clear without cloud . . . [11]

When I read these lines I am charmed first by their ceremonial tone, for I have always liked rituals involving animals, especially predators that are beautiful—as most predators are—but I am not sure that I want any more from the passage than that: that and the fine, forceful, authoritative sound of it. The supposition that the lynx has or can have something to do with keeping the edge—the *edge*—on someone's cider is enthralling, and I would put up a fight rather than have someone bring in a complex mythology—a *literature*, books—to explain it. What I like in Pound is exactly the opposite of what the world has taken him to represent. I like the maker (the *fabbro*) of the clean phrase and the hard-edged, imaginative image, and am tempted to let most of the rest of Pound go.

And yet I know I should not, and will not. There is a great deal more to Pound than I have been able to appropriate for my own conscious uses. What of his approach to translation, for example, and his own translations (particularly from the Chinese) that are more original poems than translations, and are better poetry than *their* originals?

> March has come to the bridge head,
> Peach boughs and apricot boughs hang over a thousand gates,
> At morning there are flowers to cut the heart,
> And evening drives them on the eastward-flowing waters.
> Petals are on the gone waters and on the going,
>   And on the back-swirling eddies . . . [12]

When one has come to that passage, when one has come to that rhythm, when one encounters these things, when one stays with them, especially the fifth of these lines: "Petals are on the gone waters and on the going," then a permanent value has been added to a grateful and growing sensibility: water is alive with inevitable and beautiful movement, the words that bear the flowers bear it like a river, and the whole heartbreaking marvel of time—time and seasons long past and time but recently past, time at this very moment passing but still, *now*, trembling with its own pastness not yet come, but passing into, passing—the gone waters and the going . . . well, I must break off, for my words are no match, and above all, no substitute, for Pound's. Neither Li Po nor Rihaku (Li Po's Japanese name), nor the scholar Ernest Fenollosa nor indeed the whole of Oriental culture itself ever wrote so well, or at least so well

Orientally, in English as this, so that we can not only see but *feel* it: what the East's way of sensing and experiencing existence has been, is, and must be. The sheer *excitement* inherent in the cross-fertilization of languages, cultures, writers has been made ours by Pound. I shall never forget the first wild rush of possibility that flooded me when I had finally learned a few hundred words of French and at the same time began to read Pound, and I realized that the second language constituted a kind of magic in which all kinds of new writers existed, new insights and images awaited me. I have never since stopped dwelling in that adolescent raptness, for, after all, Pound never did, and his example has been before me ever since that time, always opening new doors, giving me new writers, new lines, new sources of imaginative joy, new access to the stealing of the fundamental Promethean fire, the living flame of poetic insight: the true spark, no matter in what language, what place or writer or work.

When I came to *The Cantos* after reading the *Cathay* poems I was certainly stumped. I would have liked, at that time, to have had my confusion not only aided and abetted but in a measure justified by something Katherine Anne Porter wrote, reviewing Pound's *Letters* in 1950, a year after I had finished at Vanderbilt:

> The temptation in writing about *The Letters of Ezra Pound: 1907-1941* is to get down to individual letters, to quote endlessly, to lapse into gossip, to go into long dissertations on the state of society; the strange confusions of the human mind; music, sculpture, painting, war, economics; the menace of the American University; the weakness of having a private life; and finally the hell on earth it is to be at once a poet and a man of perfect judgment in all matters relating to art in a world of the deaf, dumb, and blind, of nitwits, numbskulls, and outright villains.[13]

The temptation "to quote endlessly, to lapse into gossip, etc." is not only Miss Porter's; it is Pound's as well. One might say with some justice that *The Cantos* are composed almost entirely of quotations—often seemingly endless, though fragmentary—of gossip, and above all of dissertations. Some of these are on subjects which entertain Pound's interest only slightly, but others, as we know, such as economics and the virulent nature of credit, are nothing less than obsessions, not to say manias. As a college boy I wondered, and I still wonder at the mind that could take itself with such humorless and utter seriousness, and at such patience-consuming length, as the mind which rambles through *The Cantos* in at least seven languages, ranting obscurely, lulling into poignant and piercing lyricism, leaping from one historical figure, one era, one event to another, seeming to draw all kinds of inferences but making none clear, never out of breath and, though claiming to be, never really conclusive. Yet I had this comfort: moments like those in the *Cathay* poems appear all through *The Cantos*; they are there; you just have to dig for them. And I keep believing, with this fact as a base, that little by little, line by line, reference by reference, culture-image by culture-image, I may be able to come into possession of more of Pound than I have now: that he will keep opening things up for me: things I would never have known without him. After all, he has not really failed me yet, though confuse me he certainly has.

Pound's practice of quotation and cultural cross-reference has had a profound and far-reaching effect on the composition and reception of poetry, but I believe that effect to be lessening. The use of the out-of-context quotation is supremely effective in the work of T. S. Eliot and Marianne Moore and perhaps that of David Jones and the black American M. B. Tolson, but it is disastrously bookish and hit-or-miss in the *Maximus Poems* of Charles Olson, in William Carlos Williams's *Paterson*, and in the lyrics of Robert Duncan. *The Cantos* and *The Waste Land*, by authority of the weight of commentary made upon them, have made the quotation-haunted, cross-pollenized poem the only kind of structural organization that poets have allowed themselves to employ in forms longer than the brief lyric. Compared to the layers of reference of *The Cantos*, say, the straight narrative verse-novel, such as any of those by Edwin Arlington Robinson, seems pathetically thin and one-dimensional. Delmore Schwartz comments on *The Cantos*:

> Taking this long poem in itself, we must of necessity see it not as an integral part of a literary period, but in the

company of other long poems of like ambition. The first lack to be noticed from this standpoint is the absence of a narrative framework such as sustains every long poem which has become a portion of the whole corpus of poetry. Pound himself has declared that it is above all by its story that a literary work gains its lasting interest, and it is difficult to see what basis for unity in an extended poem would be superior to that of plot . . .

. . . The Cantos have no plot, although as the poem continues, the repetition of key phrases, characters and situations, makes more and more clear the kind of unity which the Cantos do have, a wholeness based upon certain obsessions or preoccupations, deriving itself from the character of Pound's mind, and displaying itself not in conjunction with the numerical order of the Cantos, but, so to speak, against the grain of continuity, which itself seems to be determined by the requirements of musical order, *melopoeia*, as Pound calls it. Or to put the whole issue differently, here we have a long poem without a hero, such as Achilles or Odysseus or *Virgilio mio*, or Agamemnon or Hamlet. Or if there is a hero, it is not Thomas Jefferson, Sigismondo Malatesta and the other letter writers, but it is, in fact, Pound himself, the taste of Pound, above all his literary taste, that is to say, his likes and dislikes among books and the men who in some way have had to do with books or documents of some kind.

And when we examine the texture of the verse, we find lacking, amid much beauty of language and observation other elements which have been characteristic of great poetry. The Cantos, as others have noted, consist of many surfaces, presented with great exactitude, but with nothing behind them. We get what is upon the surface, whether the idiom of a text which Pound is translating or the particular quality of sunlight upon the water which Pound is describing; but we do not get anything more than this.[14]

It is at this point that I take issue with Mr. Schwartz, as brilliant and useful a critic as he is, and perhaps with Pound as well, for it is in just these "surfaces, presented with great exactitude," that

I find the Ezra Pound that I can most truly, effectively and permanently use. Certain of these passages have had for me what amounts not so much to a "shock of recognition" but a shock of *possibility*: the possibility of catching an observable or imaginable part of the world in fresh, clean language that would be simple without being thin and ordinary: that would have the forthrightness of assertion, and be given in language having a strongly marked rhythmical pulse, somewhere near the Anglo-Saxon, and consequently the sound of a voice saying something both simple and extraordinary, the tone of a thing *meant*, which is also the tone—the *tone*—of a delivered truth:

> Blue dun; number 2 in most rivers
> for dark days, when it is cold
> A starling's wing will give you the colour
> or duck widgeon, if you take feather from under the wing
> Let the body be of blue fox fur, or a water rat's
> or grey squirrel's. Take this with a portion of mohair
> and a cock's hackle for legs.
> 12th of March to 2nd of April
> Hen pheasant's feather does for a fly,
> green tail, the wings flat on the body
> Dark fur from a hare's ear for a body
> a green shaded partridge feather
>   grizzled yellow cock's hackle
> green wax; harl from a peacock's tail
> bright lower body; about the size of pin
> the head should be. can be fished from seven a.m.
> till eleven; at which time the brown marsh fly comes on.
> As long as the brown continues, no fish will take Granham
>
> That hath the light of the doer, as it were
> a form cleaving to it.[15]

Now that's *fishing*! That's not Renaissance Italy, or Jefferson's or Mussolini's political theories or the economic theories of Major Douglas. The passage is from the fifty-first Canto, in the midst of one of Pound's otherwise inchoate and violent fulminations against usury. It occurs as an illustration of one of Pound's favorite doctrines, that of dedicated and loving and above all *personal* craftsmanship: the activity performed well, the object made well, because of dedicated expertise employed for the love and honor of the thing performed, the thing made. The quality that makes Pound a good and sometimes great poet is that, though he is a great, buffoonish hater, he is not so great a hater as he is a lover. His love of what he deems excellence in all its manifestations he has ever encountered amounts very nearly to paranoia, and, though as strong and overriding as that love is, it cannot help seeming to the reader of *The Cantos* that Pound is attempting to place him under a species of cultural house arrest: that the poet is forcibly enlisting him in a totalitarianism of the excellent, as Pound defines it. The profit I have had from reading *The Cantos*—profit as a human being and a poet—has come largely from picking through those heavy-laden and earnest pages for startling, isolated shocks of possibility: conjunctions of words that opened up my own rather unbookish but very word-sensitive mentality to what I might come upon in my own memory and set forth with a corresponding imaginative forthrightness, strong rhythm—rhythm using rather more double-stresses, spondees, than is usual—and an unhesitant sound of authority, a tone of truthfulness and "no nonsense": a tone of "this is it, and don't argue." I like that kind of assertiveness, especially when it is personal and imaginative as well as assertive, and Pound's example has been of immense help to me in formulating passages in which these qualities were dominant.

All this is an admission, of course, that I do not really *know The Cantos*, and that I am missing most of their real intent, the real totality of the poem. Searching for Pound's best shots—his best shocks—of insight, I have been able to come closer to that totality than I was when I first started, and I have in the main disliked what I have found. Once more to quote Delmore Schwartz, and argue with him:

> The obscurity of the Cantos, their dependence upon quantities of information which are not readily available is at once another definition of the poem, and yet not at all as

> important a handicap and burden as some suppose. The amount of learning necessary in order to understand the manifold allusions of the Cantos can easily be exaggerated, and could quite simply be put together in one supplementary volume such as has already been provided for Joyce's *Ulysses*. Pound is not as learned as he seems to be—the scattered impression of his learning leads to the mistaken impression—and at any rate the amount of information which must be acquired is nothing compared to what must be done in order to read *The Divine Comedy*, or the effort we make when we learn a foreign language. It is curious, of course, that a writer of our own time and language should require so much external help, but the only question is: is the poem good enough? It is.[16]

Well, Delmore, it is and it isn't. One of the main troubles with it is its lack of actual concern with people. Every person that Pound brings to our attention is an *example* of something: that is to say, a symbol, an effigy, a stand-in for an abstraction: good government, bad government, artistic excellence, economic right-mindedness, and so on. Even the anecdotes about people Pound has known, such as the famous one about Henry James, are more *illustrations* than they are anything else; there is no true human encounter. Perhaps this is not a valid criticism; I don't know. But there does seem to me, despite Pound's hectoring enthusiasm—or love, as I choose to call it, though of an often forbidding kind—that there is a distressing erector-set mechanicalness about *The Cantos*, a complex in-group snobbery, a very off-putting air of contemptuous intellectual superiority, and I'm afraid one part of me will never get over it. There are various kinds of bullheadedness in literary criticism, of course. One kind is Pound's and another kind is J. B. Priestley's:

> For all his long and deep concern for the art, [Pound] has been a bad influence on modern poetry. It is he more than anybody else who has encouraged an unnecessary obscurity, not arising from the flashing broken images of passion, but too often from a cold cleverness working away at compression. For a line can be so loaded with meaning that it can only be understood if the reader regards it as part of

> an exceptionally difficult crossword puzzle; but at what moment, in this puzzle-solving atmosphere, does aesthetic experience arrive, when does poetry begin? It is he who has encouraged too many younger poets to collect savory and rare ingredients, but then to ruin the dish because the oven, the poetic feeling, is too low to cook it properly. Following his example, they have offered us too many recondite allusions, too many scraps of other languages (for a poem is a performance on one instrument, not one of those "musical acts" in vaudeville), and too many of these cold flat statements, filled with polysyllabic abstractions, that read like quotations from legal documents. What may have originally been conceived in passionate intensity too often somehow loses, through too much concentration and cool brainwork, real poetic feeling, and ends by suggesting an over-self-conscious intellectual sneering and showing off.[17]

There is that side, too: the clean, sharp, hard-edged and forthright statement-in-depth, the insight voiced with strong and compelling weight and memorable rhythm is buried in ill-digested philosophy, economics, history and politics: that is a simplistic statement, but it seems to me to be exactly true. The Hugh Kenners and Donald Davies of the world, the professors, will continue to find great profit in their studies of *The Cantos*; Pound is already an industry in academia, and will be more and more of one in the future, comparable in the volume of its products, perhaps, to Milton, Melville and Kafka, to say nothing of Joyce and Eliot. Meanwhile I will continue to hunt through Pound's work for those isolated but indispensable shocks of verbal possibility that only his example affords me, and to honor his effort to make the *paradiso/terrestre* for which he so strenuously wished and worked in all his doctrines and poems but most particularly in *The Cantos*. "I have made a heap of all that I could find." So says Nennius, so says the author of the *Historia Britonnum* if it wasn't Nennius, so says Pound's disciple David Jones, and so says Ezra Pound, by implication and example.

An extraordinary heap. Pound's wish was always for more insight, more understanding, more consequentiality: in a word, more *life* for us. What he wanted for each of us, and for all human culture, was highly relevant personal experience: the guarantee of this within ourselves and our culture's guarantee that such experience should be ours. A sense of the consequentiality of things, actions, men, ideas and civilizations is what we most want, and what we most sorely lack. Pound was on the right side of the question, as confused and confusing as he often was and is, and as elitist as his stance is. "What thou lovest well remains." It does. What remains to me as a working poet are the water-bug's mittens, there in live observation from a living world, in believable, extraordinarily releasing, clean, powerful statement: those shadow-garments, but of marvelous shadow: the everyday hand-garments of children now indicating the invisible, water-walking feet of miraculous, real creatures, the world of nature observed and lived and recorded and transfigured for oneself as the sun transfigures the position of the water-bug: those shadow-feet, those mittens, on the beautiful fact, the bright rock.

NOTES

[1]David Jones, *The Anathemata* (London: Faber & Faber, 1952), p. 9.

[2]Lionel Johnson, cited by Ezra Pound in *Literary Essays of Ezra Pound*, edited by T. S. Eliot (New York: New Directions, 1968), p. 362.

[3]Basil Bunting, *Collected Poems* (Oxford: Oxford University Press, 1978), p. 31.

[4]Ezra Pound, *The Cantos of Ezra Pound* (New York: New Directions, 1970), p. 800.

[5]Hugh Kenner, "Pound, Ezra (Weston Loomis)," in *Contemporary Poets of the English Language*, edited by Rosalie Murphy (Chicago: St. James Press, 1970), p. 872.

[6]Pierre Reverdy, *Le Gant de crin* (Paris: Librairie Plon, 1927), p. 32.

[7]John Updike, cited by Stanley Edgar Hyman in *The Critic's Credentials* (New York: Atheneum, 1978), p. 111.

[8]Henry James, *The Portable Henry James*, edited by Morton Dauwen Zabel (New York: Viking, 1951), p. 426.

[9]Yvor Winters, *In Defense of Reason* (New York: Swallow Press / Morrow, 1947), p. 480.

[10]Randall Jarrell, *The Third Book of Criticism* (New York: Farrar, Straus & Giroux, 1965), p. 304.

[11]Pound, *The Cantos*, p. 491.

[12]Pound, *Personae* (New York: New Directions, 1949), p. 131.

[13]Katherine Anne Porter, *The Collected Essays* (New York: Delacorte, 1970), p. 40.

[14]Delmore Schwartz, *Selected Essays*, edited by Donald A. Dike and David H. Zucker (Chicago: University of Chicago Press, 1970), pp. 109-110.

[15]Pound, *The Cantos*, p. 251.

[16]Schwartz, p. 111.

[17]J. B. Priestley, *Literature and Western Man* (New York: Harper, 1960), pp. 406-407.

IMAGINATION AND PAIN

Virginia Woolf once observed that it is

> strange indeed that illness has not taken its place with love and battle and jealousy among the prime themes of literature. Novels, one would have thought, would have been devoted to influenza; epic poems to typhoid; odes to pneumonia; lyrics to toothache. But no; with a few exceptions . . . literature does its best to maintain that its concern is with the mind; that the body is a sheet of glass through which the soul looks straight and clear, and, save for one or two passions such as desire and greed, is null, and negligible and nonexistent. On the contrary, the very opposite is true. All day, all night the body intervenes.

Figure it: a young English writer-biologist lies dying—dying for years—of disseminated sclerosis, which deadens him inch by inch. He has kept a kind of journal since he was a child, and recently he has also written a few essays, some of them printed in local periodicals, a number of scientific papers, a good many letters. But by the time he is twenty-eight or nine it is quite apparent to him that he is going to die, and that nothing can be done about it. The body has intervened. He decides to live all-out—or at least insofar as his limited mobility will let him—to marry, to have children, and to do whatever he can as a writer.

> I might be Captain Scott writing his last words amid Antarctic cold and desolation. It is very cold. I am sitting hunched up by the fire in my lodgings after a meal of tough meat and cold apple tart. I am full of self-commiseration—my only pleasure now. It is very cold and I cannot get warm—try as I will.
>
> My various nervous derangements take different forms. This time my peripheral circulation is affected, and the hand, arm and shoulder are permanently cold. My right

> hand is blue—tho' I've shut up the window and piled up a roaring fire. It's Antarctic cold and desolation. London in November from the inside of a dingy lodging house can be very terrible indeed. This celestial isolation will send me out of my mind. I marvel how God can stick it—lonely, damp, and cold in the clouds. That is how I live too—but I am not God.

The only large possibility for his writing is the journal, and he begins to edit it, add to it, change it. He works on style, presentation, metaphor, self-analysis, psychodrama. Later, when the journal begins to take on the lineaments of an existence-justification, he remarks, with the *brio* of the talented and dying that, "The world has always gagged and suppressed me. Now I turn and hit it in the belly."

After three years he does indeed die, but before that happens he has seen his book, *The Journal of a Disappointed Man*, through the press and into the hands of the public. It is variously praised and attacked (H. G. Wells, for example, called it the work of "an egotistical young naturalist"). The slight notoriety pleases him, there on his truckle bed in the nursing home.

He has killed himself off in the *Journal*, but lives on in the actual and tormented flesh for another two years after its appearance. His gentle, faithful brother, Arthur Cummings, gets hold of all the miscellaneous jottings that aren't in the *Journal* and publishes them after Bruce's death as *A Last Diary*. Bruce has instructed him to end all his writings, with the Hamlet quote "The rest is silence," and he obeys.

Silence indeed; it is a true story, and it ended on the final day of 1919.

Issued under the pseudonym of W. N. P. Barbellion (the initials with heartbreaking bravado standing for Wilhelm Nero Pilate), the journals and diaries are among the most depressing books ever written. Sickness, particularly excruciating, wasting, humiliating sickness, is very hard for the reader to live with for long; the feeling of identification with the sufferer is too powerful, too unsettling: the beholder cringes from the opportunity to batten on his own hypochrondria.

And yet, never has a slow death been so lively as this one! Barbellion was not merely *interested* in things; he was absolutely enchanted by anything and everything created by an Agency other than man. Even more than Blake, he was entitled to say "everything that lives is holy." He was completely self-educated, and made of himself a good enough biologist to win scholarships and museum jobs over hundreds of candidates trained specifically for the examinations. And in the pages of the *Journal* we encounter what surely must be the ideal scientific attitude of all time. Wonder, knowledge and love are Barbellion's tools. Every sentence pulsates with inquisitive vitality, and it is not the febrile and panic-stricken overresponsiveness of the moribund. The effect of his writings is of abundant and delighted accessibility, openness of an almost sexual intimacy with the sheer miraculous facts of nature whose intricacies and *actual* workings must be understood for the witness to be able to grasp the full wonder. Barbellion dissected Sea Urchins in joy, humming Brahms as he dealt in the difficult specifics of awe.

> Dissected the Sea Urchin (*Echinus esculentus*). Very excited over my first view of Aristotle's Lantern. These complicated pieces of animal mechanism never smell of musty age—after aeons of evolution. When I open a Sea Urchin and see the Lantern, or dissect a Lamprey and cast eyes on the branchial basket, such structures strike me as being as finished and exquisite as if they had just a moment before been tossed me fresh from the hands of the Creator. They are fresh, young, they smell new.

He felt "in there" with all living, created things.

> How I hate the man who talks about the "brute creation," with an ugly emphasis on *brute*. Only Christians are capable of it. As for me, I am proud of my close kinship with other animals. I take a jealous pride in my Simian ancestry. I like to think I was once a magnificent hairy fellow living in the trees and that my frame has come down through geological time *via* sea jelly and worms and Amphioxus, Fish, Dinosaurs and Apes. Who would exchange these for the pallid couple in the Garden of Eden?

We see all this energy cut back, cut down, as the disease widens and deepens. Naturally enough, Barbellion spends more and more time thinking about his body and its condition, but it is not egotism. The point—to *him*—is not just that he is dying: he is dying of definite causes that produce definite symptoms: he is a scientist as well as a strong, restless spirit whose clay house is crumbling; he becomes his own experimental subject, and with humor as well as detachment. The nursing home has no one like him.

> May 24th, 1919—My legs have to be tied down to the bed with a rope. A little girl staying here lends me her skipping rope.

And earlier,

> November 26th, 1918—My old nurse lapses into bizarre malapropisms. She is afraid that the Society for the *Propagation* of Cruelty to Animals will find fault with the way we house our hens; for boiling potatoes she prefers to use the camisole (casserole)!
>
> . . . Yesterday, in the long serenity of a dark winter's night, with a view to arouse my interest in life, she went and brought some heirloom treasures from the bottom of her massive trunk—some coins of George I. "Of course, they're all obsolute now," she said. "What! Absolutely obsolute?" I inquired in surprise. The Answer was in the informative.

As pervasive as it is throughout these two books, disease is not the salient fact about them. That fact is Barbellion's mind, with its fascinated, unsatisfied, enthusiastic imagination. At no time does one have the sense of dealing with exacerbated, done-in nerves producing last-ditch insights. The writer-reader encounter has to do with an abundant sensibility grievously taxed by chance and body-chemistry, and with a stranger's awakening; a combination which makes a remarkable, shared thing of courage and imagination on the sick man's part and sympathy on the reader's.

Certainly Barbellion's work is depressing. But it is a depression out of which you leap, straight up, and higher than ever. This odd, intelligent fellow is better than anyone you know. He will help.

> June 1st, 1919—Rupert Brooke said that the brightest thing in the world was a leaf with the sun shining on it. God pity his ignorance! The brightest thing in the world is a Ctenophore in a glass jar standing in the sun.

And there it is; the man has taken the trouble to know. The little sea-beast has become a sacramental emblem. A Ctenophore, according to the *American Heritage Dictionary*, is "any of various marine animals of the phylum Ctenophora having transparent gelatinous bodies bearing eight rows of comb-like cilia used for locomotion. . . ."

We might rechristen the Ctenophore Barbellion's Amulet, taking it from a tidal pool, as he did: a tiny fragment of sun-enhancing radiance, and alive.

THE WEATHERED HAND AND SILENT SPACE*

In the excitement of young men coming together to form a new group of poets—later to be known as the Nashville Fugitives—Allen Tate wrote to Donald Davidson in 1924 of the latest and youngest Fugitive, Robert Penn Warren, "That boy's a wonder—has more sheer genius than any of us; watch him: His work from now on will have what none of us can achieve—power." That estimate was accurate then, and it has, as they say in the South, "proved out" several hundred times over in poetry as well as in remarkable fiction.

The source of Warren's stunning power is *angst*, a kind of radiant metaphysical terror, projected outward into the natural world, particularly into its waiting waste expanses: open field, ocean, desert, mountain range, or the constellations as they feed into the eye a misshapen, baffling and yearning mythology bred on nothingness. He is direct, scathingly honest, and totally serious about what he feels, and in approach is as far as can be imagined from, say, Mallarmé, who urged poets to "give the initiative to *words*." Warren gives the initiative to the experience, and renders himself wide open to it. He is not someone who "puts a pineapple together," as Wallace Stevens does, constructing its existence by multiple perceptions, by possibility and caprice rather than by felt necessity; he is not interested in the "ephemeras of the tangent," but in the unanswered sound of his heart, under the awesome winter presence of the hunter Orion.

He plunges as though compulsively into the largest of subjects: those that seem to cry out for capitalization and afflatus and, more often than not in the work of many poets, achieve only the former. To state things in this fashion may make it seem almost necessary to charge Warren with being rhetorical in some kind of wrong way, and

*Robert Penn Warren, *Being Here: Poetry 1977-1980* (New York: Random House, 1980)

indeed in his on-going intensity he does not escape some of the implications of the charge. Balzac said to a friend bent on Art that the truth is emphatically *not* in the nuance, but what matters in a piece of writing is that it "possess a force that carries everything before it." This Warren certainly has. He is a poet of enormous courage, with a highly individual intelligence; he is fully aware of the Longinian pit that yawns for those who strive for Sublimity and fail to attain it. Precariously in balance, he walks straight out over the sink-hole of Bombast; his native element is risk, and his chief attribute, daring.

The odd tone—utterly Warren's—is compounded of southern dialect, Elizabethanisms overstaying into country speech ("set foot") and always present in rural areas where mountains have gathered and preserved them, and a sometimes rather quaintly old-fangled scholastic vocabulary. The life-beat of the lines is predominantly Anglo-Saxon, as one can see—no; hear—as soon as the first hard stresses fall into place beside each other, and continue, as in "Recollection in Upper Ontario, From Long Before":

> Zack's up, foot's out! Or is it? A second she's standing,
> Then down—now over both rails—
> Down for good, and the last
> Thing I see is his hands out. To grab her, I reckoned.
> Time stops like no-Time. . . .

I like to imagine Warren's reading, and approving, Phelps Putnam's request that the god Chance "make us tough and mystical." Warren is very tough, with the farmer's hard, work-cramped hand everywhere over the field of the page, and he is also very mystical, particularly when he turns toward the great, contemplative expanses: broad fields, the sea hazing with curvature, deserts that do the same, or rise and dissolve into mountains, themselves half-in half-out of reality, stars—spread patterns of total emptiness—blinding vistas of snow and ice, as when Warren is "Snowshoeing Back to Camp in Gloaming":

> So I stood on that knife-edge frontier
> Of Timelessness, knowing that yonder

Ahead was the life I might live
Could I but move
Into the terror of unmarred whiteness under
The be-nimbed and frozen sun.

Warren is a speaker who "alone has returned": a voice out of primitive starkness, with his only defenses—and these only occasionally usable—a gallows wit, scatological irony. He is above all a man who looks, and refuses to look away.

The best time to read Warren is at night. That is when the heart's sheer physicality is most deeply felt, most inescapable, most inexplicable. Night is the time when great distances can live for the beholder, and be lived by him; when the blood and the stars have relevance to each other. Despite three hundred-odd years of "progress," things may yet turn out to be as the physician William Harvey had them, when he said: "There is a spirit, a certain force, inherent in the blood, acting superiorly to the powers of the elements . . . and the nature, yea, the soul in this spirit and blood is identical with the nature of the stars." The Warren of this book is starry-blooded, a night-walker, a night-watcher, a searcher lying motionless. And perhaps this is the best Warren of all, remembering other nights, darknesses, a cave from his childhood, in his "Speleology":

Years later, past dreams I have lain
In darkness and heard the depth of interminable song.
And hand laid to heart, have once again thought: *This is me.*
And thought: *Who am I?* And hand on heart, wondered
What it would be like to be, in the end, part of all.

And in the darkness have even asked: *Is this all? What is all?*

It is his ability to state psychic dilemmas of this kind, and in this way—the grim, exalting light of self-education shining through the thick, correct, and sanctioned Other books onto the actual world—in a homecrafted idiom as sinewy as it is unforeseeable, that makes Warren the passionate and memorable artist that he is, and the greatest of our "impure" poets. If Wallace Stevens—to take Warren's most notable and obvious opposite—is "pure," Warren is impure; if Stevens changes reality by changing the angle of his eye, Warren fixes himself into it in wonder, horror, loathing, joy, but above all with unflinching involvement; if Stevens plays with it, tames it and "understands" it, Warren encounters it nakedly, and without pretense, dallying, or skillful frivolity.

Once, in connection with a movie I was engaged in making, I met with the film director Sam Peckinpah in London to talk over possibilities. Although, as it turned out, he did not direct my story, I remember that as we parted he said to me, "Don't worry; everything'll be all right. No matter what happens, we're both trying to do the same thing. I do it with the pictures I put up on the screen, you do it with your words, but it's all the same: We're trying to give them images they can't forget." I have come to think of this, now, not in relation to movies, but as a characteristic of Robert Penn Warren's poems; they have given many such images to me. John Berryman asks of Stevens, "Why does he not wound?" No one would ever pose such a question in Warren's case. He wounds deeply, and he connects deeply; he strikes in at blood-level and gut-level, with all the force and authority of time, darkness and distance themselves, and of the Nothingness beyond nothingness, which may even be God: Pascal's "infinite spaces" laid—or laid open—on the farmer's page.

THE UNREFLECTING SHIELD
F. Scott Fitzgerald's Poetry

Poetry is either something that lives like fire inside you—like music to the musician or Marxism to the Communist—or else it is nothing, an empty formalized bore . . . The Grecian Urn *is unbearably beautiful with every syllable as inevitable as the notes in Beethoven's Ninth Symphony or it's just something you don't understand. It is what it is because an extraordinary genius paused at that point in history and touched it. . . .*

Knowing those things very young and granted an ear, one could scarcely ever afterwards be unable to distinguish between gold and dross in what one read.

This is eloquent; one believes it, and is moved. Scott Fitzgerald said it to his daughter in a letter written in the last year of his life; it is one indication of his involvement with poetry and of his belief in the use of poetry—read, memorized, revered—as a criterion by which imaginative language is to be measured. Matthew Arnold had no better notion of the touchstone; no, nor as good.

But there is a mystery about Fitzgerald's own verse, and one enters it by asking the most obvious question that his work in verse demands. Why aren't the poems better? Really, why aren't they? Granted that more than half of the pieces collected here are juvenilia, and mainly consist of song lyrics, musical comedy doggerel, and rhyming banter of a personal nature, there are still a good many poems that were seriously intended, and most of these are no better, or very little. One notes in passing, also, that even after he had done with college shows, Fitzgerald continued to write scrappily in this idiom, which indicates a perennial fascination with the externals and superficialities of poetic form, a great deal of the time tending toward glibness, and worse still the kind of period glibness that dates rapidly—what we would now call cutesy or even smart-ass. Nothing is more depressing than this, surely, and seldom has a greatly gifted writer been more unfortunately served by a medium he revered and trusted.

It is quite probable that Fitzgerald's unfortunate emphasis on received form was a result of his friendship with John Peale Bishop, an elegant, skillful, derivative but sometimes genuinely valuable poet, who understood Fitzgerald's gift very early and is an exact and imaginative commentator, though an indifferent model.

> None had such promise then, and none
> Your scapegrace wit or your disarming grace;
> For you were bold as was Danaë's son,
> Conceived like Perseus in a dream of gold.
> And there was none when you were young, not one,
> So prompt in the reflecting shield to trace
> The glittering aspect of a Gorgon age.

The verse of Fitzgerald's college days, that seriously intended as poetry, is even more painfully derivative than most such. The main influences are those of the Nineties, Wilde and especially Dowson. Swinburne is heavily and rhythmically present, and, oddly enough, Kipling. The influence of Bishop also surely accounts for the echoes of Verlaine—from translations. Bishop, a thoughtful, better educated, and consciously literary young man, was much influenced by then-current fashions, mainly by the French symbolists as popularized by Arthur Symons, and thus by their expatriate American followers like Ezra Pound and T. S. Eliot. This was unfortunate for Fitzgerald, as evidenced by his attempts to write in the more exercise-like modes of Verlaine and Moréas. When he became more sophisticated and read Eliot and Rimbaud rather than Swinburne and Dowson and cribs of Verlaine, you would think, given his extraordinary literary intelligence and the superb tact of the word-choices in his fiction, Fitzgerald's gift for verse would deepen and solidify, and that the verse would have some chance of turning into real poetry; yet except in the case of a few isolated lines this did not happen. Again, one wonders.

Is there such a thing as lyric insight? If so, what is it? Fitzgerald himself, in his definitions for Sheila Graham, seems to limit the meaning of lyric to that of song, or words in some kind of song-situation. I would suggest another interpretation, perhaps one more useful in defining Fitzgerald's essential talent. The lyric instinct is out of time, timeless: a kind of immobilization, a penetration into an instant of perception, fixed in words that illuminate the perception and make it possible in terms of those words and those only. I suggest that the best of Fitzgerald, mainly in the prose, but to some small extent also in the poems, has the quality of penetration and memorability that we associate with lyric success. In his use it has what I am tempted to call a "heartbreak" quality, in which a delicate irony and a kind of intelligent ruefulness are balanced by a strong sense that circumstances, given these people and these events, could not be otherwise. Fitzgerald's best phrases have these characteristics, and they come out of the scenes of his novels, such as that in which the ruined Dick Diver blesses the Riviera Beach:

> "I must go," he said. As he stood up he swayed a little; he did not feel well anymore—his blood raced slow. He raised his right hand and with a papal cross he blessed the beach from the high terrace. Faces turned upward from several umbrellas.

One finds good things of this kind on almost every page of Fitzgerald's novels, stories and sketches: the description of the curtains calming-down when the windows are closed in the Buchanan living room and the roll-call of the colors of Gatsby's shirts, and Dick Diver's interpretation of the World War I battlefield in *Tender Is the Night*, which ought to convince anyone of the truth of Coleridge's dictum that the most valid test of poetic power in a writer is his ability to write well about events in which he has not participated.

> See that little stream? We could walk to it in two minutes. It took the British a month to walk to it—a whole empire walking very slowly, dying in front and pushing forward behind. And another empire walked very slowly backward a few inches a day, leaving the dead like a million bloody rugs.

Fitzgerald's lyricism is deeply embedded in a sense of drama, and to employ it he has need of situations in which the drama has been built up by the preceding interaction between people. This approach needs development, it needs characters, it needs a setting, it needs length, and the drama—and in his case the penetration of lyric intuition—depends on these elements: the elements, the materials of fiction. The paradox is this: that Fitzgerald's lyric gift, his gift of the heartbreak phrase, the unforgettable, intrinsically poetic choice of words, needed not the structures and formal manipulations peculiar to versification, but those of the novel and the story. The notebooks give much evidence of this. Indeed, many of these observations, intended to be worked into fictional situations, are better than anything in these poems. "Stifling as curtain dust" is one example, and there are others.

These poems are the concretions of an extraordinarily perceptive, wry, slightly sardonic and highly self-conscious mind, poetic in its intuitive verbal grasp, its individual linguistic apprehension of reality, but committed to the craft of verse in only an obvious and superficial way, and seemingly not more than slightly aware of the real expressive potentialities of verse form; not aware enough, in any case, to work out the embodiment of its sensibility on those terms.

One might conclude, then, that Fitzgerald's work here, his random reflections, verse-letters, jokes, momentary satires, parodies and song lyrics, as well as his attempts at "serious" poetry, were, if not exactly a tragic waste of time, then a more or less complete one. But though there is some truth in this assumption, it leaves out of account things worth considering. To begin with, the evidences of an unusual mind are never completely worthless, no matter whether the mind is in its true groove or out of it. It is of course saddening that a medium which Fitzgerald loved did as much to hide his gift as any form of composition might be expected to do; it is disconcerting to find so very little of sustained value in an idiom in which a gifted man placed so much importance. That is part of the bafflement of Fitzgerald, but it is an important part. Yet here too, even in the corny lyrics, the private jokes for friends (in one of these he calls Gary Cooper "the tall muleskinner," which is better than perfect), the curious telegrams and communiques like some private code, there are occasional random sparks of the uniquely Fitzgeraldian insight. Beneath everything here, even the most trivial, there is the flicker of a fine unmistakable consciousness, and one could do worse—a lot worse—than to give each item the attention reserved for the inimitable. "It is what it is because an extraordinary genius paused at that point in history and touched it."

BLOOD ZERO

"Primeval" is a word often used to describe Jack London's work, his attitude toward existence, and his own life. From the beginning of the intensive self-education he undertook early in his adolescence through the end of his life at the age of forty, he prided himself on his "animality," and identified with his chosen totem beast, the wolf. His gullible friend, the California poet George Sterling, called him Wolf, he referred to his wife as Mate-Woman, named his ill-fated mansion in the Sonoma Valley Wolf House, and created his most memorable human character, Wolf Larsen, in *The Sea Wolf*. Larsen exemplifies all of the characteristics London admired most: courage, resourcefulness, ruthlessness, and above all, a strength of will that he partly bases on that of Milton's Satan in *Paradise Lost*. Larsen's favorite lines from Milton are "To reign is worth ambition, though in hell:/Better to reign in hell than serve in heaven," a sentiment with which London certainly concurred.

This attitude toward the *figure* of the wolf—a kind of Presence, an image, a symbolic and very personal representation of a mythologized human being—is pervasive throughout all of London's Arctic tales and is implied in many of his other fictions. The reader should willingly give himself over to this interpretation of the wolf, and conjure the animal up in the guise of the mysterious, shadowy and dangerous figment that London imagines it to be. We should encounter the Londonian wolf as we would a spirit symbolic of the deepest forest, the most extremely high and forbidding mountain range, the most desolate snowfield: in short, as the ultimate wild creature, supreme in savagery, mystery and beauty.

The mythic wolf that London "found" in his single winter spent in the Canadian North during the Klondike Gold Rush of 1897-98 and imbued with strangeness and ferocity bears in fact little resemblance to any true wolf ever observed. In studies by biologist Adolph Murie and researchers like L. David Mech and Boyce

Rensberger, the wolf emerges as a shy and likable animal with a strong aversion to fighting. There is no evidence that any wild wolf has ever killed a human being in North America. As Rensberger notes, "It has a rather playful, friendly nature among its fellows. Research findings to date show wolves to exhibit many of the behavioral patterns that should find favor among the more sentimentally inclined animal lovers."

And yet London's wolf is very much a part of the consciousness of many people, and as the wolf's habitat continues to shrink under the pressure of oil pipelines and other industrial encroachments, its mystery and its savage spirituality increase, now that vulnerability has been added. We need London's mythical wolf almost as much as we need the wildernesses of the world, for without such ghost-animals from the depths of the human subconscious we are alone with ourselves.

That Jack London, the Klondike, the wolf and the dog should have come together in exactly the circumstances that the gold-fever afforded seems not so much a merely fortunate conjunction of events but a situation tinged strongly with elements of predestination, of fate. Born in poverty only a little above the truly abject, London displayed almost from the beginning such a will to dominate as might have been envied by Satan himself, or for that matter, by Milton. His early years were spent as a boy criminal, specializing in the piracy of oyster beds in San Francisco Bay, as a tramp on the roads and railroads of the United States and Canada, and as a laborer—or what he called a work-beast—in various menial and humiliating jobs, which fixed his mind irrevocably in favor of the exploited working classes and against any and all forms of capitalism, at least in theory.

During his later travels and his battles for survival in the economic wilderness, he came quickly to the belief that knowledge is indeed power. In his case, knowledge was more than the simple and too-abstract word "power" implied; it was muscle, blood, teeth, and stamina; it gave the force and direction that the will must take. When he landed in the Yukon in 1897, he had already read, with virtually superhuman voraciousness, hundreds of books and articles, principally in the fields of sociology, biology, and philosophy. He was alive with ideas and a search for ultimate meaning that amounted to an obsessively personal quest, and shared with the pre-Socratic philosophers—Thales, who assumed that water is the basic substance; Anaximenes, who believed the same thing of air; Anaximander, with his space or "boundlessness"; and Heraclitus, with process and fire—a belief that the great All is single and can be known. As he moved farther into the winter wilderness of the northern latitudes, he came increasingly to the conclusion that the "white silence" of the North is the indifferently triumphant demonstration of the All, the arena where the knowable Secret could most unequivocally be apprehended and, as the conditions demanded, lived. The snowfields, mountains, forests and enormous frozen lakes were to London only the strictest, most spectacular and unarguable symbols of the universal abyss, the eternal mystery at the heart of nothingness, or the eternal nothingness at the heart of mystery, as Herman Melville saw it in *Moby Dick*.

> Is it that by its [whiteness's] indefiniteness it shadows forth the heartless voids and immensities of the universe, and thus stabs us from behind with the thought of annihilation, when beholding the white depths of the milky way? Or is it that as in essence whiteness is not so much a color as the visible absence of color, and at the same time the concrete of all colors; is it for these reasons that there is such a dumb blankness, full of meaning, in a wide landscape of snows—a colorless, all-color of atheism from which we shrink?

London's whiteness, though its similarities of meaning are strikingly close to Melville's, has also some basic differences.

> A vast silence reigned over the land. The land itself was a desolation, lifeless, without movement, so lone and cold that the spirit of it was not even that of sadness. There was a hint in it of laughter, but of a laughter more terrible than any sadness—a laughter that was mirthless as the smile of the Sphinx, a laughter cold as the frost and partaking of the grimness of infallibility. It was the masterful and incommunicable wisdom of eternity laughing at the futility of life and the effort of life. It was the Wild, the savage, frozen-hearted Northland Wild.

London's scattered but deeply *felt* reading had so imbued him with Darwinian principles that he looked on the landscape of the Yukon as a kind of metaphysical arena in which natural selection and the survival of the fittest were enacted unendingly, illustrating (though to no perceiver but the casual) the "Law." The North is a background that determines character and action, bringing out in men certain qualities from the psychic depths of the race of all living beings. London does not attempt, as Melville does, to strike through the "mask." The "mask" in London's tales is more the classic mask of the actor, the mask that each participant feels rising to his face from the setting of the drama, the frozen features that *rerum natura* has always reserved for it.

As George Orwell has remarked, London's instincts "lay toward acceptance of a 'natural aristocracy' of strength, beauty and talent." Few writers have dwelt with such fixation on superlatives: "the strongest," "the biggest," "the handsomest," "the most cunning," "the fiercest," "the most ruthless." One cannot read these stories without agreeing with Orwell that "there is something in London [that] takes a kind of pleasure in the whole cruel process. It is not so much an approval of the harshness of nature, as a mystical belief that nature *is* like that. 'Nature red in tooth and claw.' Perhaps fierceness is the price of survival. The young slay the old, the strong slay the weak, by an inexorable law." London insists, as Melville does not, that there is a morality inherent in the twin drives of animal evolution; brute survival and the desire of the species to reproduce itself are not primary but exclusive motivations.

In this savage theater of extremes, the vast stage of indifference, where "the slightest whisper seemed sacrilege," London felt himself to be a man speaking out of the void of cosmic neutrality and even to it and for it, wearing, really, no mask but his half-frozen face, from which issued in steam and ice the truth of existence: the way things are.

The actors are men and dogs.

> Down the frozen waterway toiled a string of wolfish dogs. Their bristly fur was rimed with frost. Their breath froze in the air as it left their mouths, spouting forth in spumes of vapor that settled upon the hair of their bodies and formed

> into crystals of frost. Leather harness was on the dogs. . . .
> In advance of the dogs, on wide snowshoes, toiled a man. At the rear of the sled toiled a second man. On the sled, in the box, lay a third man whose toil was over—a man whom the Wild had conquered and beaten down until he would never move nor struggle again. It is not the way of the Wild to like movement.

In the Arctic and particularly in the Gold Rush Arctic, the dog was of paramount importance. Men could not cover the great distances involved, much less carry their food and equipment, on foot. There were as yet no machines, not even railroads. Horses would have bogged down hopelessly in the snow and could not have lived off the food, such as fish, that the environment supplied. The solution to the finding and mining of gold was the dog, because of its physical qualifications, its adaptability, and even its kinship to other creatures occupying the "natural" scheme of things in which it was to function.

London's anthropomorphizing of animals is well known, and the instances in which he overindulges this tendency are frequent and sometimes absurd. He was no Rilke or Lawrence, seemingly able to project his own human point of observation into another entity, either living or inorganic, and *become* the contemplated Other. He could not and certainly would not have wanted to know, as Aldous Huxley said Lawrence did, "by personal experience, what it was like to be a tree or a daisy or a breaking wave or even the mysterious moon itself. He could get inside the skin of an animal and could tell you in the most convincing detail how it felt and how, dimly, inhumanly, it thought." London had no wish to negate himself in favor of becoming an animal; the London dog or wolf is presented not as itself but as London feels that *he* would feel if he were embodied in the form of a dog or a wolf. The self-dramatizing Nietzschean is always very much present. In the canine battle scenes, for example, London analyzes with an almost absurd and quite human confidence the various "tactics" employed by the participants.

> But Buck possessed a quality that made for greatness—imagination. He fought by instinct, but he could fight by head as well. He rushed, as though attempting the old

> shoulder trick, but at the last instant swept low to the snow and in. His teeth closed on Spitz's left fore leg. There was a crunch of breaking bone, and the white dog faced him on three legs. Thrice he tried to knock him over, then repeated the trick and broke the right fore leg.

Anyone who has ever seen dogs fighting knows that such subtleties as "the old shoulder trick" do not occur; if the affair is not merely one of a good deal of threatening noise, then one dog just goes for the other in any way possible. When London describes what dogs *do* rather than what they "think"—how they *look* when listening, how they appear when in repose, how they pace when restless or hungry—he is very good. When he makes a primitive philosopher of the dog in the same sense in which the author is himself a primitive philosopher, the result is less convincing. One believes of Bâtard that in five years "he heard but one kind word, received but one soft stroke of a hand, and then he did not know what manner of things they were." It is quite conceivable that a dog that had never received such treatment would not know how to respond. On the other hand, Buck's mystique of racial fulfillment, his metaphysical musculature, are so plainly impossible that one is tempted to forgo passages like:

> He was sounding the deeps of his nature, and of the parts of his nature that were deeper than he, going back into the womb of Time. He was mastered by the sheer surging of life, the tidal wave of being, the perfect joy of each separate muscle, joint, and sinew in that it was everything that was not death, that it was aglow and rampant, expressing itself in movement, flying exultantly under the stars and over the face of dead matter that did not move.

Likewise, White Fang's encounter with the Californian electric streetcars "that were to him colossal screaming lynxes" is not the product of a first-rate imagination. London merely knew that, since White Fang had lived in the Arctic and lynxes also lived there, and since lynxes sometimes make noises and streetcars also make them, he could feel justified in combining these items in a figure of speech the reader would be inclined to take as reasonable because neither reader nor lynx nor London nor streetcars could prove it was not. A moment's reflection, however, should disclose how far-fetched the image is; the dog would simply have been bothered by the utter *unfamiliarity* of the machine, would simply have apprehended it as a large noise-making *something*, though assuredly no lynx.

White Fang was conceived as a "complete antithesis and companion piece to *The Call of the Wild*." London averred that "I'm going to reverse the process. Instead of the devolution or decivilization of a dog, I'm going to give the evolution, the civilization of a dog—development of domesticity, faithfulness, love, morality, and all the amenities and virtues." Yet, why is *White Fang*—more than twice as long as *The Call of the Wild* and a good deal more virtue-bent in the human sense of intention, a story in which the animal protagonist ends not as the leader of a pack of wild wolves but crooning his "love-growl" amidst a chorus of city women rubbing his ears and calling him the Blessed Wolf—why is it so markedly inferior to the story of reversion? Largely, I think, because the events depicted in *The Call of the Wild* are closer to what one *wants* to see happen: because we desire the basic, the "natural," the "*what is*" to win and not the world of streetcars and sentimentalism that we have made. Thus, in a sense, if we accede to London's narrative we also are approving of God and his white, mocking malevolence, his "Law" maintaining sway over all the irrelevances and over-subtleties of mechanized life. We like the author for putting the perspective in this way, and especially in a way as forthright, inexorable, exciting and involving as he commands.

The key to London's effectiveness is to be found in his complete absorption in the world he evokes. The author is *in* and committed to his creations to a degree very nearly unparalleled in the composition of fiction. The resulting go-for-broke, event-intoxicated, headlong wild-Irish prose-fury completely overrides a great many stylistic lapses and crudities that would ordinarily cause readers to smile. As Orwell notes, "the texture of the writing is poor, the phrases are worn and obvious, and the dialogue is erratic."

True, but it is nonetheless also true that London has at his best the ability to involve the reader in his story so thoroughly that nothing matters but *what* happens; in this sense he is basic indeed. His primary concern is action, with no pause to allow the savoring of verbal nuances or subtleties of insight. "La vérité, c'est dans la nuance," said Flaubert. London would have left that notion behind in the dog blood crystallizing on the ice floc, the eddying plume of a miner's frozen breath. His style is in presenting what *is*, and that only. As a writer London is at his most compelling in "presentational immediacy"; the more the passage relates to the nerves and feelings of the body, the more effective it is.

> As he turned to go on, he spat speculatively. There was a sharp, explosive crackle that startled him. He spat again. And again, in the air, before it could fall to the snow, the spittle crackled. He knew that at fifty below spittle crackled on the snow, but this spittle had crackled in the air.

He is an artist of violent action, exemplifying what the American poet Allen Tate meant when he said: "I think of my poems as commentaries on those human situations from which there is no escape." Once caught in London's swirling, desperate, life-and-death violence, the reader has no escape either, for it is a vision of exceptional and crucial vitality. London's most characteristic tales have the graphic power of the best cinema, and I for one hope that the film medium has not exhausted such possibilities as the latest adaptations assayed seem to encourage. Be that as it may, the quintessential Jack London is in the on-rushing compulsiveness of his northern stories. Few men have more convincingly examined the connection between the creative powers of the individual writer and the unconscious drive to breed and to survive, found in the natural world.

THROUGH THE WHEAT

First of all consider the title of this novel. It is obviously the work of a poet, though perhaps one who had probably never written a line of verse. It is a war book of the most striking and moving kind, and its poetic qualities are evident everywhere from its title to its extremely matter-of-fact but sensitively realized details. The book is not called *Over the Top*, or *The Last Patrol*, usual titles for war revelations. It is called *Through the Wheat*, and that should tell us something about the attitude and ability of the author.

War comes down to practicalities. *Through the Wheat* is a vision of war that is as profound as any vision of any war has ever been, from the tribes of the caves to the ambushes of Vietnam. The spirit is the same: men trying to kill each other for well-defined reasons or undefined ones. The story is the odyssey of an individual soldier in a particular battle in World War I, but such are its implications that the effect of warfare on the individual is so universal that it extends through all time, to all places and in all histories, quite simply, as warfare. The men of the Fourth Brigade are Marines—men not very well trained for this kind of experience because this was the first war of its kind. They expected the disciplined war-practices of nineteenth-century Europe, and found themselves inescapably entrapped by a new barbarism and military chaos.

I once asked myself in a journal entry why World War I is fascinating to the people in our time. There are various possibilities, but I am not sure that any of them is satisfactory. I personally believe that it is because, in a world continually at war, *that* war is the worst war, as far as the individual soldier was concerned, ever to have been fought. There is never again likely to be a war that is so degrading, so dirty, so heartlessly tiresome and confusing and confined as that one.

Modern warfare consists of confused men handling mighty weapons. Private Hicks, an automatic rifleman, is one of these. The men of Private Hicks' company are not sure of what they are doing, or why they are doing it, but, because of modern technology coupled with the inexplicable nature of the human soul, they are loosing almighty destruction in a field of wheat: part of a farm.

These are no idealists. They are not theoreticians of war. Private Hicks would not have understood Frederick the Great on the art of war. He is a created automatic rifleman, and his destiny rests with that function. He would have no comprehension of a statement such as

> Though the actions of our hero shine with great brilliancy, they must not be imitated, except with peculiar caution. The more resplendent they are, the more easily may they seduce the youthful, headlong and angry warrior, to whom we cannot often enough repeat that valor without wisdom is insufficient, and that the adversary with a cool head, who can combine and calculate, will finally be victorious over the rash individual.

No; the men of the Fourth Brigade, United States Marine Corps, are not advancing through a wheat field by means of theory. The whole point of *Through the Wheat*, and the whole point of modern warfare, is that they do not have the slightest notion as to why they are engaged in this murderous occupation. Tennyson's "Theirs not to reason why" hovers like a crow over the wheat field through which Hicks and the others advance, being fired upon, and firing at will with awesome weapons. Thomas Boyd has caught the whole mania of modern warfare: the all-encompassing sense of power embodied in a precision-steel weapon of devastating effect on the fragile body designated as an enemy. Think of the delicate organization of a human body: the intestines, the heart, the lungs, the eyes. Think of what one of these weapons can do to such vulnerable organs. Think too of the power that men have always hungered for over the bodies of other men: such power now made possible by a single weapon in the hands of a single soldier. Also consider the fear that such destruction may be visited upon one's own body, under conditions of incomparable uncertainty and horror, and you have *Through the Wheat*.

Eye-witness novels of war are made by one of two kinds of men.

The first and most predictable of these is the writer who purports to tell the "truth" about warfare. There are many of these, and some of them have been momentarily well-known. The second kind of writer who deals with warfare is the artist: he who raises carnage to the level of vision. Such is Tolstoy, such is Stendhal, such is Stephen Crane.

And such is Thomas Boyd. He is dead now, and will never give us another book, but this one is proof enough that he was a writer of the first rank, operating in his grisly arena with the powers and truth and poetic transcendency of a master. There is no battle scene in Tolstoy's *War and Peace*, no conflict in Stendhal's account of Waterloo, to equal the drama and terror of Boyd's account of Private Hicks' advance through the wheat. It is one of those miracles of fiction that this book should exist at all: that such a sensibility as Boyd's, subjected to the roaring uncertainty of battle, should have emerged to write—be *willing* to write—a book, and that the book should be of this caliber. Crane's *The Red Badge of Courage* is a fine novel dealing with warfare, but from the standpoint of the sense of participation in a crisis situation, the identification with the participants in the horrifying experience of modern warfare, Crane's novel pales considerably beside the hot, sweaty ordeal of Boyd's protagonist. Crane may talk of cannons "arguing on distant hills." There is irony and a fine artistic detachment, but when Boyd says of Private Hicks, " 'Last night he got to talkin' to dead men, and when they didn't answer he shook them as if he thought they was alive,' " the reader comes into a new dimension.

Whether Private Hicks knows it or not, he is of the company of the mythic Eternal Warrior. What he went through, so that he tried, in the delirium of battle, not so much to awaken as to converse with the dead is the stuff of warfare in all times and in all places, among all men. As Ernest Hemingway, an Eternal Warrior himself, has said,

> When you read the account of St. Louis IX's Crusade you will see that no expeditionary force can ever have to go through anything as bad as those men endured. We have only to fight as well as the men who stayed and fought at Shiloh. It is not necessary that we should fight better. There can be no such thing as better. And no thing that can ever happen to you from the air can ever be worse than the

> shelling men lived through on the Western Front in 1916 and 1917.

But the greatness of *Through the Wheat* is in showing that a young unprepared boy, thrown into a situation in which there are terrible deaths, wounds, endless explosions, terrible smells, decomposing bodies of friends, eaten alive by lice, always hungry, can emerge from the golden deadly wheat field, his automatic rifle dangling without ammunition from his slack hand, his young eyes vacant with horror, and still find something to affirm, even though it is only the miraculous preservation of his own life. There is something human to be found there, even there, in the terrible field of wheat.

THE GEEK OF POETRY*

"The same light that had played over the stones in his hand began to play over his mind. . . . The revolution within had really begun. A new declaration of independence wrote itself within him. 'The gods have thrown the towns like stones over the flat country, but the stones have no color. They do not burn and change in the light,' he thought."

Though the small Midwestern towns of the early part of the century did not, for Sherwood Anderson's Hugh McVey in *Poor White*, "burn and change in the light," they strangely and confidently did for Nicholas Vachel Lindsay; in fact, they *were* the light, glowing with every imaginable color, giving off the odd-angled and essential glimmers of New-World "promise" from a smouldering bed-rock communality, a combustion always latent, and always—especially under Lindsay's own ministrations—capable of leaping into full, vital flame, warming, entertaining and explaining us all. His birthplace, Springfield, Illinois, was for him this quintessential town, the rapt, chanting keeper of the Christian-Populist flame, undevious and irresistible, in whose light all things look and sound as they are: obvious, clumsy, crazy, good-hearted, vigorous, outgoing, and above all, loud. Lindsay's *Golden Book of Springfield* is the Book of Books of this ideal, its Platonic frame and fire-cave.

Have we really buried foolish, half-talented, half-cracked Lindsay in the textbooks—the very oldest and most mistaken ones—of literary history? Have we settled him in the dust of provincial libraries, in the unimaginable oblivion of metropolitan bookvaults? Was there ever anything, really, in all his wandering, his "gospel of beauty," his "higher vaudeville"? In those forgotten audiences

***Selected Letters of Vachel Lindsay*, edited by Marc Chenetier (New York: Burt Franklin, 1979)

hungering for him, providing thunderous feedback for his poems? Or in his curious, exasperating, self-enchanted, canny, bulldozing and somehow devilish innocence? Can any of him be saved, or is it better to move on: on even farther?

When one arouses Lindsay's shade, as Mr. Chenetier devotedly has done, four main settings rise with it: "The road," the carnival sideshow, "zeal" (in the eighteenth-century religious sense) and mass hypnosis. Secondarily, there came ambition, the question of sincerity, then failure, suicide, and the particular kind of sadness attendant on the sickening-away of exuberance, as well as the equally sad one of bearing witness to a well-meant put-on that goes on too long. The flim-flam man is fun only while you are not yet on to his game. But not much even then, and none at all when you are.

It seems to me, however, that Lindsay's career and example raise some interesting—if not exactly crucial—questions about the relation of the poet and his audience, and also about the desirability and danger of self-delusion in the artist. I have always felt that Lindsay provided a kind of focus by means of which we might, if we so chose, gauge such questions and to some extent resolve them, each privately. But beyond a few superficial assumptions gleaned from the authors'-notes of anthologies, I had never, before reading these letters, known much of what sort of man Lindsay actually was, or how he lived and worked. I use this last word advisedly, for Lindsay was very consciously a *worker* in the cause of his version of poetry, and for some mysterious entity he and his Campbellite mother called "art": for example, his accounts of the means he used to get his poems and graphics—"his Christian cartoons"—before a public are not only enthralling in themselves, but show a kind of crank ingenuity that is quite impressive and even heartening in its single-mindedness. One would like to have the guts, the *chutzpah*, to do some of the things he did to reach people, and these not in isolated circumstances but as a mere matter of course.

> Powlinson has decided to broaden his policy, and by his direction I took the tickets into every saloon on the route, and after asking the bartender's permission, placed a little pile of them by the cigar lighter, where men might pick

> them up as they went out. My route is over the most interesting part of New York, and the theatre section of Broadway runs across it, and the experience is rich, absolutely great. I am going to endeavor to carry all the tickets I can, and dodge the sign-painting, which wears out my soul.

One thinks, what energy! What high-minded foolishness! And in what a cause! Why, if American poetry had a thousand of *him* . . . ! The letters after these early ones are an erratic reverse Pilgrim's Progress through successive states of eroding self-delusion, a raw account of the manner in which a man of compassion and odd-ball, shamanistic insight was fashioned into a freak—or, better still, into a carnival geek. For Lindsay, what seemed at first to be the incredibly fecund native ground of the American village turned into a tangled, sterile wilderness of hamlet-studded, boob-haunted railroad track, once the mere novelty of his personal presence and his "message" had been worn off by over-exposure, until, just before his suicide in the home of his birth in "golden" Springfield, he confessed that both he and his "dream" had failed utterly, that he had wasted himself, and spoke of " . . . my best years . . . simply used up in shouting."

If I had the power, I should like very much to save Lindsay, to hold on to at least some aspects of him, if for only one reason. He lived naturally in a condition that many greater poets never had, or if they had it, were embarrassed or diffident about: a total commitment to his own powers of invention, a complete loss of himself in his materials. To his fantasies, to the absurd figures he made—not a whit more convincing than Disney's—by trying to mythologize American history and legend, he gave himself in unthinking abandon: he invited and gloried in seizure, and as a result possessed total immersion in his creative element, no matter what might be the end result. Perhaps that is not much, but perhaps it is more than we think. The best of Lindsay's poetry seems to me unique, its innocence not only real but unified and valuable. The letters, too, make available the same kind of right-or-wrong totality, the hell-with-it and *go*-with it.

> Whatever happens, the sun still shines, and every girl in this school has promised to teach me to swim next month when

> I get out of the doctor's care. I am going to learn as slowly as possible, one girl at a time.

A good foolhardy heart said that in a letter, even though it was written near its death; in it we have no difficulty in recognizing the same force, the same undiscriminating responsiveness, as that behind

> I heard Immanuel singing
> Within his own good lands,
> I saw him bend above his harp.
> I watched his wandering hands
> Lost amid the harp-strings;
> Sweet, sweet I heard him play.
> His wounds were altogether healed.
> Old things had passed away.

DEVASTATION IN THE ARROYO

Joe Simmons—no one ever called him Edgar, that I ever heard—first wrote to me when I was at Reed College in Oregon in 1963, and had had a poem called "Cherrylog Road" published in *The New Yorker*, I think it was. I remember that he claimed to know the actual place where the events of the poem had occurred, but he didn't, and neither did I, for it was fictional. That didn't matter; a correspondence ensued in which all kinds of things poured out: war experiences, his notion of alcohol as a divine form of human fuel, sex, extreme violence, delirium tremens as "a kind of glory," a fascination with music—he was a drummer, semi-professional—and above all endless frenetic pages about poetic technique. He believed in "discontinuous bursts of verbal energy," and claimed to see this in some experiments I had been doing. He sent me the manuscript of his book, *Driving to Biloxi*, in which clusters of words were similarly spaced, or as he said, "spark-gapped." From the beginning I was struck by Joe's manic governor-less energy with language; I sensed that he was an authentic—as opposed to a would-be—wild man on the page. I liked this; I still like it. Hit or miss as Joe is, when his wildness means, it *really* means. It comes to something, a something which could come only to him.

My one meeting with Joe Simmons was for three days, and they were deep and lasting ones. He had moved from the small Mississippi school from which he had first written me, and was now at the University of Texas at El Paso. At his invitation I went out there for a reading, and formed what physical memory I have of him. He was a vital, fast-aging man, seriously balding and exuberant, and every word he said to you came out of some rooted and shaken place of supreme importance. Despite his fixations—or perhaps in part because of them—he was a wonderful companion, and for a short-circuiting visionary he had a surprising interest and even influence in civic affairs. No one could have been more surprised than I when I stepped off the plane and discovered that by some means Joe had arranged for me to be "honorary mayor" of El Paso for one day, with an ornate key to the city and a date with the current Miss El Paso, a dark, humorous, diffident girl half my age with great propriety of manner and a large store of information about beauty contest competition techniques. The "date" was ostensibly for a party at Joe's house after the reading, but before that was the Visit to the Arroyo.

I went with Joe gladly to a dry creekbed, arroyo—some would call it a wash or even a gulley—down the street from his house, which was in a pleasant suburb backed by hills. Where the suburban grass gave out and the desert powder began, I sat down on the floor of the stoneless gulch with him, staring into the white crumbling wall and wondering what I was doing there. We crouched for at least half an hour, and I began to develop a fondness for a particular branch of some plant—perhaps mesquite, but probably not—which was growing sideways toward me. Out of the edge of one eye I glimpsed a lizard, but Joe did not believe in turning the head while on duty, and so I did not, and caught only that one dusty flicker from the Upper Jurassic. At what seemed to him the right time Joe got up and I with him, and we walked back to the house, beating the desert off ourselves, the conversation flooding with topics. "That's where I get all my images of velocity," Joe said. "Speed, power, movement controlled and uncontrolled. That's where I see it: on that wall: on it, through it. Everything comes right at me." He was then working on "Osiris at the Roller Derby," a poem of fortuitous craziness and a sense of imminent destruction, like a human demolition-derby presided over by myth. It came, literally, right off the wall.

I love to remember that afternoon, and Joe's curious and eloquent introduction at the reading, the guitar-and-drums we played alone in his house except for his fine-looking boy Jess, and the party, during which a bunch of us went up and sat on the hill overlooking Joe's house and out into the valley, Miss El Paso dominating the conversation with esoterica about the end-of-runway turn, ideal height-weight measurements, and something she called, with sinister exultation, "the final smile."

Before I left, Joe told me of his belief that with the help of his wife and son and poetry he had made "a real life out of the wreck of a life." But he had made more than that. I know of no poet who took more chances, and though there is a great deal of bungling in his work, the transcendent moments would not be possible without it. Simmons's poems are the quintessence of the 1950s, from World War II blues and the terrors and dread three-day pass exaltations, the disastrous sexual encounters, the alcoholic remorses, the political uncertainties; all these. They are in a sense "confessional," but they were not composed under the dark and semi-official aegis of Robert Lowell and his circle of ghoulish norns, displaying professional wounds. Simmons is larger than they, freer and more reckless, open-ended in form, metrically experimental, full of guts, willing to be wrong. He writes off the white-hot spur of the moment—seems, even, to be writing *with* spurs—and his obsessive and terrifying poems are visionary in the sense that they make hallucination exhilarating at the same time as self-murderous. They are a masterful ruinous projection of a strong, demoralized man of the American neon fifties, replete with lost weekends, dreary Hitchcock play-yards, frowzy hysterical mistresses about whom there nevertheless hovers a fitful aura of what might be real love, the glare of the U. N. going up, Paris after the dry-outs, the whole curious over-reactive life of those years so lividly painful to remember and impossible to live down. The whole of the period is not here, but in the best of Joe Simmons's jagged, searing strokes the essence of it is; his poems will last, for they are better than the materials they come from.

I have my own private joke about Joe, as I think of the ultimate judgment of writers, never delivered but always hanging over us, and of Joe's vision of speed and collision coming at him, hurtling from the soft wall of the arroyo. And think also, after dropping Miss El Paso off somewhere among the other muses, of transference, and of Joe and his other kind of beauty, with the final smile.

VISIONS IN THE INVISIBLE DIMENSION

My oldest son's ex-wife's sister, who is a professional, took part a few years ago in a group show of infrared photographs, and asked me to write something for the catalogue, and for a book to follow. She sent me a boxful of slides, and I looked at them with high interest, and wrote an introduction to a volume which the group intended to produce with money obtained from the sale of the pictures. But, though the show was evidently a critical success, not enough money resulted to finance the book, and it was never brought out. I adduce these remarks not as proof of any degree of professionalism in photography, but for what they attempt to say about the connection between artistic vision and science, particularly scientific paraphernalia.

My first experience with infrared photography was off the earth, in the air over the South Pacific, where in an earlier self (that unlikely, true dream) I was flying with a nightfighter squadron in World War II. After the missions we would run the film—infrared film—of what the gun-cameras had half-seen or dreamt: a few deadly flickers, a palsied guttering; perhaps, rarely, an unexpected distant fireball, the end of certain metal and fabric, gasoline, human lives.

That was then, and the death-cameras, I am told, have since been greatly improved, and are waiting. But the structure of light is still the same as it has been all the time, and will be: the spectrum was also waiting, from end to end, red to violet. To see the world through the camera and the long red rays—that part of light which is most penetrating, mysterious, and dark-seeing—is an experience made possible by applied science, and one falls to musing about the possibilities in the alliance between scientific techniques and art, and would doubtless continue such speculation did not these extraordinary photographs make it seem beside the point.

The places, objects and people of these photographs are seen as in an intensely clarified dream, a kind of spiritual fourth dimension; nothing beheld in this way can conceivably be insignificant. William Blake said that "We are led to believe in a lie/When we see *with* not *through* the eye." Infrared photography is another perspective of "through," a quiet and stunning revolution of vision whose scientific basis tends to be forgotten when one comes by means of it into a dispassionate Eden, a new order of spatial perception, where things are so oddly isolated and standing-forth, assured and unfathomable, that the mind has trouble adjusting to the ease and rightness of this sort of reality, with its cast of the foreordained. One is here in a relationship of superhuman cleanness and delicacy to the objects of experience, again remembering Blake: "If the doors of perception were cleansed everything would appear to man as it is, infinite." Here, deep in the red rays, is a painless, haunting clairvoyance, a new immediacy which is also timeless—weightless, tinted, mostly shadowless. Wherever the eye turns, a long-hidden long light from the Nature of Light plays starkly and subtly over Essences: which are mysteries still: unknowable, but enchanted, shown-forth, spell-answering.

BARE BONES: AFTERWORD TO A FILM

When it was first resolved that *Deliverance* would be made into a film, I was engaged to do the screenplay. Outside of two small documentaries I had written for the government when I lived in California, I had no experience of film writing, and certainly none in the area of "novel-into-film" that, together with much horrifying evidence, I had been led to believe was a kind of ossuary or elephants' graveyard of the integrity, trust, and efforts of a good many novelists, some of whom I knew.

To begin with, I had no idea of format, and I asked the functionaries of Warner Brothers to send me some sample scripts, which they did. Among these I remember *A Clockwork Orange*, which seemed unduly skimpy and altogether too easy; this sort of thing was not at all in line with what I had in mind to do. On the other hand I had been told that James Agee turned in—preliminary to the final shooting script from which the films were made—long, almost excruciatingly-detailed "treatments," which were "as good as literature." That was more like it, I thought, so I got hold of *Agee on Film*, volume 2, and read the treatments very carefully. I came up somewhat confused, though with much more of an idea of the procedure I wanted than I had had. I could not see any reason why the film script, or the treatment, should not be a valid art form in itself; I did not then and I still do not. Since the writer of screenplays, particularly in the earlier stages of the development of material, is quite literally not limited by anything, he is free to visualize in ideal terms the story as he would like to see it: that is, *his* ideals as they have always existed in connection with the story, or as they develop from instant to instant as he works. With this in mind, and with the eye of imagination making the movie I would like to see come up on the screen shot for shot, I opened my novel and began. There was no reason to suppose that the sequence of events in the book needed to be altered in any way from what it was on the page; the main concern was the transference of the essential story from one medium to another, and so the writing of the treatment became an intense and extremely stimulating sort of game in which, with a camera in the hands of God rather than those of any mortal cinematographer, I wrote the scenes one after the other as I would like to have them be, all things considered *sub specie aeternitatis*, and with completely unrestricted resources, some from the actual world and some from my mind, imagination, fancy, or somewhere else private but accessible. The story had been with me for such a long time, and I felt that I knew each detail of it with such intimacy, that nothing anyone else could do could bring a dimension of understanding to it that I could not easily better. Perhaps this sort of egomania is necessary to creation in any form, but one is particularly susceptible to it when turning one's own material from a medium which may reach a few thousand into another which may reach millions. The only thing to do, I thought, was to go ahead with the treatment on my own terms and see what happened. But the idea of creating a work in the medium of the film treatment that would stand on its own as a work of art, utilizing the techniques and qualities of the medium, underlay my intent from beginning to end. An audience capable of both reading the novel and seeing the movie was being offered two versions of the same story, and I hoped that, with luck lasting, these would strengthen, enhance, and deepen each other, so that the overall experience of *Deliverance* would be just that for the beholder or participant, and would say certain things to him. For this reason I tried to visualize every nuance, every flicker of light of every scene. I left almost nothing to the actors—to whatever actors there would be—to the director, to the cinematographer, to the sound technicians, or even to the safety crew on the river. I had Platonic, ideal working conditions, and no one to tell me what I had done wrong. I had a thousand ideas I thought not only workable but positively inspired for every scene, every camera angle, every movement, every transition, every fortissimo or diminuendo of sound, every change of chord in music, every birdcall. When I sent the completed initial screenplay to Warner Brothers, I was convinced I had put down on paper what I wanted to have happen on the screen, no matter who the director was, or the actors, or any of the rest of the crew. After all, it was my story, and no one else on earth could know it as I did.

The various details of what transpired between my starry-eyed completion of the screenplay and the actual 105 minutes of running time of the released version is not the intention of this Afterword to record. But I feel I should say what a good many other writers must have felt and some perhaps have said. The writer quickly discovers that, well-intentioned as he is, as intimately involved as he may be with his own story, or whatever commitment either artistic or emotional he may have in the transference of his material to the screen, his opinion, after a certain quickly-reached point, will not count for much. The first thing he is told by any number of people is that, though his story is "film material," and though he is supposed to have credit—or *a* credit—for the script, he himself does not "know film." Sadly this is true; he does not know film and he realizes little by little and then more by more that he is not going to learn film, either, to his or anyone else's satisfaction during the time that his story is being made.

The essentials of the writer's situation are these. First of all, he has sold his material to the film medium, and consequently and presumably to those who "know film." It is useless for him to speak of his ideas for a scene; an opening scene, say. For such and such a reason, he is told, such an idea is unfeasible. He is told that specific scenes cannot be filmed as he wishes them to be because of considerations known to the makers but unknown to him, and these are never sufficiently explained, or at least not plausibly. By the time the film begins to move into the actual production process, the writer has begun to feel like the pig in Randall Jarrell's parable of the Poet and the Critic. The filmmaker, like the Critic, like the judge of pork at the county fair, says to the pig-poet-novelist-screenwriter as he pokes him contemptuously in the ribs, "Huh! What do *you* know about pork?" Though he *is*, unfortunately, pork, the novelist can in fact find little by the way of answer. The director first, then the actors, then the technicians and other functionaries set things up to be filmed in a way which is congruent with the director's version of the dramatic and scenic possibilities of the story and whether or not this is consistent with the writer's is strictly immaterial, irrelevant, and in the end something of an embarrassment, at least to the writer. Details are changed, whole sequences are changed, dialogue is altered or improvised until, though something which resembles the original idea of the story remains, the texture, the field of nuance, the details, characterizations, dramatic buildup and resolution as originally conceived, are lost; nothing but the bones are left. The writer wanders around the set, among the bones, wondering with vague but fascinated impotence what is going to be filmed that day, what compromise or invention will be deemed necessary. There is a certain amount of interest accruing to this position, but eventually the role of faintly-embarrassing specter gets as old, predictable, and tiresome as any other, and after some time spent in this unprofitable way and after seeing his own opinions, suggestions, ideas, convictions, his notions of psychological and dramatic propriety as the first considerations to be dismissed in favor of approaches he believes not only hopelessly but even laughably inadequate, and after being given every encouragement to leave the location and the making of the picture, the writer indeed does leave and simply sits back to wait until the film plays his own local theater, where he can watch it with only a little more of an inside knowledge than those anonymous creatures of public darkness around him.

And yet I don't want to end this on such a funereal note, for as it turns out, the director, John Boorman, the actors, and the crew did, I think, their honest best to come up with what they believe is a credible film version of the novel *Deliverance*. All of them ran considerable risks, and qualify as brave and dedicated men. But the movie, enormously successful as it was and with a longevity given to few films to achieve, is not the film as I would have it. That version is still only in the wide screen of my head, and in these pages; it is still Platonic and possible; it is still in the making. And I like to think that someday, long after I have departed this and all other scenes, it will be made, with the full implications of the story restored, the delineation of character as I have indicated it, the dialogue as I have written it, and the dramatic emphases as I have placed them. I like to think that any reader or viewer who encounters this treatment of the story will enter into Plato's cave with me, will show it in the wide-screen theater of his mind, and will compare it with the version he has seen in actual theaters, or on television.

The main entity the two versions will necessarily have in common is the river itself, and here I do not believe that my imagination or anyone else's could improve on the Chattooga River used in the film, or on cinematographer Vilmos Zsigmond's handling of it. The river in the film is fully the equal of the river in the book, and the sweep and amplitude of the actual running current, the slow stretches, the cliffs, the stones, the rapids, and the force of the water are everything, in Zsigmond's handling, that I could have wished. But the psychological orientation—the *being*—of the characters, their interrelations, their talk with each other, the true dramatic progression, are only hinted at here and there. If these things were to be realized in another version of *Deliverance*, my later, true ghost—not the one that wandered apologetically and impotently through the thickets and over the clifftops of the sets of the movie—would be pleased. For anyone who wishes to imagine or "see" the film as the author wished it to be experienced, it is in the words of the original screenplay and in the imagination.

CONVERSATION ON A DOCK*
with Bill Moyers

DICKEY: I'm essentially a writer of long poems, which is a form not in favor at this time but will eventually come to be in favor, I think. What I want to do, what I try to do, is to reclaim for poetry what it used to have: to reclaim for it some of the territory that it has relinquished unnecessarily to the novel, and the short story.

MOYERS: What territory is that?

DICKEY: The narrative. Something with a narrative thrust, a story thrust. I've a new long poem coming out. I'll just read a little section of it. It's a kind of vindication of the drunken poet who tries . . . who's making one last-ditch effort to relate himself to the Universe, to the stars, to the solar system, to everything.

MOYERS: Tonight a conversation with James Dickey, a Southern boy who tells God how to rearrange the Universe.

You've got to remember that my old man
Was an astronomer, of sorts, and didn't he say the whole night sky's invented?
Well, I am now inventing. *You've* got *a crab. Right?*
How about a Lobster *up there? With a snap of two right fingers*
Cancer will whirl like an anthill   people will rise
Singing from their beds and take their wheaten children in their arms,

Who thought their parents were departing
For the hammer-clawed stars of death. They'll live

And live. A Lobster*! What an idea! An idea God never had. Listen, my God,*

*WNET, 25 January 1976.

That thing'll be great! *He's coming into my head—*
Is he inside it or out? No, *I can* see *him!*
The DT's aren't failing me: The light of Time shines on him
He's huge he's a religious fanatic
He's gone wild because he can't go to Heaven
He's waving his feelers his saw-hands
He's praying to the town clock to minutes millenia
He's praying the dial's stations of the Cross he sees me

Imagination and dissipation both fire at me
Point-blank O God, no NO I was playing I didn't mean it
I'll never write it, I swear CLAWS claws CLAWS

He's going to kill me.

MOYERS: Why did you choose to live in this particular place? Was it just an accident?

DICKEY: Well, in a way, but the main point for anybody is to come to rest somewhere: where you want to lay your bones down. When you come to my age, you have great fun composing your own epitaph.

MOYERS: Have you done that?

DICKEY: I have indeed.

MOYERS: What is it?

DICKEY: I don't want to be buried in a coffin. I don't know whether the State of Georgia or the State of South Carolina would stand still for this, but because we made a movie up on the river, the Chattooga River, what I would ideally like is to be dumped into the ground on the west bank of the Chattooga River right by the wildest of the rapids, which is a place called Woodall Shoals, and covered up . . . and have somebody to play "Dueling Banjos" over my grave, and have a very simple stone erected, maybe a woodcarved thing, that said, "James Dickey, 1923-1990 . . . or whatever it would be . . . American poet and novelist, here seeks his Deliverance."

MOYERS: James Dickey is the sum, and more, of all the

contradictions that appear in the powerful, terrifying and tender poetry which has made him famous. That's because he writes about the experiences he has lived—from college football star to fighter pilot, to hunter, woodsman, teacher, guitarist, and dreamer of things not possible and already present.

From his booklined study near the campus of the University of South Carolina where he's poet-in-residence, Dickey ranges into a world he embraces lustily, even as he yearns for an order it refuses to yield except in the Poet's mind.

He has read and lectured widely and served as Consultant in Poetry to the Library of Congress. In 1966, he received the National Book Award in Poetry. His first novel, *Deliverance*, was a huge success, as a best seller and as a movie in which Dickey appeared as a rural Georgia sheriff. It was a fitting role. He still seems most at home in the Southern wilds whose passion, camaraderie and violence recur again and again in the works of this most original man.

MUSIC: "Wildwood Flower"—Guitar solo.

MOYERS: Why is there in so much of your work so much obsession with violence and the cruelty that men do to each other?

DICKEY: I don't know why, except that I'm essentially a creature of the War; my most formative years were taken up with waging war against an enemy, not one face of whose I had ever seen.

MOYERS: You were a pilot?

DICKEY: I flew in the Pacific. And I had some terrible things happen to close friends of mine. And this cannot but breed hatred. MacArthur, who was my commanding officer, said to the air crews of the Fifth Air Force, "Bring no ammunition back. If you can't find your primary target, find your secondary target. Expend your ammunition. Find something. Find a train depot, a marshalling yard. If you can't find that, find a sampan, a fishing boat. But blow it up. Shoot something. Put the fear of God, the fear of America, into the enemy."

MOYERS: Did you enjoy being God?

DICKEY: In a way I did. And so would anybody else.

MOYERS: You wrote that terrifying poem . . .

DICKEY: "The Fire-bombing," which is about exactly that.

MOYERS: Well, in there you talk about the pleasure of the power and the flame. Was it real pleasure?

DICKEY: Yes, because you were never faced up with what you did. You were attacking, say, from nine or ten thousand feet, at night. You never saw what you did. You never saw the families burned alive in their homes. You never saw the children mutilated. All you saw was this God-like explosion of flames that you caused, and you knew you would never be able to command that sort of power again, under any other circumstances.

MOYERS: One of your critics says: "Dickey is sweet; he's winning. He's high-minded, even while writing about bestiality and violence and lust. He confronts reality, but he's never touched by it."

DICKEY: I'm not sure what that means.

MOYERS: Were you touched by what happened?

DICKEY: Yes, I was. And I wouldn't have written that particular poem if I had not been, because it stayed with me for years and years and years. Why didn't I feel guilty? The main emotion of our time is guilt. And if you don't feel guilt, there will be plenty of people around, especially in intellectual circles, who will say, "Why the hell don't you?" But when you're an airman, the ultimate guilt at what you've done is the guilt of the inability to feel guilt, because you have not seen the results.

MOYERS: How can a man be a killer and a poet?

DICKEY: Well, there are plenty of examples in literary-history where they have been. Good Lord, Villon was a murderer, and I'm not sure that Marlowe was not. Some poets need violence, or at least excitement.

MOYERS: You think that's essential to us?

DICKEY: Not essential, but I think many feel this. Norman Mailer and other writers of our time: Hemingway, James Jones, William Styron, and many another.

MOYERS: Well, do you agree with Camus that the only question worth asking is the question: does a man have the right to take his own life?

DICKEY: Well, in a way I do. And such an eloquent and persuasive writer as Camus is, it's very hard to argue with him. The only time I ever saw him, I heard him lecture at the Sorbonne, and he was talking about the Existentialist proposition that we no longer have any supernatural sanctions. The belief in God, except in a few enclaves and so on, is pretty much gone from us. We no longer have a medieval society where everything we do is related to the future world and our particular road for getting into it. This is what Camus was talking about that night: that man no longer has to depend upon any kind of supernaturalisms, nor *can* he rely on them: that man is essentially what he has made of himself. The famous Sartrian formula—Man is free to act, but he must act to be free—is pretty much the subject of that evening's lecture.

There was a French Catholic boy down the row from me. I was sitting there spellbound at Camus' eloquence, but this boy, obviously very much on the religious side of the question against Camus' humanism, his Existentialism, bounded to his feet with a huge silver crucifix around his neck, and challenged the speaker. They do these things well in France. I love to be in on that kind of a discussion.

MOYERS: Yeah, that was a part of where I come from.

DICKEY: Right. The boy shouted to the speaker, "What can I do to start a new religion?" And Camus, looking like Humphrey Bogart with his raincoat slung over his shoulder, mused for a moment, and then said, "Get yourself crucified, and rise from the dead."

MOYERS: Well, I can guarantee you that's one new religion that was stillborn, right there.

Jim, if you take the Existential thought that man is free to act, but he must act to be free, it then makes permissible anything. It even makes permissible the violence.

DICKEY: That assumption depends upon the quality of the action and also on the quantity, I should think. We have to be guided by some principle that determines the direction of the action that we take, don't you think?

MOYERS: Is this what you mean by the unity you've been searching for in your work?

DICKEY: Yes; violence and all, I share Aldous Huxley's belief in kindness. We need more kindness.

MOYERS: Well, is that enough?

DICKEY: Is it? Again, I don't know, Bill. But I think it's a large part of what we need. We need a little less . . . or a *lot* less self-serving, a lot less exploitation of other people.

MOYERS: But Camus was saying that night that that's the fundamental principle, self-serving.

DICKEY: Yes, but that's not all he meant.

MOYERS: You'd be free. And isn't that what made the '60's and made the early part of the '70's? Wasn't that behind Watergate and Viet Nam?

DICKEY: Perhaps so. Or as Somerset Maugham, one of the great cynics of our time, much less a humanist than Camus, said, "If it were possible for the individual human being to prefer somebody else's good to his own good, the human race would have perished long ago."

MOYERS: One of the intriguing characteristics of your life is that you admire men like Hart Crane and James Agee: men who were consumed by themselves and who ended tragically.

DICKEY: I do. They are great, weak, tragic and indispensable people. If I were to furnish you with a suicide roll of the *best poets* of my time, it would read like a roll call of the best poets of my time. Every one of them killed himself—Berryman, Crane—though he's a little bit before me—Robert Shelley at Iowa, Weldon Kees, Delmore Schwartz . . . suicide is a kind of occupational hazard of American poets. Randall Jarrell was another; Ted Roethke was a virtual suicide.

MOYERS: Why do you think it is?

DICKEY: I think their minds eat them up. Anybody who can write like Randall Jarrell has got to live in hell all the time, because the intensity of his mental activity is such that it gives him no rest; he cannot hide from his own mind.

Incidentally, I love what Randall said about the death of Big Daddy Lipscomb, the huge tackle for the Baltimore Colts, who died from an overdose of heroin. Randall says at the end of his poem, "The world won't be the same without Big Daddy . . . or else it will be." You could say the same thing of Randall, or of anyone. The world won't be the same without Randall Jarrell . . . or else it will be.

MOYERS: Some of your friends are worried that your obsession with Agee and Crane and men who were consumed by themselves is . . .

DICKEY: . . . it's going to get to me.

MOYERS: . . . is a self-revelation.

DICKEY: It is. I understand those men; I feel it is an honor to read them. I don't understand the moderates. I understand the excessives.

MOYERS: Are you capable of suicide?

DICKEY: No, I don't want that. But death by violence perhaps.

MOYERS: Do you seek it out sometimes? Your bow and arrow hunting? Your canoe trips?

DICKEY: Sometimes. In some ways I really want to get killed by a grizzly bear!

MOYERS: Why?

DICKEY: Well, what can you say? What a way to go, though!

MOYERS: I thought . . . if anyone had said to me, how do you think

Dickey wants to die, I would have said by drowning because of his fascination with the water. What was it you said, "When a man drowns, he joins the dead."

DICKEY: Yes, my second book was called *Drowning With Others*.

MOYERS: You say that the war . . . was a terrifying shape . . .

DICKEY: Yes, it shaped my values, such as they are.

MOYERS: I can accept Huxley's imperative about kindness. I'd like to be kinder and I'd like for people to be kinder to me.

DICKEY: Especially *that*!

MOYERS: And I can understand the impact of being in the war and being a pilot on you, but what I still am grappling with is why today, 30 years after the fact, there is less kindness and violence still is at the theme, not only of your work but our lives.

DICKEY: Well, I'll tell you what I think, Bill. I think that the affluent society has created a state of boredom which can only be characterized by the word "crushing."

MOYERS: Boredom.

DICKEY: Boredom, right. So intense that people will do anything to get out of it. The business of running rivers, say, like the people whom I characterized in *Deliverance*: four decent suburban fellows who go up-country to run a wild river before it's dammed up, before it disappears forever—seems to be some kind of an index to the way people feel. People can sit down and have a martini and look at television and the Bill Moyers show, and the suburban life comes out to be a kind of condition of inconsequentiality; you feel that you live with your head packed in cotton. There's no reality. You don't have any touch on the world.

MOYERS: You talk about *Deliverance* being about the suburban dweller fulfilling his potentiality for violence.

DICKEY: He's trying to.

MOYERS: Do you have that potentiality?

DICKEY: I have had it. But no, I think I'm getting a little bit past it now. But it seems to me that Lewis, who heads the expedition . . .

MOYERS: In *Deliverance*.

DICKEY: . . . in *Deliverance*, the one who was played by Burt Reynolds, has a baleful fascination for the soft-jowled suburbanites that he leads into the expedition to go on the river. He's full of pseudophilosophical platitudes, and these people who work in counting houses and advertising agencies and insurance firms, and so on, have never heard anybody talk like that before, at least not in *these* platitudes. When Lewis says, "I think the machines are going to fail. I think the system is going to fail, and a few men are going to take to the woods and start over."

MOYERS: Don't you think some people wish that were so?

DICKEY: I do; that's my point.

MOYERS: But how does this apply to Sarah Moore, an anonymous creature out of nowhere taking a gun and . . .

DICKEY: I think it all links up, because you would rather be *something*, even if murder is involved, than nothing. The Lee Oswalds of the world would rather be murderers than be the nothings that they are.

MOYERS: Then is a gun the only way to make a statement today?

DICKEY: Not the only, but one of.

MOYERS: And easily available.

DICKEY: Yes; easily.

MOYERS: Another kind of poet.

DICKEY: Do you mean Oswald? Well, I wouldn't credit him with that distinction. In order to be a poet you've got to be able to put down memorable words on a page. You just don't pull a trigger.

MOYERS: Is there a madness at the center of things today that's characteristic . . . ?

DICKEY: I think there's a certain kind of terror, and the terror is played off against respectability, which is an intolerable match-up.

MOYERS: Explain that.

DICKEY: Well, on the one hand you have the need for some kind of activity that will activate adrenalin in your own body, and give the sense of living on the edge, give significance to things—or at least the illusion of significance. On the other hand you have security which militates against going out and crashing cars against light poles or being in demolition derbies and hunting the giant elk with the bow or hang gliding. But the fact . . . the fact that hang gliding . . . I'd like to do that, wouldn't you?

MOYERS: I'm . . .

DICKEY: Contemplating . . . ?

MOYERS: I'm tempted. I think I shall summon the ability to . . . resist the temptation.

DICKEY: Well, maybe I won't.

MOYERS: But what is there in us that wants to do such things?

DICKEY: I don't know; I really don't. I suppose it's the possibility of walking a tightrope between life and death. If you have nothing but life, the suburbs, you have nothing but affluence, you become aware of the truth of what the French philosopher, George Bataille says, "There is at the heart of the human experience a principle of insufficiency." And action would supply that, maybe: at least part of a principle of sufficiency. Maybe it would, maybe it wouldn't.

MOYERS: Do you think that principle of insufficiency has been at the heart of the region . . . the history of the region that we're both a part of, the South?

DICKEY: Yes, I think it is. I once said something in a poem on a football coach, Vince Lombardi, that indicates the feeling I have about the South.

MOYERS: What?

DICKEY: "Love/hate is stronger than either love or hate." Do you find that to be true in your experience?

MOYERS: I do, particularly with this part of the country that won't let us go. And the fact that it won't let us go makes me think that we've romanticized its hold on us.

DICKEY: We have romanticized, but there are certain things about the South that are good, very good. Now about *real*, nobody knows what real means. Plato didn't, Aristotle didn't, Heraclitus didn't, Einstein didn't. Nobody knows what is meant when you say real. But there are certain things, characteristics, qualities about the South, that are important to me personally.

MOYERS: What are they?

DICKEY: One of them is the courtesy of most people here. I remember riding on a train in New England where there was a family. And they were trying to get the little boy to eat his dining car meal. And the father was saying to the little boy, "Look, it's good. Don't you like it? It's good. Eat it." That would never happen in the South. You would never hear a Southerner speak to his child that way, with *that* kind of impatience.

MOYERS: But I know that in the midst of all the civility and kindness and courtesy and beneath . . .

DICKEY: There's a terrible violence.

MOYERS: As men spoke with drawls, they lynched Negroes.

DICKEY: They sure did.

MOYERS: So, I'm not sure . . . I'm back again to Huxley.

DICKEY: Or to love-hate.

MOYERS: To Huxley: Is kindness enough? No, it isn't enough. The South is kind. People love each other. They're gentle with each other. But they'll hang you.

DICKEY: Yes, they will.

MOYERS: And then, talk about it at supper.

DICKEY: And you talk about violence: the violence of the Southerner, of a certain type, say, the red-neck type, is more terrible than anything that you will encounter on the streets of New York with a hold-up gang. Like the two fellows on the river bank in *Deliverance*, when they say to you, "I don't give a goddamn about you. Back up to that tree. Just don't do nothing. Back up." Voight says, "Now, is it a matter of money?" "No, if we want money, we'll take your money." The bone marrow chills; the violence of those people is terrible because they mean what they say. They are not fooling. If they want to pull the trigger on you and blow your brains all over those woods, they'll do it.

MOYERS: But I'm just as dead if a mugger in the subway who doesn't give a damn about me . . .

DICKEY: You might bluff him, but you won't bluff the Southerner.

MOYERS: Well, why did you choose to stay here? You could have lived anywhere in the world.

DICKEY: Because of the virtues of the place.

MOYERS: The vultures?

DICKEY: Hah! Though I like *them*, too! There's nothing in the air more beautiful! No, not the vultures: the virtues of the place. There are a lot of things about the South I don't like, but one of the things I do like about being a Southerner is the tale-telling ability of most Southern people, and the jokes. I love Southern jokes. Don't you?

MOYERS: Yes, I . . .

DICKEY: They have a flavor to 'em that you just don't find anywhere else. I'll tell you one: There was this ole' boy that worked in Ball Ground, Georgia. He loved clothes, and saved up all his money every year working in the filling station to go to Atlanta to Robert Hall's to buy a suit, a new suit every year. So, he went up there and he went to Robert Hall's and he found this green suit that he liked. It really looked good on him. So, he went back down to Ball Ground and walked down the street in his suit, hoping somebody'd notice him. A friend of his came up and said, "Jack, boy, that is some kind of good looking stack of threads you got, boy. That *really* looks good. It brings out the color of them strange eyes. But the left sleeve is too long. I must tell you. The left sleeve is too long." So, he went back to Robert Hall's, and to the salesman said, "All right, look. You sold me this suit . . . $75. But the left sleeve's too damned long." The salesman said, "Don't worry about it. We don't have to alter it. It's too long. Why don't you take your hand and kind of shoot it out like *that*? Then nobody'll notice the difference. It'll be all right."

So he went back down to Ball Ground, and he walked down the street with his arm like this. And another friend stopped him in front of the drug store. He said, "Jack, I like your suit. I think it's great. It really . . . everybody's talking about it. But the right sleeve is too short." So, he said to himself, "My Lord God Almighty, $75, a whole year's savings. And the damned thing don't fit. I'm going to get that damned suit altered. It's gonna come out all right, because the color's so good." So, he went back up to Robert Hall's with all those bare racks, and no overhead, and all that. And he said, "Look, the right sleeve is too short. What am I going to do about it." The salesman said, "All right, you just take that sleeve and you bring it in like *that*. You shoot this one out like this, you bring this one in like *that*. And it's going to be all right. Wear your suit! Enjoy it!" He went back down to Ball Ground, and walked down the street again. Another friend stopped him, and said, "Look, that's a great suit, Jack, it really does look good. But the pants are too long." He went back to Robert Hall's one last time. He said, "All right, now, do something." The salesman said, "You've got it solved on *this* side, you've got it solved on that side. What you do is, you take this hand and pull up the pants like that and you hold this sleeve like this, and nobody's gonna know that the damned thing is out of proportion." So, Jack walked down Main Street on Sunday morning, and he met a man and his wife, and passed the time of day with them. After they got out of earshot, the man's wife said, "Did you see poor Jack Simpson? You went to high school with him. Now he's staggering down the main street of Ball Ground, Georgia, all crippled up with arthritis like that." And her husband turned to her and says, "Yeah, but don't that suit fit him good!"

MOYERS: I don't know whether the story is Southern, but the telling of it'll do.

DICKEY: It's all the same.

MOYERS: It's all the same? Who was your favorite Southern author, Faulkner?

DICKEY: Oh no. I never did care for him very much.

MOYERS: Why?

DICKEY: He's too prolix for me, too uncertain-sounding.

MOYERS: Prolix?

DICKEY: Long-winded. Doesn't get enough said, for all those words.

MOYERS: He might have told a story quicker than you told that one.

DICKEY: No doubt! The whole point of the Southern story-telling is that you draw the story out. And the length of it is part of the effectiveness. But there are ways and ways of doing this; some are good, some are boring.

MOYERS: Bruce Catton, the great historian, said to me once, "I'm not sure that I'd want to know the South when it isn't any longer a lost cause."

DICKEY: Yes, because that's in a sense, what makes it; that it *is* a lost cause.

MOYERS: Haven't we made a myth out of that? Haven't we reveled in being the victim or the loser?

DICKEY: Well, sure. But did not Homer make a myth of Troy, which is the greatest poem of all time, the *Iliad*? And is it not about a losing cause? Hector is the real hero, if not to the Greeks, to us.

MOYERS: But I think sometimes the rest of the country finds us, well, boring because we live always in that past when the glory of the possibility became the dust of Atlanta, the fires . . .

DICKEY: In a way that's true, but the South is a region which is important to mankind, nonetheless. The industrial East doesn't have what we have, the Far West doesn't have it, the Middle West doesn't have it. There's something that causes people to come to the South, and when they come, they stay. The climate may be part of the reason, but it's not all of it.

MOYERS: Yes, and they bring with them the very industrialization, the very generalities, the very anonymities, the very blandness and homogeneity that makes other regions less interesting.

DICKEY: That they do. To get around more or less to the center of what you're talking about, Bill, it comes back to our initial consideration of Camus and Sartre. Camus says that the main thing is as to whether a man has the right to take his own life. You and I say—I hope you'll agree—that the main proposition is how you *live* your life: every one of us comes from an anonymous and fortuitous concatenation of genes. Your mother and your father married, and they were a product of thousands of years of other people which led up to you. Myself, the same. Anybody the same. You and I were born into *this* region.

The only philosophical proposition that's worth anything at all to consider is how to live your life, what you want it to contain, how you want it to be. For example, do you want to be an internationalist . . . not you, maybe, but does *one* want to be an internationalist or does one want to be rooted in a single region? To stay in one place and do forays—or my word, sorties—out to Europe and other places, but still have a place to come back to? Or does one want to be kind of a nomad? These are questions that are important.

MOYERS: Well, you didn't want to be a nomad.

DICKEY: I was for many years a nomad, but I came back.

MOYERS: I know.

DICKEY: Place has got to matter.

MOYERS: But did what you came back to turn out to be what you wanted it to be?

DICKEY: Yes, I think principally it did because I insisted on making it as I wished it to be, within the circumference of the Southern ethos. The ethos has something to do with rootedness. You should be rooted, I do firmly believe, as a Southerner—as a born Southerner and—what would you say—as a voluntary Southerner. I believe that you should be rooted in a place, but you should also be able to make sorties out from that into the Other, into some of the variety of the world.

MOYERS: The home place has much going for it, though. Cookery, for example.

DICKEY: Yes! I think that fried chicken is a great contribution to world culture. Don't you?

MOYERS: I do, and I think the same is true of grits.

DICKEY: When you eat a Southern meal, you know that you have supped among the gods, because who other than a god could invent the divine fact of okra?

MOYERS: What else do you like?

DICKEY: To eat?

MOYERS: Yeah.

DICKEY: I like the cooking of Louisiana. I like the rice dishes that they do. I like the seafood along the Maryland shore, the oyster dishes and that sort of thing. I like New England lobster. New England has got a little bit of a look-in on the regional cookery scene, but not nearly so much as the South.

MOYERS: I'm glad to see you concede something.

DICKEY: They have a little something; I concede it. I *eat* it! But *cornbread*! Do you like it?

MOYERS: Oh, of course.

DICKEY: Good!

MOYERS: I went out to see my 90-year-old grandmother recently. She was about to be operated on for the first time in her life. In fact, it was the first time in 90 years that she had been to the hospital. And she went to the surgery still complaining that she hadn't been able, because she became ill as I was arriving there, she had not been able to cook me her cornbread.

DICKEY: Well, the South has got that cookery, and everybody's trying to get in on it. We've got our cookery, we've got our stories, we've got our writers that come from the stories and that tell the stories. And we've got a certain courtesy which may be dying out, but it still exists, because it has existed. We have a certain tradition of family in the South.

I was shocked when I went into the service in 1942, and found I was in there with a lot of Pennsylvania and Ohio boys who did not even know their first cousins' names. Now that, to a Southerner, has a certain degree of immorality about it. Do you feel strongly about your family?

MOYERS: Oh, sure. Some of my cousins that I . . .

DICKEY: I hate some of mine! I hate 'em, but I *know* 'em! I had one relative . . . this is another tall tale! He was not *a* drunk, but *the* drunk!

MOYERS: Every town has to have one.

DICKEY: Right! And almost every family! But you should've seen *him*! The family was in despair of him. They finally contrived to get him into Alcoholics Anonymous. You know AA has the buddy system, where they team you up with a cured alcoholic who comes out and commiserates with you and is with you through your bad time when you've got to have a drink, and you have to resist it, and all *that*.

And this fellow came out to my relative's house regularly, and they'd play cards, and that sort of thing. But my relative was not only one of the few people who was not cured by the Alcoholics Anonymous buddy system, but succeeded in getting his buddy *back* on the bottle. So, instead of gaining one they lost two.

MOYERS: Little setback for the cause, there!

DICKEY: They go on.

MOYERS: Here we are in 1976. We're celebrating 200 years of a revolution. Everybody's having his say, the politicians, the editorial writers, the President. What does a poet say about this American experience?

DICKEY: Well, the American experience, my Lord . . . there are many different ways of saying things about the American experience from the poet's point of view, but I would say that the new world offers to the poet, as well as to the person, the citizen and so on, an almost infinite range of possibilities of experience, but that he had better choose carefully.

When you look at your relationship to your country, you realize that you are born of a certain time, and of a certain place, and the accidents of fortune. The accidents of fortune got me born, to a genial, low-key father and an invalid mother who tried desperately, during the Depression, to maintain the genteel tradition of the South.

Yours were different. You were out there in the plains of Texas . . . in Marshall.

MOYERS: Piney Woods.

DICKEY: Your circumstances are quite different from mine, and yet, in certain ways they link up. This is our version of America. It's Bill Moyers' version of America and James Dickey's version of America because we came into an historical period and we were nurtured by it and defeated by it and if we were any good, we rose above it, transcended it, and used it.

MOYERS: As you live it, as you travel the country, as you do your readings at college campuses and for groups, do you come to any kind of insight about what we the people want to be, what you think we collectively aspire to be?

DICKEY: Well, if I could solve that problem, I could raise up the American nation singing hosannas unto the most High. Everything would be solved. But I can't, any more than the politicians can. I would say this: every man wants to be himself within a situation which allows him to be so. Everyone has many selves, and it seems to me that in our country and in our time, or in any kind of time, in the historical era, that we live our only human lives in, it's necessary to energize as many of your selves as you can.

Wilbur Mills, for example, with the girl jumping into the fountain! Everybody thinks that's a terribly reprehensible act yet I applaud it.

MOYERS: Why?

DICKEY: Because he had had a repressed kind of personal situation and this was a release for him, and I don't begrudge him that at all. I would vote for him because of the incident, not in spite of it. There are many people who have situations, life situations, in which they are trapped; and their truest and most instinctive selves are negated. They need a release. I'm on Wilbur Mills' side. Aren't you?

MOYERS: I'm on the side of that fundamental, undeniable mystique of self.

DICKEY: Yes, that fundamental, undeniable right to make a fool of yourself if you need to. There's nothing wrong with that. I mean, one of the things about America, Bill, is that we're all expected to be saints when our neighbor and everybody's neighbor knows damned well that we are not. So, we're supposed to maintain a mask. And that's wrong because nobody—Wilbur Mills or anybody else—can do that successfully. And he should not be asked to.

MOYERS: Why did you choose, Jim . . . why did you choose *Jericho* as the title for your last book?

DICKEY: I'm a long-term hit-or-miss reader of the Bible. I think some of it is marvelous rhetoric, and beautifully stated. It seems to me that there's something like the possibility of a Promised Land that bears a certain analogy to the South. We may have had slavery; we may have had lynchings, and of course we did. And we fought an American version of the *Iliad* where we were the losing side, we were Troy instead of being Achilles' faction, the Greeks. We lost. But, as John Peale Bishop says, somewhat arrogantly, we "had arrived at a manner of living somewhat more amiable than any other that has ever been known on this continent."

MOYERS: I wonder if it didn't achieve it, though, in its own mythology? We may not get to the Promised Land if it ever existed for us to get to, but . . .

DICKEY: Well, it exists in the mind. Perhaps only there.

MOYERS: And it's obvious to me that you don't want your sense of being Southern to disappear.

DICKEY: No, and neither do you. Again, again, one of my Vanderbilt teachers, a great teacher, Donald Davidson, who was the mentor of the Fugitive Group at Vanderbilt in the late '20's and '30's, used to lecture to us most eloquently. He said, "What gives variety and richness to life is *difference*. You don't go to Spain or to Italy or to France because it'll be like what you've left in America. You want to go there because it's different." There are places in Europe, even today, where you have to do no more than cross the street and the wines change, the food changes, the clothing changes, the folk songs change, everything changes. This is because these things are rooted in a particular area, and they have been that way for hundreds and in some cases thousands of years.

Flamenco music, guitar music, is a Spanish thing. It's not a French thing; it's not an Italian thing. It's a Spanish thing. You take Southern music. The two greatest musics that the New World has ever produced both came from the South. On the black side, the blues, from which came jazz, and from the white Southern Appalachian tradition, blue-grass and country music, the "Nashville sound."

MOYERS: But for all the chords that you resonate in me as you talk about that, I still think it's talking about another lost cause. Don't you?

DICKEY: I agree. And it's too damned bad. But I think that certainly these things can be preserved on records, they can be preserved in recipes. They can be preserved in certain modes of clothing, and so on. They can be preserved, in a way, but only in attenuated versions. I'm not idealizing things. I know the skeleton in the Southern closet as well as you do, as well as anybody does. I know that slavery was a disgraceful thing. But so are the New York ghettos.

MOYERS: I couldn't have made that . . . I couldn't make that . . . and I'm reminded of what Lincoln said, "Anytime I hear anybody recommend slavery, I suggest he try it first."

DICKEY: I don't recommend it either. Let Lincoln try the ghetto, too, though.

MOYERS: What about James Dickey: What's going to be his deliverance?

DICKEY: I don't know. It'll involve doing my work and living my life and taking care of my people, my family, and getting them educated and trying to experience what there is. I think I can make it to 85. So whatever I do will have to be done by then.

One of my favorite writers is Robert Penn Warren, a Southerner from Guthrie, Kentucky; and I'll finish up with something of his. What I believe in, more than anything else, is delight, ecstasy. Some of this will come out of a region as the flowering plant comes out of the ground. But you have to be there. Feelings of this sort could happen to you in a city when you are about half drunk, for example, with a pretty girl. I don't knock that. They could happen as you were just walking along. I believe in both caused and causeless joy. You can see a flight of birds fly over and your heart will be filled with a nameless delight. The poet strikes his spark, at least this kind of poet does.

This is just a few lines from Warren, Robert Penn Warren, about being a boy in the country in Kentucky, as he sees a flight of geese go over, and he is filled with an unnamable emotion.

Long ago in Kentucky, I, a boy, stood
By a dirt road, in first dark, and heard
The great geese hoot northward.

I could not see them, there being no moon
And the stars sparse. I heard them.

I did not know what was happening in my heart.

It was the season before the elderberry blooms,
Therefore they were going north.

The sound was passing northward.

Tell me a story.

In this century, and moment, of mania,
Tell me a story.

Make it a story of great distances, and starlight.

The name of the story will be Time,
But you must not pronounce its name.

Tell me a story of deep delight.

MOYERS: You remember what Zorba said standing at the window there at the inn . . . What?

DICKEY: "Men like me should live a thousand years."

MOYERS: I hope you do.

DICKEY: I do too. But probably eighty-five. That's when everything will begin.

AN ACCEPTANCE
National Book Award in Poetry, 1966.

On occasions such as this, writers are not so much invited as summoned, called up. They are called up, surely, in the sense of being called up for jury duty or for military service; but they are also called up in the sense that ghosts and spirits are summoned. Most of you have never seen me before, and very likely you will never see me again. I appear on just this one occasion out of a kind of forest of print, or a never-ending rain of words written in the forms—or no-forms—of verse and hoping to be poetry. I appear as a result of having had a few such verses printed in a book—one among thousands—which you have chosen to honor on this occasion. I have come out of certain lines of print with my name attached to them, and yet I stand here for a moment or two as a man: a man who awoke, if not exactly to find himself famous, at least to find himself slightly notorious among his fellow craftsmen. The main change in my immediate life, however, is merely the addition of a new word to the family vocabulary. Last year's description of the poet—graciously contributed by my fourteen-year-old son—was "decadent." This year's, thanks to the National Book Committee and the Poetry Judges, is "insufferable," coming this time not from the son but from the wife, who is certainly in a position to know. And here I am, no ghost yet—thank God—but a middle-aged man (*early* middle-aged, as one continually and a little desperately points out to oneself), and I have this occasion to tell you a couple of things.

It might not be to the purpose here to make any sweeping statements on the nature of poetry; or on that much-agitated question, the Place of the Poet in Society; or to dwell on the arduous labor of love that poetry must be in our time. And yet I will generalize, even so. What comes through to me continually as I go on writing poetry is the infinite renewability of the individual human life, both as it is lived and enhanced by the poetry that one knows and reads, and as it is relived in memory. I once read in the *Journals* of Julien Green that the one thing for which death may not be forgiven is the destruction of memory. And yet, how extraordinarily vivid and alive memory is while we have it! How many images and events, how many anecdotes, fantasies, wish-fulfillment daydreams (ah, *those* are magnificent!), how many *selves* we carry around with us! And each time one dips into that increasingly full reservoir, one notices that everything that comes from it brings to the surface not only itself, but an implicit meaning. To discover that, to invent it, to transmute it into language, is the beginning of things for the poet, and the end as well. I find that I write poetry because I want to *know* something—to *come* to know it, even if I have to invent what I know—by living with it on as many levels as I can, by being intimate with it, severe with it, angry with it, baffled by it, in love with it. But what always emerges is the sense of its *importance*, or at least its importance to me, being quite literally all that I have.

And really, that is why you have asked me here tonight: why you have called me up: not so much to honor but to recognize one human being's story, the events and meanings of his life. At this particular moment of time, when I stand publicly honored for my private life, I am filled with the kind of wild hope that can come only from such occasions. This is the belief that one person's life, through the medium of his art, has at last succeeded in getting outside of himself and has come to rest in others. It would be egotistical for me to assume that this is in any sense a special case—that my life is any more valuable than another's—and I take great delight in affirming that it is not, and also in affirming that the lives, the events, the memories, the total existences of the bodies and brains of all men are infinitely valuable to the world, the more valuable as they are the more deeply known. If I could, I would make the few minutes that I stand here—for once in a lifetime—simply a reiteration of this belief; and I would add to this the assumption that poetry, through its own means, moves toward an affirmation of this kind, taking on faith that what meaning *is* can sometimes be *said*, and that the very saying has the peculiar grace of being able to raise one's random perception of a blade of grass bending in the air to a kind of *nth* power of fragile significance. It is this that we have, in the end, against the "silence of the infinite spaces." We don't have it forever, but for a while we do have it; and it is, because we are human beings, and because this is our condition, magnificently enough.

Some Statements on Poetry

PREFACE TO *THE EARLY MOTION*

This volume brings together all the poems in my first two books published with Wesleyan University Press. The poems are a complete and I hope valuable record of the early phase of my writing life, and represent my attitudes toward the subjects, and toward imagery, rhythm, and form, at the time of writing, roughly from 1959 to 1965.

The themes, which have been expanded and explored in my later work, are in these poems announced and given such treatment as my abilities allowed. These poems emerged from what I call a night-rhythm, something felt in pulse not word. How this anapestic sound was engendered by other poetry, good or bad—by Tennyson, Swinburne, and also by Poe, Kipling, and Robert Service—I cannot say, except to assert that I had read these poets, and I have always liked heavy recurrence of stress. First I heard, then I wrote, and then I began to reason; when I reasoned, I wrote more of the same. The reasoning ran something like this: suppose you have lines like "There's a land where the mountains are nameless,/And the rivers all run God knows where;/There are lives that are erring and aimless,/And deaths that just hang by a hair," and you decide that the level of meaning, compelling as it may be to saloon-keepers and retired postmen, is not good, but that the surge of the rhythm *is*, what then? What if images, insights, metaphors, evaluations, nightmarish narratives, all of originality and true insight, were put into—or *brought* into—the self-generating on-go that seems to have existed before any poem and to continue after any actual poem ends? What if these things were tried? What then might be done? What might become?

On some such assumption, more or less dictated by the blood, by the nerves' hunger for unassailable rhythmic authority, most of these poems were written. At one end of the spectrum of possibility lay the auto-intoxication of Swinburne and Poe, and at the other end the prosaical flatness of William Carlos Williams; these are the obvious but by no means the utter extremes. In the poems of *Drowning With Others* I edged toward the end of sound over sense, toward the foreordained hammering of ultra-rhythmical English, and tried to make the concepts, images, and themes of my life conform to what the night-rhythm had caused to come through me.

The themes that poured into the night-sound were memories of warfare, particularly the air and island combat of the South Pacific, and also (perhaps related in some way) hunting with bow and arrow, which I discovered and began to practice at this time. Also, themes of animals in their alien and instinctive existence, of European travel, which I had first experienced in the mid-fifties, and the continuities of blood and family. I found that although I liked the concentration and single-impact penetration of the short poem, I also liked the expansiveness and opportunity for multi-level development afforded by the long one. In *Drowning With Others* I experimented with poems in several parts, such as "The Owl King," in which a single action is given from three points of view. In *Helmets* I worked toward longer, more inclusive presentations, as in "Approaching Prayer," for example, and in "Drinking from a Helmet," which I considered my most ambitious effort up to that point, I splintered the experience undergone in the poem into nineteen fragments of varying lengths, and by this means tried to get the lyric "timeless-moment" intensity and the enveloping structure of a narrative into the same format. In *Helmets*, though I still relied on the night-rhythm, the sound-before-meaning, I also wanted to give more play to narrative movement, the story-value of what was being said, and consequently I toned down the heavy bombardment of stress and relied more on matter-of-fact statement and declaration; I went toward the flat end of the spectrum, where narrative—or long narrative, anyway—usually lies.

If you add to these elements not only the sound of the folk-guitar, the simple chordal structure of the music I was just beginning to learn when I wrote these poems, together with the ballad-themes often dealt with by Appalachian musicians, you have pretty much what I was about in these two books, or thought I was about, and the principal ways that led to my getting whatever it was I got, may have got, here.

The method of treatment is, I think, consistent, and the emphasis on the rhythmic component of poetry is more salient here than in my later work, a fact that may interest some readers. What I have done subsequently depends in an integral way on these poems; in the "early motion" can also be seen and heard the later motion, and doubtless, when all the poems are done, the whole motion as well.

PREFACE TO *FALLING, MAY DAY SERMON, AND OTHER POEMS*

For years, as I read and wrote poetry, a strange kind of object was forming in my mind. Sometimes it was barely present, but at others it seemed almost three-dimensionally real. This was the shape of a solid bank, an on-end block or wall of words, solid or almost solid, black with massed ink, through which a little light from behind would come at intermittent places. Gradually I began to construct such a wall outside myself, at first with words typed and then cut out with scissors and placed in various combinations on a piece of cardboard from a shirt come back from the laundry. The shape of the cardboard was the shape of the poem, and I moved the words around as in a game of metaphysical Scrabble, with the payoff coming in images and new directions of thought from lucky combinations. There was no theme to the first of those poems, but since I had typed and snipped many words that were related to water—or *were* water—the final version had something to do with rain. Though it was not successful enough to publish, I felt that it was promising enough to keep and learn from, which I tried to do. Since cutting out individual words was too laborious and time-consuming, I began to build the walls directly on the page from the typewriter, and spent more and more time erecting them and pushing against them, and trying to peer through them at the place that let the light through. I began to conceive of a poem presented in this way as a confrontation for the reader just as a real wall would be, or one of the paintings of Mark Rothko: a strange and solid obstacle which the reader would not be able to go through, but would have to climb down. Of course one has to "climb down" any page of print—prose or verse—but since I wanted my walls to be rhythmical, to include the recurrent and varied stresses, pauses, onrushes and sound-continuities of a recognizable prosody, the descent would be markedly different from the run-of-the-mill climb-down of a page of prose, or at least I hoped it would. I tried to make it memorable step by step, intending the intermittent light to come strongly and unexpectedly through the places I left blank.

To this concept of the poem-as-barrier, the poetic line is crucial in another sense than it usually is. One of the main virtues of the line is that it increases by a very great deal the memorability of what is being said. I wanted this memorability factor to be powerful, but I thought at first that this might be difficult to assure, since the line went all the way across the page, and was composed of many smaller lines set apart by spaces. But as I continued to work with this form of organization, it seemed to me that in just this fact—the fact that each long page-wide line was comprised of several short "internal" ones—lay the solution to the problem, for the reader could fasten on one fragment within the main line as readily as he could on the whole linear unit, or perhaps even more readily. For example, in the following passage the words, though grouped and spaced irregularly, are presented in their own association within their specific isolated groups and at the same time are contributary to the general structure of the narrative of the girl's fall:

> . . . for her the ground is closer   water is nearer   she passes
> It   then banks   turns   her sleeves fluttering differently as she rolls
> Out to face the east, where the sun shall come up from wheatfields   she must
> Do something with water   fly to it   fall in it   drink it   rise
> From it   but there is none left upon earth   the clouds have drunk it   back
> The plants have sucked it down . . .

Working in this way, I saw that what I wanted was to give each cluster of words its own fierce integrity, and that I was perhaps inadvertently seeking a way to make manifest the characteristics of thought when it associates rapidly, and in detail, in regard to a specific subject, an action, an event, a theme. I envisioned the mind as working by associational and verbal fits and starts, jumps, gaps, and the electric leaps across them: in successive shocks, rests, word-bursts, stamp-printed or lightning-stamped images, crammed clusters. Though I had employed this approach, or something like it, in some of the poems in *Buckdancer's Choice*, I now meant to go the whole way with it, and launched into the two long poems which give this book its title, one the hallucinated version of a girl's fall from an airliner and the other an equally hysterical improvisation on a folk theme from north Georgia, both poems of madness, death, and violent affirmation.

From here, where? I am trying now to work not so much with blockforms and walls of words, but with balance: the balance of the poem on the page which is in some sense analogous to the balance given to the trunk of a tree by its limbs, or by the twigs to the stem. Obviously, all kinds of arrangements of balance can occur, from the obvious to the more irregular and delicate. Around a central bole, sometimes hidden but always present, any number of balancing units can be arranged, and if these are successful in the poems I am writing now and those I plan to write, I hope that the experience of this central stem will be a part of the reader's hidden pleasure: that, and a sense of precariousness, of swaying.

AFTERWORD TO *BABEL TO BYZANTIUM*

Most of the criticism I have written is in this book, and was done originally as reviews for various magazines. It is interesting and a little shocking to reencounter some of the things I said, some of the opinions I made public at those times, in those places, and any effort to make my judgments at the present time dovetail with those of my younger self must necessarily be foredoomed. In fourteen years I have set, settled, changed, changed around, changed back, changed again. Yet I have not varied from the opinion that if a critic locks himself into fixed positions on a writer and on works, positions he considers it a moral necessity to maintain, he thereby surrenders his openness, his accessibility to experience, the moment-to-moment responsiveness of his life-situation, and indeed part of himself. I realize that these assumptions are hopelessly vague as the basis for any sort of permanently valuable criticism, and yet change is a part of my or anyone else's makeup, do what anyone will.

I now feel that I was partially wrong in some of these judgments, partially right in others, totally wrong in a few, and exactly right in an equal few. The rightest assessment I made, I think, was that of W. S. Graham. Everything I said about the poems is in the poems, and is just as I said it was. In fact, if I had it to do over again, I would write a whole article on Graham's work and focus on the extraordinary new approach to prosody he has made possible. I would quote a lot more, particularly from poems like "The Thermal Stair," his elegy for the painter-pilot Peter Lanyon, killed in a gliding accident in 1964. As it is, I can quote a little of this now, from the part where the poet and the artist, dead in a thermal climb, drink, listening to the sea, in a pub.

> Climb here where the hand
> Will not grasp on air.
> And that dark-suited man

Has set the dominoes out
On the Queen's table.
Peter, we'll sit and drink
And go in the sea's roar
To Labrador with wallis
Or rise on Lanyon's stair.

I was wrongest in my grotesque overestimation of the work of Nikos Kazantzakis, and I feel that the essay on him was more an exercise in effusiveness on my part than responsible criticism. And yet I still like what I say about existence, about the creative mind, using Kazantzakis as a pretext, better than almost anything I have written about poetry, and I am grateful that Kazantzakis's *Odyssey* gave me the opportunity to say it. I must conclude that there is some imaginary poet named Kazantzakis who exemplifies this effusion on my part, but the real one doesn't. *That* one now strikes me as a rather tiresomely obvious, self-serving and humorless man, pompous and somewhat unpleasant in the self-aggrandizing and pseudophilosophical manner of the worst of Nietzsche.

Regrettably perhaps, I no longer feel it necessary to pay any sort of lip-service to William Carlos Williams, who in my opinion is a poet of no merit whatsoever. A good doctor, I am sure, a reasonably good observer of some aspects of American life, a good human being, generous and well-intentioned, but as a writer flat, obvious and uninteresting beyond the telling.

I would stand by my remarks on Yvor Winters, and on his school, exemplified here by Ellen Kay and Donald Drummond. If asked I would say the same thing again, except that I would be even harsher, I expect. Even so, I have come around on Thom Gunn, whose approach is essentially the same as theirs. The difference is talent; Gunn has it and they do not. I think now that the best case that can be made for neoclassical verse in our time is made by Gunn. I should have seen the possibilities of this in my review, and this failure is probably the most flagrant in the book, if my section on Kazantzakis or my absurd overestimation of Hayden Carruth is not.

On two of these writers I am still as divided, as uncertain, as before. These are Robinson Jeffers and Randall Jarrell. Since writing these pieces I have read almost all of both writers over again, and I don't believe I will ever be able to make up my mind, so glaring and extreme are the defects and virtues. For example, the sweep of Jeffers is impressive, as I noted. As the world dwindles, computerizes and plasticizes, it is even more impressive; one looks through Jeffers's dark, long lines at the Carmel coastal hills as though at the Lost Paradise itself. And yet his metaphors, his actual linguistic insights, are second-rate, almost invariably. If a defense could be made for poetic technique that ignores or cannot command the actual essence of poetry, which is the highly individual apprehension of some aspect of reality or fantasy fixed in disturbing, inimitable and releasing words, then Jeffers would be worth defending. But this will have to be done by somebody else. I am finished with Jeffers, except in classrooms, or alone, late at night.

To me, Randall Jarrell is one of the most curious cases in all literature. I have a provisional pantheon of three never-fail poet-critics by whom I measure others. These are John Peale Bishop, Conrad Aiken, and Delmore Schwartz. To these, and at that level (though they are not practicing poets), I would be inclined to add Dwight Macdonald and Stanley Edgar Hyman. But far above that reliable professional class is Randall Jarrell; he is in a class by himself; he is something *else*, as they say in the South. Both when he is wrong (or when *I* think he is wrong) and when he is right he is full of so much intelligence, so much ebullience and involvement and concern that he makes other critics, even those I have cited, appear to be suffering from some unnecessary terminal illness, compared to his superb, open-minded, bright, resourceful, enthusiastic, healthy example. But the poems . . . the poems.

It is impossible for me to understand how a person like Randall Jarrell, with the gifts of intellect and discretion and daring and wit that he had, with his devotion to the life of art and especially of poetry, with the leisure and the will to write as voluminously and at the same time as carefully as he wished, could not, for all these bestowings, write truly memorable poetry. It may be that he gave away too much to the situation itself, to each of the dramatic episodes he wrote about, to the "human situation" in which he was so deeply involved. That may have been it; I don't know. But the fact is that Jarrell's language does not truly and deeply live for me. I can't remember any of his *lines*, or the actual words in which he says a thing. I can remember some of his situations, and almost all of his attitudes, but not his words. The essay, the dialogue, I wrote about Jarrell was the first critical article I ever published in a national magazine, and between then and now I met and corresponded with Jarrell, and came to prize his example and his life, his wit, his commitment and enthusiasm, more than ever, and consequently I have strange and mixed feelings about what I said a long, sincere, confused, stupid time ago; I feel now that I overrated the poetry and underrated him. And there the matter rests. For now, anyway.

As a kind of free-ranging hindsight, an inventory of changed and unchanged opinion, here are some other self-critiques, regrets and assertions.

I wish I had had more to say about John Berryman and the poetry of the will, and about affectation and mannerism as it pertains to this, for I think that the inventive use of the will is important in Berryman's approach to composition, and is perhaps more important, generally, than we might have thought.

To Robert Frost I was not unkind enough. What I said in favor of his poetry I said by an extreme effort of self-delusion, and under what I must have felt as the heavy pressure of critical—rather than popular—opinion. In reality I have never been able to abide Frost's work, with its dreadful meeching self-righteousness, its attitude of sullen cringing, of a kind of triumphant skulking. To finish off New England, I can also say that I overrated Edwin Arlington Robinson, whom I now find unreadable, though in the penance of the long introduction I did for a *Selected Poems* I discovered something in Robinson's enormous doorstop of a *Collected Poems* that I would not forego: one line: "And Lingard, with his eerie joy."

On Cummings I would say exactly the same thing, though less raptly; on Roethke the same, and on Wilbur.

There are smaller figures than these that I seem to have taken wrongly in one way or another. Though in the main I was favorable to Winfield Scott's long poem *The Dark Sister*, I no longer care much for it; it is not nearly up to the best of Scott's work. On the other hand I have since read Scott Donaldson's biography, *Poet in America*, and as a result came to read most of Winfield Scott's verse and whatever of his prose I could find. I now think Scott one of the better poets of our time, and if Donaldson had not already done so—and if the late George P. Elliott, a likewise neglected and good poet, also had not—I would be tempted to say why. Of the self-ruinations of American poets, Scott's is the most typical, and the saddest, and he deserves the recognition for the lack of which he quite literally died.

Charles Olson is like William Carlos Williams, whom he very much resembles: well-meaning and congenitally unable to say one memorable thing. However, someone put me on to Paul Christensen's book about Olson, *Call Him Ishmael*, which turns out to be far more interesting than Olson is, and valuable.

William Stafford is even better than I said he was, and if I had more room I should like to talk about the wonderfully individual, off-beat and convincing tone he brings into poetry.

I like Robert Penn Warren's work and Edwin Muir's more than I did, and Marianne Moore's and Louis Simpson's less. I can still see no merit in Robert Graves, for all his bluster, except for one or two poems that seem to have been written by someone else, or by mistake.

On Allen Ginsberg I wish I had not wasted even one sentence. The opinion reprinted here was one of the first reviews of *Howl*; and in my overcompensatory and mistaken wish to be "fair" I gave too much ground. Now, however, at the age of almost sixty, I can state with some certainty that I like real poetry, not joke-poetry. Ginsberg's influence has been disastrous, and has enabled anyone in sight to announce himself a "poet" with talentless brashness and contribute to filling the air and innumerable small magazines with forgettable maunderings, all of this resulting in a disregard for real imagination, real originality, real poetry, real being. The critics who have taken Ginsberg's kind of thing seriously are as much to blame as Ginsberg for such deprivation; all these will pass into the great compost heap of social history, and a few good poets and poems will be left, whether they are those I select or others.

As to the writers dealt with in these pages, I invite the reader to find whatever truth and permanence they may have somewhere between my extremes, or in extremes even more drastic, either way.

THE G.I. CAN OF BEETS, THE FOX IN THE WAVE, AND THE HAMMERS OVER OPEN GROUND*

I have always liked to be caught up in questions for which there have always been, are, and always will be a great many answers but never *the* answer, such as the true meaning of Moby Dick's deformed jaw, or the reliability of the repair service for the telephone in Kafka's *Castle*. One of the most perennially interesting and unanswerable of these questions, of course, has to do with the nature of poetry, and I enjoy—have for years enjoyed—rooting around in myself and others for such a definition, because many of those offered, many of those that wake one up at 4:30 in the morning, are provocative, and above a certain level one is (almost) as good as another. There are ingenuities, plausibilities and fantasies all over the place; one can pluck them out of the air, in a library or anywhere else, and after throwing out all those patently foolish and trying-for-it tries, such as Sandburg's "poetry is a combination of hyacinths and biscuits," one inhabits, doing this, a very heady realm with a good many of the finest minds ever produced by the human race floating—free-floating—around in it with you and the lesser heads. A definition of poetry: no, impossible. If Plato can't make a definition stick forever, if Aristotle can't hammer something together that can't be questioned or pulled apart, if Hume and Locke and Berkeley and Whitehead and Heidegger among the commentators can't, and Wordsworth and Coleridge and Shelley and Frost and Wallace Stevens and Lorca and Rilke and Valery and Pasternak and Kenneth Burke can't blow all the others away, *I* can't hope to blow them away, and of course wouldn't want to if I could. Nevertheless, there are certain speculations that may lead somewhere, and I like to follow those I either pull out of myself, or extend from someone else's idea that strikes me. As for my own unaided pursuit of a

*South Atlantic Modern Language Association, Atlanta, 1982

notion, I abandon myself to Hofmannsthal's epigram about the composition of poetry, that "perilous, terrible art": "This thread I spin out of my body/ And at the same time the thread serves as my path through the air." Sometimes that kind of path is good, but at times I come on things from another mind that are better than the thread, and sometimes the threadbare ozone, my own search has given me, and I'm more than happy to take off from them.

It would seem on the face of it that an attempt to say anything of significance or even of interest about poetry from the standpoint of the *intent* behind it—the intent that produced the poetry—would be even more impossible to bring to any sort of successful or usable conclusion than the effort to establish a definitive description of poetry itself. And yet I do think on these things, and I believe with some benefit, at least to myself and my own practice. There is, for example, an entry in the *Notebooks* of Winfield Townley Scott, an American poet who committed suicide in 1968—a fine poet and a great loss to us—that furnishes me the ground on which I now stand, down for once out of my own wandering atmosphere onto a place I think of some solidity and substance, a real launch-pad for speculation, a base that needs to be here. Scott says this:

> There are two kinds of poetry. One, the kind represented by Crane's line: "The seal's wide spindrift gaze toward paradise," the other represented by Robinson's: "And he was all alone there when he died." One is a magic gesture of language, the other a commentary on human life so concentrated as to give off considerable pressure. The greatest poets combine the two; Shakespeare frequently; Robinson himself now and then. If I have to choose, I choose the second: I go, in other words, for Wordsworth, for Hardy, in preference to Poe, to Rimbaud. . . . This is all an oversimplification, I know; but I think the flat assertion of the two kinds indicates two very great touchstones.

So do I. Quickly—instantaneously—it is apparent that in the Crane line, "The seal's wide spindrift gaze toward paradise," the word "spindrift" calls immediate attention to itself. It must, for the "reality-world"—as opposed to the word-world—is not well served by this word, in this line, this image. "Spindrift" is sea-foam, wave-foam, usually wind-blown along beaches, and, though the seal's eyes may be wide, and his gaze toward Paradise, "spindrift" is really not, cannot be, part of his vision: the word is word only, associational word, and in its way beautiful, but word. And it came hard; one remembers Hart Crane's search for it, day by day through dictionaries (note: *dictionaries*) on his lunch hours, when he was working on Sweet's Advertising Catalogue. The Robinson line, on the other hand, is simply factual. There are only plain words in it: a statement. Plain words in ordinary order; nothing unusual, much less exotic. The line puts the reader into contemplation of something that happened to someone, and the condition of the happening: it is the clear pane of glass that does not call attention to itself, but gives clearly and cleanly on a circumstance; that is the approach, the poetry.

Having gone this far, one is provoked to test the applicability of Scott's statement in other lines, other poets: lines and poets all over the place, in fact. Immediately, when one tries the statement out, all the poetry that one has ever read, to say nothing of the poetry one has tried to write, falls one way or the other; the poets pile up on each other like cord-wood, on either side of the fence. A partial list of the Commentary-On-Life party, the Human-Conditioners who might be called, in some sense—in many different senses—"literalists," would include Homer, Frost, Robinson, Lee Masters, Thomas Hardy, Francis Ponge and Guillevic in France, the early Gottfried Benn in Germany, Philip Larkin and R. S. Thomas in England, and my prime example, Randall Jarrell, of Nashville, Tennessee.

Magic-Language exemplars would be Gerard Manley Hopkins, Hart Crane, Wallace Stevens, John Berryman, Stephane Mallarmé, Paul Valéry, and almost any surrealist or surrealist-influenced poet: Paul Éluard, Federico Garcia Lorca, Octavio Paz, and dozens of others, these days, in almost every Western language.

So what we have here to play with is in the nature of a set of two fundamentally different approaches that exchange and interplay in thousands of mysterious, frustrating, lucky and unlucky ways. For the Magicians, language itself must be paramount: language and the connotative aura it gives off; one remembers, here, Mallarmé's injunction to "give the initiative to *words*." The words are seen as illuminations mainly of one another; their light of meaning plays back and forth between them, and, though it must by nature refer beyond, outside itself, shimmers back off the external world in a way whereby the world—or objective reality, or just Reality—serves as a kind of secondary necessity, a non-verbal backdrop to highlight the dance of words and their bemused interplay.

> Let me pass by that gate
> where Eve gnaws the ant
> and Adam impregnates a dazzle of fish.
> Give way to me, horned little man, let me pass . . .

One is quite whirled away by the possibilities of suggestion here, for a thing has been stated—*stated*—such as never happened on earth, or could happen, but can be *said*; it can be made to happen in the mind by means of words, and with this concept a whole universe of chance-taking and craziness—of freedom—opens up. If Lorca can say these things, we, too, can say them; can say, in fact, quite unimpeded, anything we want to. But freedom, too, has its rules, more mysterious than any others. Why is it that some combinations of words are in some manner more moving and acting-upon—acting upon each other, and even, tangentially, on the world—than others? Why is the startling conjunction of Adam and dazzlement and impregnation and fish as daring and truly striking as it is: an assertion that has the power of a true spell, and surely had the power to get the poet past, as he implores or orders, the "horned little man"—who may indeed be conventional reason, and the guardian of the traditional ways of poetic thinking—more memorable, more *successful* than something like André Breton's "My wife with the sex of a mining-placer and of a platypus/ My wife with a sex of seaweed and ancient sweetmeat," which is merely silly, and operates according to no secret law of conjunction, no hidden magnetism that in the true poet draws the right things together, even though initially they may be far apart, and known only to the one imagination? Why is Lorca memorable and Breton ridiculous?

Let me lay on you here, as they say, a kind of imaginative

problem, or puzzle of the imagination. It has to do with individual response, and no one can really be more right than anyone else. It was said by Van Wyck Brooks that an author can be most deeply characterized by the one word around which all his work gathers; or, as I would designate it, his "boss word." Faulkner's, for example, would be something like "doom" or "fate." The historian Francis Parkman's is "manly." Jack London's was "wolf," and Lewis Mumford's is "renewal." To digress momentarily, it was Brooks's pointing this out to me that led me to read a writer whom I previously had never felt I had cause to seek out. Willa Cather's favorite word was "splendor," and immediately I found this out, I sought *her* out. Where do you find splendor any more, with existence getting more and more crowded and inconsequential, more rat-like every day? In Miss Cather there is actual real splendor, and distance, and space, and serenity. I went where she went, in those marvellous novels, and I am still there, out on those Kansas and Nebraska prairies. But I am getting ahead of where I want to be, which is with linguistic self-sufficiency and magic-making.

Words. There are not only boss words, but boss metaphors, and of no kind of writer is this more true—with a truth tantamount to absolute—than of poets. See how you respond to a few of these, for out of any of them can be raised an infinite number of metaphorical connections not supervised by existing logic, though of course these controlling figures could also be used by the poets I have called "literalists," as well. Nevertheless, the poets I have chosen are all magic-makers, the erectors of systems of language, the central metaphors of which are the following. See which ones take you; let your own imaginations dilate around these, one by one, as though the edifice of language proceeding from the central figure might possibly become your own. Without naming the poets, I'll give you their controlling images. The first is the sheaf of wheat. God knows what one might evolve out of *that*! The second is the net. The third, simply wind, the movement of air. The fourth is the military disaster on the road. The fifth is the universal void. The sixth is the snake, whatever he may stand for, whatever words may arise from him. For one of these poets, the essential metaphor is the creek running through grass; for the last of them, it is the cry in the ravine.

Here, as I said earlier, no one can be righter than anyone else, though for my own money it would be hard to beat, among those, the cry in the ravine; simply because I am the way I am, the elements of uncertainty, fear and incipient (or possible) action appeal to me.

And of course thereby I tip my hand, for I am not of the party of the magic-language practitioners, though some of them I admire extremely, and would inhibit their freedom not to the slightest extent, for the best of them say wonderful things, and renew the imagination and the language in ways that the more earthbound and literal-minded poets cannot do, because the approach to the use of language is radically different, being more inclusive. Though there is overlap between the two practices, poems still come out, ultimately, to be more of one persuasion, one intent, than the other. The difference is still between Mallarmé and Frost, between Hart Crane and Edwin Arlington Robinson, between Vachel Lindsay and Edgar Lee Masters, between Paul Éluard and Guillevic, and, in the end, between John Berryman and Randall Jarrell. The literalists, some of them almost inventive enough and far-out enough to move into the other place, the Magic Circle, have a powerful say among us, and can't—can never be—written-off or forgotten, for the world is a powerful ally, and not a bad poet itself, as God will tell you. The Frosts and Jarrells will always be with us, even though the man of the wheat-sheaf speaks of "eyes more dangerous than moving sand," and the man with the net tells a painter friend that he must not wish that his forms "be softened by the changing cotton of an unforeseen cloud"; though the man in the wind tells us that "the most powerful lungs among us have reached true space," and the military surrealist admits that, despite his not speaking of storms, "nor of great steers skinned alive, nor windmills sugared to death on the plain," he still is fascinated by the setting where it all takes place: "behind the grayhaired conquerors, I continue to see nothing on earth/ But a road on fire." The poet who lives in the void is possibly the most delicate, for against the void he has only love, sexual love, and "it is there that vertigo/ folds on itself like a bird." These are remarkable insights, and so are many others so conceived. The poet whose chief image is the snake says "deported from the yoke and from the nuptials, I strike the iron of invisible hinges." He of the net, again, says "lobsters that sing are Americans," and the watcher of peaceful water in meadows says to the "soul submitted to the mysteries of movement,/ Pass, carried by your last wide-open look:/ pass, transient soul no night can stop, neither in your/ passion, nor your smile, nor your ascension." The poet who hears the cry in the ravine has the same tone, for he is the same man who watches the creek: "a bat/ is lost in daylight,/ lost every day, torn apart by his black/ wings. . . ."

In World War II Randall Jarrell was in the Air Force, and, though he was never overseas, his human empathy and compassion and his dedication to the world, to a Reality which can only be hinted at but never really reached by language—being what it is and sufficient to itself—made of him one of the very best interpreters of warfare ever to write, able to fix unerringly on the most truthful and revealing observations and insights of other men, of combatants, and of war reporters like Ernie Pyle. But for Jarrell's singling out this episode, I would never have known something about the helplessness, and at the same time, of the grotesque resources, of the human spirit in warfare, that now, forty years later, I think it not only desirable but necessary for me to know.

> I stooped over the form of one youngster whom I thought dead. But when I looked down I saw that he was only sleeping. He was very young, and very tired. He lay on one elbow, his hand suspended in the air about six inches from the ground. And in the palm of his hand he held a large, smooth rock.
>
> I stood and looked at him for a long time. He seemed in his sleep to hold that rock lovingly, as though it were his last link with a vanishing world . . .

That rock *is* the world, is the universe, is the earth of living creatures and their existences, and Randall Jarrell held to it as unthinkingly and as lovingly and as desperately as that sleeping boy was doing after the Normandy beach-head. If it is over-weighting the scales on the side of the Human-Condition poets for me to quote Jarrell as much as I do here, I am not apologetic, for I intend my remarks as a kind of tribute to Randall, from whom I believe I learned more about what really matters in poetry and in literature than from anyone else I have known. As a poet, he might have tried a little harder for the magic, for the inescapable oddness of an idiom perhaps not based so entirely on what he thought to be the actual patterns of American speech. It is rare that you remember the actual words in which he says a thing. There are exceptions to this, however: wonderful exceptions in which language, in Randall's use, catches both the commonplace and the unusual, the inevitable, the miraculously necessary, all in a few words, a kind of blind blurted list in which, just the same, there is a rueful incisiveness. He invokes Woman, "Before the world's eyes narrowed in desire,"

Now, naked on my doorstep, in the sun,
Gold-armed, white-breasted, pink-cheeked, and black-furred . . .

Now *there* is the touch of the world! We men have known such creatures! Each of us has known at least one, and she is truly, as Randall says, "the last human power."

Here, then, are two extreme extremes, almost as though the proponents of either were using different media rather than the same medium. One orientation is bent on generating, for whatever sake, the proliferation and dance of words themselves, among themselves; the fascination is in the sometimes selective, often highly unselective action of words upon each other, for whatever meaning or sensation they may throw off, evoke. The other faction, of which Jarrell seems to me the most eloquent and persuasive defender of my time, believes in words as agents which illuminate events and situations that are part of an already given continuum, and which are only *designated* by means of words. According to this view, this practice, the poem is something overseen, *supervised* by life: by what, as Jarrell would say, we all know, we all have felt. The ultimate critic, which is to say not only the ultimate judge of value and interpreter after the fact, but the ultimate Virgil or Dantean truth-guide as the poem is composed, is its relation to lived actuality. If the reader is tempted to ask "lived by whom?" I would answer, defending as much as outlining the point, by all of us insofar as mutual human emotions and reactions are concerned: those, like fear and hunger, rooted in our common animal nature, and those like greed, and causeless anxiety, that are uniquely human. This is the world of "flesh-and-blood objects and their flesh-and-blood relations, the very world, which is the world/ Of all of us,—the place where, in the end,/ We find our happiness or not at all."

Poetry thus conceived is largely though not invariably scenic: scenic and "thing-y."

These are transient barracks, at an Air Force Base, in 1944.

> Summer. Sunset. Someone is playing
> The ocarina in the latrine:
> You Are My Sunshine. A man shaving
> Sees—past the day-room, past the night K.P.'s
> Bent over a G.I. can of beets
> In the yard of the mess—the red and green
> Lights of a runway full of '24's.
> The first night flight goes over with a roar
> And disappears, a star, among mountains.
>
> The day-room radio, switched on next door,
> Says, "The thing about you is, you're *real*."
> The man sees his own face, black against lather,
> In the steamed, starred mirror: it is real.
> And the others—the boy in underwear
> Hunting for something in his barracks-bags
>
> With a money-belt around his middle—
> The voice from the doorway: "Where's the C.Q.?"
> "Who wants to know?" "He's gone to the movies."
> "Tell him Red wants him to sign his clearance"—
> These are. Are what? Are.

It's real, all right; the poem is set as solidly in the details of an actual situation as it can be by means of a simple listing and connection of the items that make up a time and place. If you believe in the G.I. can of beets, you believe in everything that is mentioned; there is no need to lie, for the man who set down these items, who composed this scene out of a very real memory, would not lie, because he believes that the poem and the Truth it refers to are not separable from each other: if there had not been that scene, there would not be this poem; the poem refers us to a part of what has happened to someone—to what, in 1944, happened to many. Is this reference to reality, to things as they are, to things as they have been, to things that seem so much to be what they are that they cannot be anything else, entitled to be the limiting factor for all imaginative use of language? The Magicians say no; that there *are* no limits, or that the limits are defined only by personality, only by the individual poet's creative reach, only by the laws he makes for himself, and by means of which he operates. Speaking of contemporary painting, abstract expressionism, Jarrell says that "much of the world—much, too, of the complication and contradiction, the size and depth of the essential process of earlier painting—is inaccessible to Pollock. It has been made inaccessible by the provincialism that is one of the marks of our age." Then he says to us, later in the essay, as he says he says to his wife, " 'What a pity we didn't live in an age when painters were still interested in the world.' " And yet, here too is a kind of provincialism, and it seems to me that very good poets of a certain kind cannot for long be held by it, will not allow their imaginations and their metaphor-making hungers to be confined, limited, and finally judged and condemned, exalted or forgotten by the ordinariness—or even the strangeness—of the strictly observable part of existence, either anybody's or everybody's. Empiricism, as others than Jarrell have noted, yields—no, *is* itself a kind of poetry, but it is not the only source and the only strength.

Recently I have tried, as the athletes say, to work out with the magical side of language: to break away from an approach that I felt was tending toward the anecdote, and depending too much upon it for whatever value this dependency might give it. Perhaps, in the latest poems I have done, this has been a mistake, but even if it has, I can still say that by the attempt I have been made aware of ranges of expression, of possibilities, of departures, of "new thresholds, new anatomies," that I previously had no idea existed, or certainly had no idea that I might explore. Excitement over the new is the life-blood, the guts of any kind of creativity: something, some way as yet untried.

I have shared this excitement with a good many poets of my time, some a little older, some the same age, but most, younger than

I. A great deal of translation work has been undertaken during my lifetime, and at least since the success of Ezra Pound 's *Cathay* poems there have not been the restrictions on translation that had, previously, demanded certain fixed standards, such as fidelity to the original text, and—despite Pope and Dryden and Homer and Virgil and the heroic couplet—something approximating the metrical and linear form of the original. Pound's renderings changed all that, as, for better or worse, Pound changed a lot of things. If you go to a quite good popular anthology of Chinese poetry, like, say, Robert Payne's *The White Pony*, you may find there a quite respectable poem by Li Po called "A Song of Chang Kan." Most of us don't read Chinese, but if we read Payne's translation we are likely to feel that it is a good, feeling poem that projects a human situation with modesty and a certain power. I won't text-creep here, won't compare—but I expect you would agree with me that Payne's transliteration has produced something readable and even moving. "A Song of Chang Kan," before us in this way, is definitely a good poem. But Ezra Pound's version, made possible to some degree by Ernest Fenollosa's research but mainly by Pound's intuition, tact, resourcefulness, and daring, is not a good poem; it is a *great* poem, up there with the best our time has produced: utterly clear, tonally just right: a depiction of female love in deep and modest language that must be with us as part of us, from the very first encounter. But, as any good Sinologist would tell you—if he likes scholarship better than poetry, tell you gladly—Pound's version is not strictly accurate; in fact, to scholarly scrutiny, it is not accurate at all; even the name of the village is wrong. Much has been left out of the original, and words, lines, images have been changed. Where does this leave Li Po, long dead, some say, from getting drunk and trying to embrace the moon in the Yellow River? Long dead, but the writer of the poem? What happens to the English-tongue greatness of the poem, as it emerged forever from passing through Ezra Pound's hands? It is a great poem. Whose is it?

I can no more hope to solve the problem of what constitutes a true, just, accurate and at the same time poetically-valuable translation than I can solve the one I started with: what poetry itself, is. I am convinced, however, that any given translated poem should be a good poem in its own right in the second language. It need not be a better poem, and can even be a worse poem, but the experience of poetry itself, as the beholder of it takes it in, is similar in all cultures, I suspect, and among all people: it must be a real poem, and not some classic or contemporary author in another language embalmed or petrified: or, to use a phrase I like, to describe *some* translations—doubtless accurate and scholarly—as "laid-out in English." Whatever your opinion, and whatever my opinion, it is a fact that translation—accurate translation, inaccurate translation, half-translation, half-assed translation, "imitation," free-form "improvisation from," pseudo-translation, intuitive translation, having-nothing-at-all-to-do-with-the-original writing—which should not be called translation at all—and many, many other forms of poetic mediation between languages—is now probably the paramount influence on poetry in English. Americans do more of it, but the English do plenty, and the Irish, some. What amounts to an international style is emerging from this. The cohesive poem, the structured poem, the classically-overseen poem, the reasoned-out and yielding-to-reason poem, the poem of scholarship and wit, the ironic poem, the New Criticism-ed poem, the satirical poem—which depends on a line of argument—the light-verse poem (except for the *New Yorker*!), the narrative poem, all these are rare; you will find few of them in the magazines, or in the hundreds of books of poetry, of would-be or aspiring-to-be poetry, that come out each year. What, instead, do we find?

We find writing which is largely, in each poem, and from poem to poem, discontinuous, alogical, and arbitrary. For example, this is the kind of writing aimed at; it happens to be German, and is by Paul Celan, and called "Flower." The translation is by Michael Hamburger, who is very accurate indeed, having German as much to hand as English. This is what Celan says.

> The stone.
> The stone in the air, which I followed.
> Your eye, as blind as the stone.
>
> We were
> hands,

we baled the darkness empty, we found
the word that ascended summer:
flower.

Flower—a blind man's word.
Your eye and mine:
they see
to water.

Growth.
Heart wall upon heart wall
adds petals to it.

One more word like this, and the hammers
will swing over open ground.

The poem, even so, is not rendered with *exact* fidelity, for Celan merely says that at the word—the one word "like this"—"the hammers will swing free." Hamburger, a fine poet himself, could not resist the "over open ground," which for my money is the best thing in the poem. Once again we are brought up against the Pound problem: among so many, the Pound problem of translation: what liberties may be taken in the interest of producing good poems based on other poems in another tongue? The more pressing question is, though, what principle should determine the items of a poem? Should their relationship to each other be strong or weak? Or should any principle of connection exist at all? The current international style in English brings in items from all over, and frequently their relationship is either so tenuous that it cannot be grasped, or it is nonexistent, the references of the poem being so discrete and arbitrary that one cannot comprehend—or worse, cannot *feel*—the poem in any unifying or impacting way except as a succession of details, some of them remarkable and a good many ranging downward from the "nice try" variety to silliness and the self-parody that is neither funny nor parody of the first-rate examples of the genre they attempt, but of the fourth- and fifth-rate: in short, of others like them.

The arbitrariness of the method, the approach, the intent, the practice, is what bothers me most. That and the fact that there is no characteristicalness, no real author, no imprint of personality in individual poems, or indeed in whole collections. It would be no trouble to take lines, phrases and images and transplant them from one poem to another without loss or gain; the same process could be employed within the same poem, with the same result. The end is a kind of poetry of interchangeable parts, sometimes interesting, but only scrappily, only point-to-point in individual observations and phrases, but not experienceable as whole poems, for all sense of progression, to say nothing of an inevitable-thing-having-been-said, has been impossible to the poem since the poet began to write it from these particular assumptions. "The essential fault of surrealism," Wallace Stevens says, "is that it invents without discovering. To make a clam play an accordion is to invent not to discover. The observation of the unconscious, so far as it can be observed, should reveal things of which we have previously been unconscious, not the familiar things of which we have been conscious plus imagination." Moreover, *drama*, here, is not so much dead; it never had a chance. This is why there has never been a great surrealist poem, as there has never been a great poem in English conceived entirely in this way; and in my opinion, there will never be. It is arguable that there have been great surrealists *poets*—some of the French would say that Éluard is one and most of them would argue that Rimbaud is one, but *Le Bâteau Ivre* is imminently logical and can be shown to be; the logic is unconventional, with elements of hallucination, but it is logic just the same: the man, or boy in the boat, or the poet seen as the boat itself, undergoes a voyage, and in it—some things before, some things after—events follow each other. Even stretching a point and categorizing Rimbaud as a surrealist, although "pre," we can still assert that aside from him, there are no great—truly great—surrealist poets, for great poets must write great poems, and surrealist poems cannot be great because they cannot *build*, and neither can the poems of the new international style. They have no armature: of narrative, of logic, of idea-development and/or idea-succession or change, or transformation; they are not thematic, or at least the theme is most of the time not publicly available. This is why, when they are not darkly mysterious or frivolous, or on-putting, the titles of international-style poems are important, for otherwise no theme could make even a weak gesture at claiming the items of the poem. In the Celan piece earlier quoted, for example, and entitled "Flower," except for the title, a repetition of it, and the one word, "petals " near the end, it could be about anything at all. "Blindness" would be a better title, or something like "Search," or even "Quarry." "Flower—a blind man's word./ your eye and mine:/ they see/ to water." Why *water*? What necessity has this? What aptness? Why not fire? Why not cloud? Why not diamond? Why not murder? Why not goose-grease? All of these would yield different "meanings," but not to a general theme, a central situation; not to flowers. It seems to me that there is a terrible inconsequentiality about poems of this kind, for the *world* is lacking, and the buzz of language and hit-or-miss-metaphor-generation is everything; the poem itself is nothing; or only a collection of fragments.

And yet, as Mr. Eliot remarked, the bottom is a great way down. Dylan Thomas would have been impossible without this approach, or something like it; as he said, he allowed one image to breed another, and the two to breed a third, of these "a fourth contradictory image, and let them all, within my imposed formal limits, conflict." His imposed *formal* limits . . . or, his *imposed* formal limits. His work too, in quite a different way from Rimbaud's, is logical, though the logic is principally that of a quasi-private symbolism held together by a magnificent and thunderously rhetorical prosody.

> For as long as forever is
> and the fast sky quakes in the web, as the fox in the wave,
> with heels of birds & the plumed eyes . . .

This has what I would call the right kind of seeming arbitrariness—what is a fox doing in a *wave* anyway?—which is Dylan Thomas's sort; the figure is not pulled, with great assertiveness and little personal sense of selection, out of an air from which one can select any two things and put them together, nor is the language, delivered as chopped-up prose with no rhythmical continuity, or what I would call "surge," shovelled off the top of the midden-heap or multi-cultured dump of a current style. Even though the poem with the fox in the wave was never used except for one line of a later poem, it is thematic, and has to do with the lives of hunted creatures, the passage of time, in which human beings, in their fear and the inevitability of their fate, suffer, live and die with the animals: "For as long as forever is . . . forever the hunted world at a snail's gallop goes." The fox was pulled out of the great world and put into an unexpected and untoward place. I am glad he is there, for he is part of a wonderful image: not only wonderful in itself but wonderful where it occurs, in this poem unpublished until Paul Ferris's biography. Dylan Thomas, I would argue, would not have been possible without the unlimited freedom that came into writing at the time of the surrealist poets, whether he drew on them or not. The point is that he used the freedom, the risk of the *merely* arbitrary, the range of his mind and imagination over everything available to him, everything he could reach or conjure up, and discovered or made—again *within his imposed formal limits*, and using *rhythm* as only he could use it—an English-speaking poetry unparalleled in our time or in any, for originality, inimitability and indispensibility. in any, for originality, inimitability and indispensibility.

So where are we? With Jarrell and the G.I. can of beets, with the fox in the wave, or with Paul Celan's hammers over open ground? I side with the world; as Kafka said, "in the contest between yourself and the world, back the world." I do, but I also want its support, *at* my back. I want, as Randall wanted, "poems in which there are real people with their real speech and real thought and real emotions."

I admit, though, to being profoundly interested in what might be the yield of absolute freedom, and hope, in practice, to be able to make metaphors I have never yet been able to achieve, bound into one poetic situation, one scene, one event after the other. The hammers swinging over the ground, detached as they are, out of nowhere and anywhere, have strong appeal to me. *What* hammers, *what* open ground? Perhaps, as some of the new poets say, it doesn't matter. But maybe it could be made to matter, in the sense that Thomas's fox in the wave matters. There may be unsuspected fortune in an approach that offers, literally, even to a literalist, any metaphorical connection that his mind can make, that offers to literature any connection that *anybody's* mind can make. What hammers, indeed? What open ground? Reality . . . World . . . what an *image*!

Lines

FIRING LINE*

With William F. Buckley, Jr.

MR. BUCKLEY: James Dickey, as you will quickly note, is a Southerner, born in Atlanta, educated at Clemson and Vanderbilt, and now he is a professor of English at the University of South Carolina and between going to school and teaching school he accomplished a great deal. During the war he engaged in over 100 combat night fighter missions. After the war, he worked as an advertising executive, but always he scribbled poetry. And then, in 1966, he earned the National Book Award for the Best Poetry of the Year, *Buckdancer's Choice.* He had already published three books of verse, and since then he has published three more. Nineteen seventy was a special year for Mr. Dickey—two volumes of poetry, one of them called *The Eyebeaters, Blood, Victory, Madness, Buckhead and Mercy*, and a stunning novel called *Deliverance*, which was nominated for best novel of the year and is currently being made into a movie. Throughout the years, he has written literary criticism for the most demanding journals. From 1966 to 1968, he was Consultant in Poetry for the Library of Congress. Unlike many poets, James Dickey is an enthusiast. He hunts with bow and arrow, canoes, weightlifts, mixes martinis, and plays the guitar, specializing in American Folk. He lives very big—a Rabelaisian—and my notion is to discuss with him the question, "What has happened to the spirit of America?'' I begin by asking him, ''Do you yourself ever feel the lure of despair?''

MR. DICKEY: I don't know whether you could call it a ''lure,'' Bill, but despair, definitely. Sure. But the spirit of America includes something like that. If we want to talk about it, though, the first thing to do is get some kind of definition. What *is* the American spirit?

MR. BUCKLEY: Well, it is easier to say what it isn't, which is a perfectly—as I understand it—conventional system and logical, too. It certainly isn't boredom. It isn't a sense of impotence. It isn't a sense of futility. It isn't a sense of misanthropy. And it isn't a sense of self-hate, either. Without saying that it is exactly the opposite of all those things, it seems to me that that litany suggests some things that are in some ways distinctive to America.

MR. DICKEY: Yes. I was in Australia several years ago, and it seemed to me—I went around and talked to a lot of different kinds of people—just on the basis of this one Australian trip, that we have developed to a point that Australia has not come to yet. Australia is like America was when we had a great feeling of hope and promise and possibility. They still have their frontier down there. Here, I think the thing that's eating us up in America is excessive introspection, and the questioning of every motive, so that you can't do the simplest thing without being made aware that there's a certain amount of suspicion and perhaps guilt that attaches to it. I think that we are being deprived of simplicity, in a very subtle way, by the news media and television. And I think that we are in a way being deprived of the motive power, the mainspring, of what has always made Americans enthusiastic and able to accomplish things: a simplicity of motive that Americans had before, and we don't have now. Everything has to be intellectualized about, and above all, every motive has to be questioned.

MR. BUCKLEY: What is your response?

MR. DICKEY: I think that this entire willingness to assign guilt to you, to me, to the American man in the street, and so on, is in a very subtle way robbing us of the possibilities of our own experience, so that we can't do the simplest thing, such as eating an ice cream cone, without somebody telling us that we are really fascists.

MR. BUCKLEY: This doubting of motives is related truly to what I started off by calling "the lure of despair." Isn't it correct that a lot of Americans, especially among the intelligentsia, do feel the nearest thing that they ever experienced to joy is when America gets into trouble? For instance, let's say that we have been whipped very badly and very decisively in Cambodia with just everybody in sight killed—I mean us. There are "X" number of people who would have gotten a certain kind of delight from that. I say that intending not to say that I am talking about perverts. I am simply talking about people who feel that there is a certain intellectual gratification that comes from their pessimism being justified.

MR. DICKEY: I could not agree with you more, and I think that so much of this stems from some personal, psychological difficulty, so that if you yourself are doubtful about your own abilities, you can always put your country down, and if you can't cut it with your country or in your country's economic sphere or social sphere, then everybody's out of step but John. There's this enormous—would you say—impulse to put the blame on somebody besides yourself. It's the politicians in Washington; it's the economic policy; it's the international policy; but don't blame me if I'm no good. They did it to me.

MR. BUCKLEY: Okay, now if that's true, what is it that happened between Australia and now that caused a people, assuming that your psychoanalysis is correct, to turn in that direction?

MR. DICKEY: Bill, the answer would be much more in your domain than in mine. I think myself, as Thomas Wolfe says somewhere, that we are lost here in America, but we will be found. But when you talk about the American spirit—and we never did, I believe, get a workable definition—we are talking about several different kinds of directions. The American spirit used to be thought of as embodied in a hardy, receptive kind of person, industrious and hard-working, who had an implicit belief in the Horatio Alger dream: Tom the honest bootblack would be able to become president of the company, which in many cases he did. I don't know how honest he was, but that's not the question anymore. The American spirit now has to do with a lot of other things. I mean people are quite willing to identify the American spirit with Lieutenant Calley, with suppression, with oppression, and with a good many things that Americans have never liked to believe about themselves. But what people must realize is that despite the inequalities—the obvious difficulties in this country—this country is the greatest thing that ever was, for people.

MR. BUCKLEY: Why?

MR. DICKEY: Because it allows the free flowering of the individual talent.

MR. BUCKLEY: Well, how do you handle the argument that, in fact the instrument, the engines of conformity, pound harder in America than anywhere else . . . that anybody who wears his hair too long or dresses oddly or is out of beat is instantly Babbittized?

MR. DICKEY: What do you mean "Babbittized"? Nobody puts hippies down any more. I think that people with long hair are great. It seems to me that the so-called hippies have added a colorful note to the American scene with their dress. In fact, the last poem I wrote was about dressing up as a middle-aged hippie. I loved doing it. All these rednecks around in South Carolina looked at me, you know. I went to a barber shop to get a haircut. I had a hat made out of three foxes, bought at Brooks Brothers, and I heard this guy down at the end say, "If there's anything I can't stand it's a middle-aged hippie." And when I got up and put on my fox hat and walked out the door, the guy in the next chair to me murmured, "Goodbye, Fox," which act I think has a great deal to do with the possibilities of human relationships. Surely I didn't expect sympathy!

MR. BUCKLEY: Well, you're saying, in effect, that contrary to the current impression, eccentricity is not only tolerated; in fact, it's encouraged.

MR. DICKEY: It's encouraged, and it's emulated. Is that the right word?

MR. BUCKLEY: It depends on what you mean to say. (laughter) What are we going to do about Susan Sontag?

MR. DICKEY: Is there something to be done about her? I don't know; I can't read her. She's unfathomable to me. What has she done that needs to be done about?

MR. BUCKLEY: Well, I'm using her as a synecdoche. It seems to me plain that she is as useful as anybody else to recall a mood about America which is very fashionable these days; a mood about America as being irrecoverably Philistine, as being as I say, conformists, as being dedicated, in the words of Howard Zinn, to death, as taking some sort of sadistic pleasure out of our enterprise in Vietnam.

MR. DICKEY: Well, that's a perfect example of what I was talking about earlier—this excessive self-questioning. If I had any advice to offer the audience or myself or you, Bill, or to any human being, I would say go out today after we leave the show and do something simple. And don't ask yourself whether it means that you really want to have sexual intercourse with your mother.

MR. BUCKLEY: Simpler than that, huh?

MR. DICKEY: Yes, do something simple, and don't bother about it. Just do it. I don't include murder.

MR. BUCKLEY: When you say, "Do something," do you mean achieve something?

MR. DICKEY: No, just some kind of simple act, something that you enjoy, something that means something to you, and you know not why.

MR. BUCKLEY: You mean drink a Coca-Cola?

MR. DICKEY: Sure. But don't say that when you drink a Coca-Cola it means you're knuckling under to the American system that condoned the My Lai massacre.

MR. BUCKLEY: Yes, yes. Or that you are an instrument of Madison Avenue which programmed your drinking the Coca-Cola.

MR. DICKEY: Well, even if Madison Avenue did, I still happen to like the stuff.

Mr. BUCKLEY: And besides, you wrote the script a few years ago.

MR. DICKEY: Yes, I *like* Coca-Cola.

MR. BUCKLEY: The notion then that America is as it is depicted, you seem to agree, we seem to agree, is wrong. On the other hand, it was you who began by remarking the differences between Australia, as you saw it recently, and America. Now, are you distinguishing between, roughly speaking, say, the New York literary bohemian set who suffer this etiolation?

MR. DICKEY: I dislike them, and vice versa.

MR. BUCKLEY: Yes, or is it the people at large who suffer from a breakdown of the spirit?

MR. DICKEY: I don't know. Again, I'm not quite sure what the spirit is. The spirit, essentially, is as it is stated at the end of *The Great Gatsby*, where Nick Carraway has this one last night looking out over Long Island Sound and thinking what this country must have meant to the Dutch sailors who first sailed into that area, pondering and wondering how they must have felt when men had a new chance. They had this whole world over here that nobody in Europe, except for just a few years, had ever known was here. I think that one of the most important feelings that men or women, or humanity, can have is that of being able to start over. This is the thing that civilization had when America was discovered. Again, if we had one of two choices, Bill . . . if we colonized another planet, or a number of selected human beings did, or if we had an atomic holocaust that wiped out almost all of the human race and there were just a few men left to start over, what would we do?

MR. BUCKLEY: To make it different?

MR. DICKEY: Yes, but would we *want* to make it different? How? I can't solve it. I wake up thinking, "Jim, if God came down through the ceiling and sat on my shoulder and said, 'Okay, we're going to do the whole thing again. We're going to start over. How would you set things up?,' " I would have no answer. I don't *know* how I would set them up.

MR. BUCKLEY: Well, I'd eliminate taxes, wouldn't you?

MR. DICKEY: There has to be something to tax first.

MR. BUCKLEY: I think you're right. And that presumably is one of the reasons why so many of the revolutionists have so little concrete to suggest, which must be why they need to sound sort of abstruse when they are talking about a vision of the order of society. Nevertheless, it still doesn't answer the question why is the—call it despair if you like, or frustration—why is it so palatable? It's there. You can feel it.

MR. DICKEY: I think it's because people don't really know what they *want* to have happen. There is so much talk about the quality of life . . . again, a sterile introspection. There is so much talk! Camus said there is only one question of any philosophical importance at all, and that's whether or not you have the right to kill yourself.

MR. BUCKLEY: Whether to commit suicide? Is that what you're saying?

MR. DICKEY: Right. This is the beginning of *Le Mythe de Sisyphe*. Whether a man has the right to take his own life. But you could extend that by saying that there's not anything that really matters to us any more than how to live on the blue planet. The philosophers have argued that out for years and years, hundreds of years, and nobody has really given any kind of an adequate answer.

MR. BUCKLEY: Yes, it's true. But some ages historically have been very robust, and people would disagree without its happening to them what seems sometimes to be happening to us. In the Renaissance, for instance, there was plenty of disagreement—plenty of everything—but no despair.

MR. DICKEY: Well, that's because, I think, that the one antidote to despair is the belief that one and one's people are going forward *toward* something.

MR. BUCKLEY: Okay. Now, to what extent would you think that our experiences in Vietnam either produced that despair or, if not, crystallized it?

MR. DICKEY: Oh, Bill, you're getting me over into your area. I must start asking you about the prosody of Elizabethan playwrights.

MR. BUCKLEY: Go ahead.

MR. DICKEY: Now this Heywood, let me tell you what he does. (laughter) No, I don't know, Bill. But one thing I would really like to get on record as saying is that I think it's maybe something of a mistake for a writer or a would-be artist like myself to be making pronouncements on public issues of which he has no more knowledge than any other private citizen.

MR. BUCKLEY: No, you see you misunderstood the question. I wasn't asking you "Are you pro or against Vietnam?" That would be a silly question under the circumstances. I'm asking you whether . . .

MR. DICKEY: I know you weren't.

MR. BUCKLEY: . . . as an artist you have presumably a keen perception of things and, therefore, you will have noticed that the affair in Vietnam, irrespective of whether it's the smartest thing we ever did or the dumbest thing we ever did, has had a terrific effect.

MR. DICKEY: Oh, yes, I think especially among the young. A great deal of this has to do with ideological reasons, and a great deal of it also has to do with young men who don't want to get drafted and sent there. I don't blame them; I wouldn't want to be sent there, either. If I were able, or if somebody were able to furnish me with cogent reasons that the involvement in Vietnam does, in fact, keep Communism from our shores; that is, from influencing or even dominating people that I love, I would think it would be worth it to have done—to sacrifice 50,000 American lives and untold billions of dollars. But I don't believe that that kind of proof is humanly capable of being given. Perhaps it is; if so, I would like to see it. I was in the service myself, and I have a serviceman's inevitable orientation toward any kind of warfare. I came up along during World War II when serving was a matter of honor—and so did you, Bill; you were in the infantry; it was a matter of honor and patriotism to be involved in your country's conflicts abroad. Since Korea, though, there seems to be something different. There was never any great objection to World War II. There were a few objectors, conscientious objectors. But there was nothing like the public opposition to the war there is in the case of Vietnam. One must pay attention.

MR. BUCKLEY: Okay. Now, is it possible to make generalities about what the Vietnam War has done to America without paying any attention at all to the question of whether or not the Vietnam War was inevitable or desirable? Let's assume it was undesirable, or let's assume it was desirable. Either way, it has nevertheless had the same impact on America. It seems to me that that impact was brilliantly and perversely expressed as a reaction to the trial of Lieutenant Calley. It seems to me that the American people don't understand the situation in which they are not permitted to win or to lose a war. If you are permitted to lose a war, that would be bad, but we could absorb it. And we've seen from the recent experience of Japan and Germany that you can lose a war and still get over it. We're not allowed to lose a war; but we're not allowed to win it either. And that has done something of a demoralizing character to America which needs to be understood.

MR. DICKEY: I agree. I think of myself again not as a political commentator at all or an expert on international policy or geopolitics or anything of that sort—just as a citizen. As I say, I'm not an expert at all. I'm sure most of you know more than I do about these things. However, I think that the business of the polarization of the young is important. The young seem to think of this as their issue, or one of their issues, in the way that they think of "their" thing being an involvement with the drug culture. Oh, not all of them, but surely many. Vietnam in a sense identifies them. They have an identity which they were afraid of being raped of by middle-class America and the situation in which most of them grew up. The war is something that's important to them because it gives them an identity both as a group and as individuals, just like the long hair.

MR. BUCKLEY: Well, the fact that it gives them an identity may contribute to our understanding that they are not for that reason completely alienated. On the other hand, what happens next? What then happens? Do they feel that they have to shrive the experience in Vietnam? What is it? Let's assume that the whole of the younger generation feels that Vietnam was a catastrophic moral venture. Let's assume that strategy stands aside and allows them to play out this particular role. How will they feel that they shrive it, in the sense, for instance, the Germans turn to Adolf Hitler, in order to undo the Versailles Treaty? What is it that when they are thirty or forty years old they will feel that the United States has to do in order to expiate Vietnam?

MR. DICKEY: I don't know; I think the opposite side of the coin from Vietnam and the Lieutenant Calleys and the My Lais and things of that nature is represented by a kind of excessive altruism, or a public statement thereof, where you . . .

MR. BUCKLEY: Undifferentiate it?

MR. DICKEY: Well, I don't know how you would "undifferentiate" it. But we could bring in another point, Bill, which is terribly interesting, especially in the literary field. What all of this complex of attitudes and ideas and actions has made possible—or one of the things it's made possible—is that it has ushered in the moral put-down: that is, the assumption that "I am more altruistic than you." In my own field, that of poetry, I have seen review after review saying that such-and-such a poet doesn't take the correct stand on Vietnam. He may be against the war in Vietnam, but he is not against it in exactly the *same way* that I am against it. Therefore, his is really a failure of morality, and his verse stinks.

MR. BUCKLEY: Is this simply an intellectual obsession or is it also, do you think, a spiritual obsession?

MR. DICKEY: I think both. I've seen a man like Kenneth Rexroth in San Francisco get up and pronounce the word "love" in a way that would make you hate your fellow man. What I think the real poets stand for and have always stood for is a position which is foursquare against cant of that sort or any sort. Love is not a program. You don't love your fellow man because it's politically expedient or literarily expedient to be more publicly loving than somebody else. You love because it's something in your nature that you can't help. Again, you don't love because it's of an advantage to love. You can *profess* love on that basis, but you don't really love. You love because you can't help it. It's because—to coin a phrase—your heart goes out in this direction or toward this person or this group, not by means of any volition on your part, or coercion on somebody else's.

MR. BUCKLEY: Well, if there is a lot of cant, then can we assume that since reality is the principle enemy of cant, all of this structure of attitudes is going to break down; and if so, what then happens?

MR. DICKEY: I think people are not going to be deluded forever by faddism or current movements or popular attitudes in certain political and social groups. So many of those things . . . they're like popular songs. They're on the juke boxes just for a few weeks and then they pass off and others come on. I think there is a basic imaginative hard-headedness about Americans that will eventually issue forth in, would you say, not exactly in programs—that's not a word I like—but in a . . .

MR. BUCKLEY: Reawakening.

MR. DICKEY: Perhaps something of that sort.

MR. BUCKLEY: Have you any idea how one would spot it?

MR. DICKEY: No, I think it's a personal and private thing, whether you agree with yourself that *this* has it and *that* doesn't. But the role of poetry, or my particular bag—is that term still in use?—I think illustrates a kind of way. Most of the language that we encounter every day is manipulative; that is, the advertisers and the politicians and the public media of various sorts have designs on you in one way or another. I used to work in the advertising business for McCann-Erickson, which was called, in the unspeakable jargon of Madison Avenue, a research-oriented agency. And I researched a lot. I was with people who researched a lot. Let me ask you a question, or somebody a question, Bill. How many advertising messages do you think you are exposed to every day?

MR. BUCKLEY: If you'd call anything that announces its own existence . . .

MR. DICKEY: I do. I do, and so do they.

MR. BUCKLEY: For instance, is 72 East 72nd Street an advertising message?

MR. DICKEY: In a way. It is selling the university.

MR. BUCKLEY: How is it selling the university?

MR. DICKEY: Because it's announcing its existence as part of this program.

MR. BUCKLEY: No, it's identifying where the students come from who take part in this program. But is that a form of advertising?

MR. DICKEY: Yes, I think the McCann-Erickson people would agree to that.

MR. BUCKLEY: Why?

MR. DICKEY: Well, again, it has something to do with the self-aggrandizement of the school, don't you think, or do you?

MR. BUCKLEY: If to identify somebody is to participate in an act of aggrandizement, then you are correct. I myself think this is something that you were taught at McCann-Erickson that you ought to have forgotten.

MR. DICKEY: Bill, you were born for controversy! But you won't get any out of me. I just want kind of a provisional answer—how many messages—well, if you drive down a superhighway you see Esso, you see Mobil, you see . . .

MR. BUCKLEY: Two names.

MR. DICKEY: Two names . . . Okay, how many of those—this is a relatively conservative estimate—do you think you run up against every twenty-four hours? You leaf through a magazine and there are scores, for example.

MR. BUCKLEY: Well, the *New York Times* is about a hundred pages. That's at least a hundred.

MR. DICKEY: That's right, but you are far short, at least according to the researchers of McCann-Erickson. They say that the average American—again, that mythological beast—is exposed to about 50,000.

MR. BUCKLEY: Fifty thousand. That doesn't allow you room to meditate much on . . . (laughter)

MR. DICKEY: No, but to get back to my point . . .

MR. BUCKLEY: That doesn't mean you tune them out?

MR. DICKEY: Well, you do, some of them, but all of them form part of the milieu in which you live. You couldn't say that they form the whole milieu, but they form a good deal of it. And the thing about poetry that is important, I think, is that it's kind of the last resort of non-manipulative language. As Auden says somewhere, "Poetry makes nothing happen." It doesn't make you want to buy something or vote for a political candidate, or anything of that sort. To use a last-year's expression, it tries to tell it like it is. It has to do with what Wordsworth called "spots of time": incidents and things which have meant something to a person, that he wants to communicate. It's kind of a communication-in-depth rather than a continual surface coercion.

MR. BUCKLEY: But why should it follow that that wouldn't be galvanizing?

MR. DICKEY: Well, it might. It might, but it doesn't have to.

MR. BUCKLEY: For instance, certainly the poem "To His Coy Mistress" was intended to be galvanizing.

MR. DICKEY: What did it galvanize? Do you mean to lead to action of some sort?

MR. BUCKLEY: Yes.

MR. DICKEY: You think it's a pornographic poem?

MR. BUCKLEY: No, no, no. That's a dirty thing to say!

MR. DICKEY: Well!

MR. BUCKLEY: It was certainly intended to be manipulative.

MR. DICKEY: Of what—to ask the lady to go out and . . .

MR. BUCKLEY: To ask her to change her mind.

MR. DICKEY: Oh, I see. But that lady's gone. I see what you mean. You could take the poem and you could use it on a latter-day lady. But, I remember hearing Auden read his great eulogy on the death of W. B. Yeats when he says that poetry makes nothing happen, which is again one of those extreme statements that Auden is so good at. Poetry makes nothing happen—"it survives in the valley of its own saying, / A way of happening, a mouth." "Earth receive an honored guest; William Yeats is laid to rest. Let the Irish vessel lie emptied of its poetry." Every time I look at *Playboy* I think of this. "Time that is intolerant/Of the brave and innocent/And indifferent in a week/To a beautiful physique."

PANEL PARTICIPATION

MR. BUCKLEY: Mr. Wafer.

MR. WAFER: Can I ask a question?

MR. BUCKLEY: In blank verse.

MR. DICKEY: It would have to be quatrains.

MR. WAFER: I'd like to pursue something. I want to preface it by saying that I admire your attitude of, I think, a simplistic view of life which I would very much like to be able to adopt. But I think the error—I think your view—is a little bit simplistic in that you termed a few minutes ago that language is manipulative and that [the] media are. Isn't this the reason that we have become so introspective? That we are essentially not so much, as you say, being attacked, but affronted on several sides by corporations, the media, etc., and we kind of have to look out for ourselves. We almost have to be introspective and analyze everything we do just to . . .

MR. DICKEY: Well, yes, I think it's kind of a paradox, as you do. Again, as Bill asked me, where is the road out of this? I don't know. I think maybe the road out is only the one that leads further in to the same sort of thing. But I do know, speaking for my personal experience, that I've had a few times in my life when whatever I was doing seemed to be the most natural, and above all, the most utterly easy thing in the world to do. Those moments I cherish because they seem to be the ones in which I was most essentially myself. This is all I mean.

MR. WAFER: To carry that a little further. . . . When we allowed or when the first persons—the white man—came to America and were themselves and in a few years had inhaled the entire country and the frontier was gone—if we allow this type of spirit to prevail again, or to encourage it, if we did start over, the error of our ways is rather obvious. We'd have to . . . I don't know what we'd have to do either.

MR. DICKEY: The thing that seems to me to underlie the whole business of the attitude of, say, man to the modern world, is economic. If we came on a new planet—even a new continent; this is in a way going on in Northern Alaska right now—there are going to be interests that want to get rich off it. And they are going to go up there and they're going to run off the elk. They don't care anything about the elk. They care about the oil. And they're going to sink those wells if they have the technical know-how to do so. Somebody's going to make a fortune off of the place, and the elk will die. Now, there are a lot of things that I don't agree with the young people about, and the one that is most distasteful to me is their involvement with drugs. I can understand, in a way, since my generation is going down the drain on liquor. I can understand why they think it might be valuable to them, in a way, or fun, to do drugs. But one issue that I really am foursquare and 100 per cent behind young people on is the ecology thing. Bill and I first met down at one of the space shots, and we were both—maybe I shouldn't speak for him but I think I can still say we were both very much moved by it.

MR. BUCKLEY: That was the day of the Homeric sky.

MR. DICKEY: Yes, it was! A wonderful phrase! I think one of the most important things that came of the business of men going out from the earth and, say, orbiting the moon or landing on the moon, is that they brought back these photographs showing the earth against its background of eternal blackness: the void. We realize that we don't have infinite resources, and we can't plunder and exploit just at will any more. There was a time when men could; when the new worlds were conquered and when the great fortunes were made. But we can't do it now. And to look at those photographs of the planet as Ed White, one of my great heroes—one of the men who was killed in that accident in the mock-up, remember; he was the first fellow to walk in space—said that whoever lives out there in space is going to have to call earth "the blue planet." We are all inhabitants of the blue planet, and these photographs taken from the moon or on the way out or on the way back from the moon show how infinitely vulnerable this planet is. I have never subscribed—despite the mathematicians with their permutations and combinations—to the possibility that there is any sentient life anywhere but here. I think it's all right here. And this makes life infinitely more precious than if it were reproducible in lots of other places.

MR. BUCKLEY: I don't think it is.

MR. DICKEY: I think that we are *it*. End of sermon.

MR. BUCKLEY: Miss Blain.

MISS BLAIN: You just said that we are it as far as sentient life goes. And also we heard you say that the American dream is gone; the American spirit has wasted itself through introspection or technologization. And so, here we are, college age. What do we have to do? We have no heroes. Why do we have no heroes?

MR. DICKEY: Again, you are of the college generation, and you would be more competent to answer that than I would. But if there is a promise in America, and if there is an American spirit worth talking about in these terms, these positive terms, it seems to me that the best thing about it is that the spirit is infinitely renewable. It may be that it would take heroes, as John F. Kennedy was to a great many people, to renew the spirit. I don't know what it would take for your generation. But I do know, and I very profoundly believe, that the American spirit—the best part of this country and this people—is infinitely renewable. The question is, what would renew it? Again, I don't know what would. Perhaps an end to the war; perhaps some kind of mass utilization of this altruistic motive that seems to be so strong in people. Some of it is false, but a great deal of it is very real, I think.

MISS BLAIN: I think this is a good place to go back to poetry. I disagree with your definition of the poet as one who does not manipulate. I think the great function of a poet is to say the new word that will define words for . . .

MR. DICKEY: Manipulate in *that* sense, maybe. All I was saying was a rather broad and perhaps a crude definition of its not leading you to perform external actions, such as vote for a politician or buy a product.

MISS BLAIN: Is it possible that poetry or some other form of art could—well, we've developed materially about as much as we can. Don't you think that we'll have to do something else—go into new realms?

MR. DICKEY: Well, your terms are awfully broad. I don't know, for example, whether or not it would be possible for me to accept your premise that we have developed materially about as far as we can. What does it mean to develop materially?

MISS BLAIN: Well, we've got enough wealth in this country . . .

MR. DICKEY: Not nearly enough.

MISS BLAIN: Oh, I think . . . well . . .

MR. DICKEY: This is the problem of a great deal of the social unrest, that the distribution of wealth . . .

MISS BLAIN: It's the distribution, though. It's not the amount.

MR. BUCKLEY: No, it is the amount.

MR. DICKEY: It's the amount.

MR. BUCKLEY: Because if you were to take everything that the Rockefellers have and give it away, it wouldn't increase by $25 the annual income of the people that you are talking about.

MISS BLAIN: Well.

MR. BUCKLEY: You can't just make people rich by taking the money from the rich . . . excuse me, Mr. Durant.

MR. DURANT: Yes. Mr. Dickey, at the beginning of this program you talked about the greatness, and you talked about the flowering of the individual spirit. What if it fades? I agree with you on your premise about the greatness of the individual and the self-sufficiency of the individual, and of the individual as being able to determine his own, in effect, destiny. But so often very contemporarily, the problem seems to be . . . well . . . what about those people who are trapped and unable to do that, whether maybe through artificial man-made institutions or whatever? But what if that individual spirit cannot flower? Do you think that maybe that's part of what we are experiencing? That while we are supposedly so free, that we're still not allowed to burst out . . .

MR. DICKEY: Well, I'll tell you one of the difficulties about America, and one of the paradoxes about it. Again, please forgive me because I really am not a political columnist. I just offer this not as a poet at all, either, but as a private citizen, which may or may not have anything to do with my work. But I would say this. One of the things that is so difficult about American life and has always bothered me so much is that American life is so tough on the losers—the people who don't have talent, who don't have drive, who really are not very well equipped for competitive life, and there are plenty of them!

MR. DURANT: Well, then let me ask you. Maybe in one sense you are not contradicting something that you said earlier, but you keep talking about the renewability. That maybe if in one avenue of life an individual fails—that maybe that failure is good because he sees immediately that that's not the avenue that he should have taken.

MR. DICKEY: To come back to my favorite phrase of the afternoon—

the thing that haunts me most when I wake up at night—is that for some, there's not any avenue, particularly. It reminds me of a wonderful joke that I once saw in the *New Yorker.* A psychiatrist is talking to a little nondescript-looking man with glasses, and he says, "Well, Mr. Burnhill, I must admit you've got me stumped; you really *are* inferior." There must be a lot of Mr. Burnhills. An intensely competitive society is not only economically hard on such individuals, but psychologically murderous to them.

MR. BUCKLEY: Well, it may be psychologically murderous to them, but it's economically a lot better off, surely, than the kind of society which because it isn't competitive, doesn't create the kind of surplus off which those who are competitively handicapped can feed.

MR. DICKEY: I agree.

MR. BUCKLEY: The poor—India does not have a competitive society, but it has misery instead.

MR. DICKEY: Plenty of that. It's just according to how you look at American society, as to whether you think it's pretty tough. But it makes at least a passable life for the losers and doesn't hold down the winners.

MR. BUCKLEY: Mr. Wafer.

MR. WAFER: Yes, I think I found—maybe not a solution—but maybe a point we could start from.

MR. DICKEY: Please tell the President.

MR. WAFER: I'll start with you. I'll try it out. You said in the beginning that you felt excessive introspection has eaten America. In so many words, that eternal questioning of everything we do has sapped the American spirit. Well, I would like to pose, as a way of using introspection, maybe in a different sense, and use an analogy of the city. The city grows normally by concentric circles. It's the easiest way to define how the city grows—from the inner city to the suburbs. They move out. And what I think might be a solution for the city is to stop here and turn around and look inside and use that sort of introspection and renew the inner city. And renew that which we are leaving behind as decline and destruction.

MR. DICKEY: As Frank Lloyd Wright said, "It all should go straight up instead of out."

MR. WAFER: I don't believe that either. But the human being must also stop and look at himself and use this type of introspection to renew himself, just as a corporation or the government. I think the human being—we lose him in there—but the larger aspects of our life should do this to renew themselves and to rebuild.

MR. DICKEY: Well, listen, I think that's a very eloquent statement indeed. But you've got so many metaphors going in different directions, I don't know exactly how they all come out.

MR. WAFER: I don't pose it as a question, but as a sense rather than—I think that's—if you're looking for a new frontier spirit, that might be better frontier spirit than the old one. We blew it last time, obviously.

MR. DICKEY: You just saw "Easy Rider."

MR. WAFER: No.

MR. DICKEY: Okay. Fine. You didn't.

MR. BUCKLEY: You sound condescending.

MR. DICKEY: I don't mean to.

MR. BUCKLEY: He's got a very good point, which is that the American habit has been like a Russian army that eats its way through and provides us logistics on its way from this point to that point—leaves a complete waste in the course of its movement, whereas, ideally, it should refine. Right? It should take whatever it is that's there and rebuild it, whether it's a slum or whether it's a bad mental attitude or neurosis or a sense of abdication.

MR. DICKEY: I can understand, as he said, rebuilding the inner city. That's possible to do, but rebuilding a mental attitude is something that's a bit different from that and much more difficult to achieve, and I would certainly question whether it would be possible to do in a good many cases. I've never really believed in psychiatry, for example, from what little I know of the subject and what little I know of people who have gone through psychiatric treatment. I'm quite willing to admit that it's efficacious in some cases. I'm sure it is. Nevertheless, it also seems to me that most of the things—the conditions that cause psychological difficulties in people—are not amenable to being treated by psychiatry. For example, psychiatry can't make you big and strong when you are little and weak. It can't make you beautiful when you are ugly. It can't make you rich when you are poor. It can't make you young when you're old. And so it seems to me that if it were possible to have a good, cheerful, happy life by having a prescribed mental attitude, which is other than your destructive real mental attitude, caused again by these external factors, it would be fine. But I just question as to whether it is possible.

MR. WAFER: I don't think I posed it in quite that sense.

MR. DICKEY: Oh, no, I just got off on something else.

MR. BUCKLEY: Well, of course, the purpose of psychiatry is not necessarily to change your body by making you grow tall or shrink down, but to make it possible for you to absorb whatever disabilities you are complaining of, and situate them in a sort of perspective . . .

MR. DICKEY: As they say, Bill, to enable you to live with it.

MR. BUCKLEY: To enable you to live with it.

MR. DICKEY: But the whole point is that you don't *want* to live with it. You don't want it to *be* that way. Of course, it *is* that way, but then where does that leave you?

MR. BUCKLEY: Well, thank you very much, Mr. Dickey, and thank you, ladies and gentlemen, and thank you, members of the panel.

A HAND-LINE: In Pursuit of the Grey Soul

A string leads into water: that is the basic situation, and of a primeval kind.

A human being is holding the string,

wearing, perhaps, hip-waders or wearing a boat. In the upright creature there is a day-glow of excitement, generally a kind of lonely excitement. What the unknown dweller in water feels is not to be understood, but the potential encounter is waiting for both. The air-dweller performs a few ritualistic actions, and waits.

He waits, usually, in lovely surroundings: in bushy creeks, in broad-flowing, inexorable rivers, in estuaries, in rice canals, or somewhere on the enormous sun-slatted mystery-mongering vistas of the sea.

There is a division between us creatures. That, too, is basic. We have different ways of breathing, those who live on the land and bring the atmosphere of the planet earth into our bodies to maintain the odd and perhaps inexplicable life that, under these conditions, we have been given, and those others who have another kind of breath. These are the dwellers in water, which exist beyond the fragile and absolute film between the earth-life and the water-life.

And I like that. Fishing is necessary to me because of the combination of practicality and mysticism that it holds. When a human being beholds a fish in its anti-human and fascinating element, there is a vibration like no other.

The poet D. H. Lawrence has worded this feeling of the man-fish encounter as well as anyone has ever done. Of the pike, he says

> I made a mistake, I didn't know him,
> This grey, monotonous soul in the water,

This intense individual in shadow,
Fish-alive.

I didn't know his god,
I didn't know his god.

I began fishing with a handline, and I still love that form of the art. This was in an estuary off the south coast of Georgia, and, though my family origins were in the mountains of the northern part of the state (and therefore my loyalty should logically be to the fly-rod and the trout), my ideal notion of fishing, of true fishing, of fishing *itself* involves the nerves of my hand as they sink by means of the line into the alien, creative darkness and wait there. It is that activity that uses a length of cheap cord, a couple of dimestore hooks (but hardy! but crookedly sharp!), two simple sinkers whose weight is of the traditional lead kind, and about a foot of ragged wood to wrap the line on. Bait does the rest: chopped-up shrimp or fiddler crabs.

Whenever I think of the sacrificial fiddler crabs I have known preparing to be sent at my behest in pursuit of the Grey Soul, I think also of Izaak Walton's feelings for the spring frog that *he* used as bait. The patron saint of all us anglers said,

" . . . use him as though you loved him, that is,
harm him as little as you may possibly, that he may live the longer."

In a rowboat one waits. The wooden stob, perhaps still half-wrapped with twine, does its own kind of waiting in the bottom of the boat. One sits with the right hand (if one is right-handed) near the string-side of the boat, keeping the cord clear of any and all contact with the gunwale, for nothing—nothing physical or metaphysical—must interfere with the sensuous encounter between the mortal forefinger over which the line is held and the Hunger materializing somewhere in the down-darkness.

There is a touch. The day-glow excitement of the fisherman radiates and haloes around him, for the depth-touch is now no longer tentative, but is a strong and recalcitrant tugging, compounded about equally of panic and rage. The fisherman is being lived by the kind of excitement that involves every iota of the body, and of the fearing and hoping imagination. Now the touch is far more than a touch, and cannot possibly be mistaken for the vicious low-morality sawing of a crab at bait, either. The tugging comes into an unseen, dancing paroxysm, and the boatman makes his move: up, quick and then steady, to assess what may be. The live, fighting weight, the sense of struggle that one may be lucky enough to master, the grasp on something hidden that gives the human being a muscular vibration of holding in hand a denizen, perhaps the very *spirit*, of an alien element, and also of holding in the palm a veritable process of nature—flowing or spreading—are the qualities that comprise the essence of fishing.

And who should miss it? It can take place almost anywhere there is water. For me fishing involves not only the salt-mirrors of the sea but also very deep woods and inaccessible places. The more trouble it takes to reach the spot where the Big One is or may be—no, damn it, *is*—the better I like it. I like to go after that Big One over logging roads, by dint of much consultation of unfamiliar maps, sweat and strangeness, and, oddly enough, by the threat of snakes. And I enjoy fishing alone. If there is talking to be done, I want to talk to the fish.

There is something at least vaguely terrifying about the sound of continual water: water that is not coming out of a tap or from a reservoir, but out of mountains, out of rain and the melting of snows. In such an environment the true—the truest—Grey Soul resides: all the Otherness you could ever ask, with all the curious dart-vectors of his subdued, other-worldly flights, his image re-combining by invocation of his own god, intense and mysterious. But he can be encountered by one with true love or true luck, and the film between land and water broken, to reseal, like an ironic wall, after the meeting.

In a wilderness creek, one comes for trout. But the fisherman is also surrounded by other forms of life, buzzing around his head, sliding through underfoot leaves, drinking shyly from the fishes' source-flowing, barely-seen and fleeing. In a creek, there is always something *else*, but most of the other forms of life around the fisherman breathe the same element he does.

In the ocean, though, there may be almost *anything* else. You don't know—you *really* don't know—what's down
there.

Hundreds of millions of creatures who all must eat dwell therein. For one's wished-for vastness of spirit, there is the ocean. For intimacy of self-communion there is the leaf-walled leg-pull of the creek, and the sense, no matter where you may be, of ownership.

In middle life I prefer the creek to the intimidation of the ocean. It makes up for its lack of infinite distances, its lack of marlin and tarpon, by its turbulent, vital movement, by the intimacy engendered in the heart of the angler by the solar-dancing roof of rhododendron and by the possible existence of the one, the only Great Trout, whose courage is a product of faroff rocky springs, of tumbling mountain rain, and whose beauty is absolute.

But the sea is there, too, from the beginning of time to the end. The trout is a brother. The marlin is a creature from another world: a being which you should not be *allowed* to catch, or even to disturb, but only to contemplate and marvel over. And yet . . . and yet . . . there is that challenge. In such an encounter the human body strains beyond any straining it has known, hooked to the fish just as surely as the fish is hooked to it. In the thrashing midst of the struggle, the fisherman battles also with himself, as to whether he ever really wanted this situation or not. But it is too late for such questions. It is life or death, and basic things are in the balance: life for the fisherman if he can boat the marlin, and life for the fish by invisible escape; death for the fish by air-breathing, and for the fisherman by coronary attack. Many human beings have so died.

The death of the fish is both the cause for impersonality in the fisherman and of deep regret. Aboard fishing boats there is never any compunction about, say, boating a sand shark and beating it mercilessly to death with clubs. Fish blood in the scuppers is only a substance to be cleaned away, and is not in any sense representative of the living creature from which it came. On the other hand, no one can have seen the dolphin come to air without a feeling of profound sorrow and loss. Here is this quivering splinter of nature turned by sullen and perverse magic from being a combination of incandescent greens and yellows into a mottled and mediocre neutral tone: yes, the thing has been done, and something taken away.

But whether in creek, river or ocean, wherever and whenever you choose to seek him out, the Grey Soul is waiting. The challenge is yours, for you are the only creature that can penetrate the mystical skin dividing the worlds and explore the depths without seeing them: the only one who can initiate the Unseen Hunt. He is waiting, that Grey Soul in the water, with his possible god, forever. You can catch him, kill him and eat him. But whatever the encounter, treat him as if you loved him.

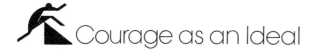

Courage as an Ideal

DELIGHTS OF THE EDGE

Henry de Montherlant, the fine, fiery novelist and essayist of the muscles, guts and sex organs, of pride and chance-taking, once said, "If your life ever bores you, then risk it." Montherlant is probably, even more than Hemingway, our philosopher of action, of the delights of the edge. He can tell you of the electric life-spark of the bull's too-close horn, of the high-jumper's controlled all-out. He can throw the body.

I thought of this a couple of years ago in North Georgia, sitting two hundred feet above a dammed river, on pinestraw with my feet at a very real edge. My wife and I were looking down onto a section of the Tallulah River where a story of mine called *Deliverance* was being filmed. Both our sons were below us, far out of the range of our voices, my oldest boy working on the shooting crew, my youngest, thirteen, just visiting. The state-run dam was closed, which meant that the great rocky fall-offs had no water to fall off them. But they had my boys.

We lay at the edge, hoping our mortal children would not do anything foolish, but also intensely interested in what they *would* do, down there beyond us. The filming was taking place on both sides of the river, and, at the edge of a ninety-foot down-river drop, there was a primitive rig where you could walk across the river holding a rope. There was also a place where you had to jump over a kind of trickling gap, presumably still holding the rope. Or not holding the rope. My movie-making son kept going back and forth, carrying spools of film, makeup kits, impossible messages to Burt

Reynolds and God knows what else. Below my son for ninety feet—I kept going up and down the rock-cruelties with field glasses—was nothing but a set of outcroppings designed by the universe eons ago to demonstrate the utter indifference of wild nature to the pain-bearing bodies of human beings; I was shook by the rage of their stillness. Any rock in any Body's descent was certain to be death- or mutilation-dealing. My wife and I said, almost at the same second, "I hope Kevin doesn't try it."

But then of course he did. The suffering, hawk-perching parents could do nothing to prevent it: could do nothing, in fact, but watch like strange pinestraw-people the adventures of a beloved creature with the sheer murderousness of Gravity in collaboration with the serious cruelty of random stone.

Our child edged out, one foot staying in front of him, along the rope. He came to the gap in the crossing-stones.

He jumped for the place his brother had mastered, and slipped. Helpless in the higher-up, the field glasses hung fire in our hands, but he had not gone over. He swayed half in and half out of life, and pulled himself back into it. There he was, still in the shaking field glasses, four-eyed from the cliff-top, and looking good. Then something broke out in him, down there. He started to dance, or do *something*: something with a lot of energy and motion. But it was not done for us: his mother and father, there at the other edge. It was a silent dance of pure delight: he was dancing with the void, and loving what had just about happened to him, and had not. We, creatures in the rarefied air of bushes at the brink, in the leaves of plants that leaned out over the vanished roar of dammed, gone water, knew that his excitement was not a show for Parent's Day, nor was it for the film crew or even for his brother. The adrenaline had hit like a Heaven-through-the-guts, and he rejoiced in the abyss, dancing back in a gangling, curious, beginning-athlete's way to safety, to his brother, to the crew, and eventually to us, who had no word to say, but only deep images, deep energies based on his.

The dance on the edge is one thing. The other, that makes the edge what it is in terms of my son's abandon, is the wheelchair. Or the bed, and hopeless immobility. It is also the coffin, the quiet plot: what Emily Dickinson called "that bareheaded life under the grass."

The principle, if one is indeed involved, has something to do with courting mutilation, paralysis and death. It is of course better to think of oneself as a being who *can* display Hemingway's "grace under pressure," but the grace you might or might not be able to display is not nearly so important as the putting of yourself into a situation in which, far from performing according to a set standard of "grace," skill or blind courage, you don't really know what on earth you *will* do, can do, or what some blind agency outside your control will cause you to do. That is when the void can be danced with.

Looked at from a certain, increasingly personal angle, all existence becomes a search for the edge: the place where one danger or the other charges the physical batteries and brings with it the will to live and search for more of the same. But behind the excitement and the momentary thrill of having done something a little special is always the threat of death, and, even more terrible, that of injury and immobilization, whereafter the excitements will all have to turn inward, and you will not—will never: that is, *never*—run that stretch of white water again, ski that slope, hunt that deer, descend beneath the reef and look the moray in his strange, challenging and somehow accepting eye. No; for the edge cuts two ways. If you beat it, you can dance with it in all your fragile mortality. But you can also fall into the indifference of the earth or into a hospital bed with your arms full of life-giving tubes that, though they give the necessary chemicals of existence, can never give you back the existence you lost on a whim: the one you gave up at the edge when you were seeking something else: the dance.

But lying—perhaps forever—in the hospital bed because the void and you did not *at that time* suit each other, you can assure yourself that the concept of the edge itself has not gone from you, and it is necessary that it should not: perhaps it is even more crucial now than before. It has become not a matter of cliffs and sports cars, of speed and the teeth of sharks, of high-powered bullets and elephants, but has changed itself into ideas and words, and these alone. The heroes of the immobilized mind, of the mind that has been reduced to the grave stillness of the body by the fatal interview, by the action of rocks and gravity, say, on human flesh, by the arm lost to the shark at the edge of the underwater pit, by the lower muscular system lost to the hope of the dance at the edge, can now have full time to take the real chance, which is that of developing something new: a strange and possible image, a metaphor, a contributing connection.

Or, again, of entering the universe. If one knows, if one has lost the dance at the edge—but not *finally*—that a philosopher named Anaximander once had the idea that the earth hung free in space, one can also, on that hope for us all, hang free in a hospital bed. And another thinker, a compatriot of Anaximander, speculated upon what would happen if one threw a spear outward from the very limit of things (What would—what *will* it strike? Where will it go?). No matter: one has had to be at the edge to throw.

Death, crippling: they are part of the risk of the dance. I have seen my son take both the risk and take on the dance. They are all part of the same life-attitude, and we need not fall, but in the risk of this possibility there is something for us. If your life ever bores you, risk it. All right.

I was somewhere near West Virginia. I had a bow in my hand and darkness coming into my face. I would see no deer this night. But it was warm, and I was not worried. I was also lost. But, double-also, I was ready. I lay down on the ground and chewed a piece of jerky, and my salt-loving saliva glands never did better. I went to sleep and woke up in the same position, remembering vaguely that a puma had been sighted a few weeks before somewhere or other around there. I cracked my eyes for no reason, and across them, in the lower limbs of about ten trees, a ghostly form went. I was not sure of whether it was something in the world, or something lean and quiet within me, or whether it was me. I could have traversed those limbs, though I'm glad I didn't have to try. That edge was the border of West Virginia and Virginia. I'm not sure which I was sleeping and waking in, or whether my left hand was in one state and the right in the other. But when that thing floated across me, I was ready to dance with the void out of which all creation comes and into which it must—hopefully with joy—go back. I got up, dirty and very hungry in the dawn-dingy forest, and looked slack-jawed at the new sun and the few birds that dared it. Here was one of the edges, and I was there. That non-beast could have torn me apart like a rotten gunny-sack, and left my ridiculous blood all over the strewn inconsequence of twigs. Mine. What I had seen was deathless, even if it had not been there. Adrenaline hit solid. Mine. I rose like the wild king of forever.

STYLE AND CHANCE

Clichés are sometimes useful; some are and some aren't. A couple of the useful ones—that is, statements that really do, even as clichés, give you an insight into how people actually think and feel—are the current "life style" and "doing one's thing." No matter what the "thing" that one does is, or the life style one has, or would like to have, the idea that human beings are thinking in these terms about themselves is important. And nobody else's life style is as important to you as your own, and nobody else's is as important to me as mine.

These matters have to do with the self, and I don't mean just the ego. They have to do with certain actions and approaches to existence that in a sense define what the self is. Like everyone else, I've seen a great many life styles, and have learned from all of them, even when the injunction was "go and do otherwise." I have never needed to ask myself what my actions are asking me, all the time: Self, what is your being? The actions that I do are telling me that. For example, I am acutely conscious of my physicality, and how my body relates to things and people is how *I* relate to them. There are writers I like who are as different as possible from myself in this respect, but the ones I like the most are those who have something like the same approach to existence, if not to the expression of it. Tolstoy is one of these. So is D. H. Lawrence. So are such diverse kinds of writers as the German poet Rilke, the French novelist and essayist Henry de Montherlant and the Japanese novelist Yukio Mishima, who destroyed, by ritual suicide, the body on which he worked so hard and mystically for so many years. Mishima speaks of his personal cult of "Sun and Steel": the pitting of the body against an obstacle, like the lifting of a weight, a barbell: the cult of open air and physical strain. That kind of thing appeals to me, though a great many of the social implications of it—such as the physique contests and what might be called the "muscle beach psychology," do not. Like Mishima, I prefer the solitude of sun and steel, and the profound contest of the individual with himself.

As for me, as a poet and one-shot novelist—that is, as an artist of some sort—I am greatly interested in the relationship between action and art. I have never been an inhabitant of anybody's ivory tower, not even my own. My interest in experience is intensely physical, as I've said; it is also intensely verbal, which is, I guess, why I am a writer rather than, say, a high school basketball coach.

Part of the physicality for me—and a great deal of the connection between things and words—is in the woods, and in the hunt. I hunt with bow and arrow, which stacks the deck very heavily on the side of the animal, and brings the hunter necessarily much closer to him than a gun would. I hate guns, as I do most machinery. As a long-forgotten nineteenth century editor, C. J. Longman, once said in a letter to one of his authors, Richard Jefferies: "to shoot with a gun is nothing; a touch discharges it, but the delight of drawing the bow, and loosing the arrow and watching its flight is indescribable." I know—and *feel*—exactly what C. J. Longman is talking about: archery is part of *my* thing.

Hunting is not a popular *subject* these days; many species of animals are becoming extinct, and the feeling is that we should not help out the process by killing them for sport, which is to say killing them for play. Theoretically I am sympathetic to that view. It is humiliating to me to think of myself as belonging to the generation that lost the earth—its animals, its fish, its rivers and mountains—and took the moon. But when I string a bow and walk into the woods, I know that there is nothing else in the world that I would rather be doing, no place I would rather be. The animals, I can tell you, are actually in very little danger. At least not from me. The important thing is to be there in just *that* relationship. And, if it is a game, it is a game of life and death. I ran up on a bear in West Virginia four years ago. There was no one with me, and he could have torn me apart. I shot and missed, and he took off. I sat down on the ground and thanked the Lord for my life. But I was filled with adrenaline, and started out to look for him. I never found him, but that experience gave me the answers to a lot of things in my life.

I don't intend all this as some kind of personal mystique of the body, assiduously cultivated and then deliberately placed in a situation which may destroy it. I would not commit hara-kiri, as Mishima did, or practice bull-fighting, a singularly disgusting sport to me, as Montherlant did. Nevertheless, in hunting, in canoeing, I have found some things, have found part of myself which I do not question. It is the same as liking a tune in music; it just appeals to one. And in that way a person is defined; he has found part of his "thing," his life style, beyond intellectualization, beyond such as I have just been doing.

UPTHRUST AND ITS MEN

University of Virginia Baccalaureate Address, 2 June 1973

An object that means a great deal to me is a photograph I clipped from a magazine. It is one of those pictures that serve to reaffirm the excitement and adventure of human daring and achievement as no painting, no mere work of art can do. The picture had been taken by a news photographer, and it was of a man who had just done something that no American had ever done before. Not even the Sistine chapel means as much to me as the picture I cut out of *Life* magazine. It hangs on the wall of my study in Columbia, South Carolina, getting a little yellow lately, it is true, and also fraying a little, perhaps because of the intensity with which I have so often looked at it. It is of the astronaut Ed White, the first American to walk in space, and killed in a training accident from which I don't think that I myself will ever recover. There he is: still in his space-walking outfit, but with the gold-headed helmet off. His head, which is losing its hair much too soon, is tousled and sweaty. He has a great, all-accepting grin on his face: a fun grin. It is a confident, excited expression; a grin of pure daring and delight. He is holding up a circle of fingers and winking at the camera—at me, you, and posterity—in a wild, conspiratorial manner. Ed White, and a few other men whom I admire, I have conceived as men of Upthrust; they are totemic to me. I like men who have the look of Ed White when he descended, in his frail, finely-cared-for human body, from the vast, uncaring, breathless wilderness of space. I like the fact that to me, if only to me, he has the look of a man who might well be thinking of the last line of Christopher Smart's great mad-poem, "A Song to David": "Determined, dared, and done."

I have never been much of a believer in false modesty—or, for that matter, in true modesty. If a man does something that requires guts, intelligence, training, self-discipline and audacity—all of which he risks against the unknown—he is entitled to that wild wink of the eye.

Ed White's exploit, out in the inhuman cold of space, among God's badly-drawn animals of stars—that is, his projection of his own mortal body amongst the stupendous beasts of the Zodiac—came as a long-term product of an intensive and creative self-cultivation. Someone characterized Ed White as exhibiting an almost maniacal—but also hilarious—self-discipline. He was, among other things that this attitude made possible to him, an Olympic hurdler. A few years ago I spent some time in the Astronaut Complex at Cape Kennedy, and one of White's compatriots told me that when they all went out to run on the beach as part of their fitness program, "Ed White would be long gone in less than five minutes. He'd be out of sight before the rest of us even got untracked." Yes indeed. Ed White did not go into space like the "galley-slave scourged to his dungeon." He went with a sense of great personal adventure: a sense of attempting—and also *tempting*—the unknown. When seen from the standpoint of an Ed White, this courting of danger, this disciplined approach to the unknown, was a kind of renewal, a bath of youth.

What I would like to do, here, if I could, is to use Ed White's gigantic spring into space as a sort of springboard for myself, and try to get over what I think it means, and what it springs toward. With examples primarily literary, I'd like to outline very broadly—I expect "suggest" would be a better word—a profitable approach to living on what we have to live on and with: what Ed White called "The Blue Planet." I call it "Upthrust." The characteristics of Upthrust are austerity and audacity, both intellectual and physical. If I had the power, I would like to produce in the people of my country and in the rest of the world a very real change of mind and heart and guts. We all hear incessantly that something is wrong with us. But what is it? When I reflect on the matter, it seems to me that the two principal feelings of the human beings of my time—including myself—are boredom and anxiety. From both of these we seek, not relief, for there is none, but distraction. The sickening quality, in the lives of modern human beings, is a paralyzing sense of futility, helplessness, frustration and sterility. This feeling, compounded in different persons of various mixtures of these emotions, is brought about by a wide variety of public and private conditions of which the citizen is made cognizant at every hour of the day and night: from which he has no relief from the beginning of his life until the end of it. The cold war, the possibility of hot war, the weapons race, racial unrest, crime and the problem of law and order, organized gangsterism, mistrust of the police and the military, the ecological situation, the extermination of bird and animal and fish species, the credibility gap, the generation gap, the problem of aging, the aged, the problem of health—cancer, heart disease and venereal disease come to mind obsessively—the rising cost of food and everything else, the depreciation of the dollar, the pollution problem, the problem of the cities and the ghettoes within them, the really hideous boredom occasioned by most industrial jobs, the proliferation of the automobile and its attendant carnage on streets and highways, hijacking, kidnapping and political terrorism, drug abuse, alcoholism, overweight, insanity, overpopulation: the list, if not endless, is certainly a very long one; the actual length is hardly more than hinted at by my very brief and largely improvised résumé. The things I have touched on are only a few of the more publicized horrors that beset us. Like Ed White's picture, they are more obsessive than any work of art could be, for they are part of the world, of the strangeness and terror—and the occasional exhilaration—that the world affords; that the Blue Planet affords.

But we are nervous. The news and communications media keep the grim and terrible constantly before us. But where *should* they keep it? After all, we as Americans, as moderns, are entitled to know. I think that the ostrich with his head in the sand will not and should not replace the American Eagle. But make no mistake: we are paying a fearful price for living on the Blue Planet in the time when you and I and the others find ourselves living on it. The price is essentially psychological.

But there is little, sadly, that we can do against the multiple horrors. We are reduced to impotence. We are constantly self-terrorized, and at the same time haunted by the very little—if indeed anything at all—that we can do about the things creating our terror. With the public and private disasters that condition our lives, what used to be called "Peace" has now become a rhetorical ploy used—again, rather nervously—by young people wandering around, vaguely altruistic, chemically somnolent, in the rapidly dwindling meadows of the countryside and in public parks, where, soon, the sight of a single blade of living grass will come, in the days that are flying faster and faster into our faces out of the future, to seem a vision of the Lost Paradise itself.

I think a lot about grass, and I think a lot about creatures. I think a lot about what the late Philip Wylie once said:

> The sum total of human works, the artifacts of savages, barbarians, medieval men and modern—all cities and towns, every hut, hovel, skyscraper and temple, everything man has made to use since the first stone tool or wooden club—does not equal, in all parts put together, the achievements of the life forms of plant and insect in a square foot of grass.

Ecology, over-population—and I believe firmly that these are the major problems ever to face mankind—are the foremost in importance among a very long list of tension and anxiety-producing conditions. But the most distressing manifestation of all this is the curious kind of passivity that has resulted from it. I refer to a helpless and rather pathetic recourse to physical pleasure, and what I myself regard as the worst of all possible results of such an attitude: the misapplication of the "Doing-My-Thing" syndrome: the "New Freedom" that guarantees the right of a person to destroy himself and others in the name of pleasure.

The culture we have created is, of course, partly to blame. We are a pleasure-oriented people. Pleasure and utility are the things we set most value upon. And we have the time and the money to indulge ourselves. That cultural condition, coupled with our anxiety, has produced us. But the really terrible danger to us—of which the drug problem and that of alcoholism are only symptoms—is the habit of mind that not only permits these things to happen, but encourages them, and in certain cases attempts to justify them intellectually.

For you can, of course, justify anything—even child-torture—intellectually. There are people who believe, say, that if a clever or even a profound writer can make a certain attitude or a certain action interesting, he is thereby providing its justification. There are a good many writers who believe in The New Freedom, some in drugs, some in induced hallucination of other sorts. Do your thing. Sure. At first sight, such a dictum seems to have nothing but good to recommend it. After all, who would want to keep someone from doing what he wanted to do, should do, benefited by doing? If it comes to that, Ed White was doing his thing, was he not?

But there are things and things. I like the hard way, myself, and the slow pay-off, in performance, of the long discipline. Doing your thing, if you are Ed White or Robert Kennedy, is of a different order of "thing" than destroying yourself in the name of pleasure, or because of a meaningless "Freedom." The do-your-thing attitude is quite often not a call to action of a self-disciplined or creative kind, but simply an excuse, an excuse for passivity—inaction rather than action: withdrawal and irresponsibility, and a terrible betrayal of the self.

I feel that a return—or the creation, really, for we as a nation have never had it to return to—the creation, then, of something like Ed White's exuberant, self-determining self-discipline might just be that bath of youthfulness and consequentiality that we so desperately need.

We need consequentiality. We must have it: the sense of things and people mattering to us. We must have it, even if we have to give to things and to people consequentiality by a brute act of will. We might start with as simple a thing as Ed White's feeling good about himself when he did three more push-ups today than yesterday. Who knows? Those extra push-ups might lead, one day—with luck and daring—to Ed White's grin: to Ed White's triumphal and unforgettable wink.

Like most of us, I have gone through my period of pleasurable passivity. A strange thing brought me out of it. I wrote a novel called *Deliverance*, and in so doing I required myself to invent a character named Lewis Medlock, played, I thought, with enormous power in the film version by Burt Reynolds. At first I intended Lewis to be a kind of physical mystic—perhaps even a little of a phony: a man trying by multiple acts of volition to make himself immortal, to rise above time. As I originally conceived him, I wanted to make him a figure both attractive and a little repellent, with his authoritarian manner and clear-cut bodily superiority to the other characters. But as I got more deeply into the character of Lewis, an odd thing began to happen to the author. I began to sympathize more and more with what Lewis was making me make him say. And what is even stranger, I began to admire him tremendously. I admired his daring, his eagerness to make giddy intellectual leaps, but above all I admired his self-discipline, which made so much audacity and excitement possible. Do-your-thing to Lewis was not an invitation to laxness, but a leaping flame of creative and physical possibility, a philosophy of sun and steel that led into the wilderness and down the rivers. It became a personal code: something to live by. In an odd way, I began to imitate Lewis, my own character, and tried to make of myself, at the age of fifty, a man of upthrust.

Upthrust encourages wild contemplation, intellectual chance-taking, and the setting of the faculty of reason on fire. It encourages bodily adventure and the testing of the body, mind and nerves against what may conceivably be mortal dangers. It makes for a certain calculated recklessness—not necessarily involving others, but not rejecting the participation of others if they wish it—and, again, danger. Upthrust encourages as great an opening-up to possibility—to chance—as one can manage, and an opening-up to such possibilities of wit, humor and imaginative style as one can come to command. As the result of coming under the domination of my own fictional character, for example, I make up about fifty limericks a day, and the crazier the better. Here's one of them.

> There was a young man with a tom-cat
>   Who mated his beast with a wombat.
> He delighted to see, with unqualified glee,
>   This strange form of sexual combat.

Limericks, weight-lifting, space-walking, poetry, archery—some of the shapes of upthrust. Many things otherwise impossible are made possible by audacity and will: many shapes of exhilarating experience: many shapes of consequentiality. That is the condition of upthrust; Ed White was deep in the middle of it, turning in his fragile mortality among the light-year animals of the Zodiac. Such a man also was Robert Kennedy. When I was in the Poetry Chair at the Library of Congress, Robert Kennedy came to represent to me the kind of man whom I would still like to see emerge as the future American: one who by his mental and physical characteristics would be capable of opening up not only the national and political life, but the personal life of anyone who had the intellectual recklessness and physical audacity to follow his example. Bobby Kennedy climbed mountains. He went down rivers. He threw excellent touch football passes to his wife Ethel, who was probably the best wide receiver that McLean, Virginia, has ever seen. He was into the very depths of political and economic theory and the mechanics of the American judicial process. He was widely and imaginatively read in literature and philosophy. And he was enormously fond of people, both as to their condition and in themselves. He was totally open to possibility, to opportunity, and to the divine unpredictability of chance. No drop-out, he. He not so much did his thing, but his *things*. And they created him.

The great modern French classical poet, Paul Valéry, who worked on his mind with a degree of intensity and resourcefulness hard to believe, once said to André Gide, "I have never been able to understand why the mass of the human race is content to have so little of itself." Amen.

As I grow older, I think of the sheer *luck* of human birth. How on earth—on *earth*: Ed White's Blue Planet—did I ever manage to get myself *born*? By a combination of chance, lust, and history. None would have worked without the others, and without hundreds of thousands of people being involved, including some that lived in trees. For some reason known only to my sister, and perhaps imperfectly known even to her, a genealogical survey of my family was made a few years ago. I liked my father's comment on the entries: "Well, Jim, take a look at all your relatives. All of 'em are in here, except the ones that were whores or hod-carriers." But the study set me thinking in weird ways of time, history and chance. Suppose . . . suppose . . . Well, suppose that back in the Middle Ages, maybe, some fellow had not turned the corner of a street in Europe somewhere and seen a girl that took his fancy. Those two people were two of the links in the not-so-great chain of my being. If it weren't for them, and for many other unknown and long-dead creatures and other manifestations of life, I wouldn't be here. Chance is luck, both good and bad. Chance is exhilarating to us would-be upthrusters.

Jorge Luis Borges, a very great writer, has a story called *The God's Script*. In it, the last priest of the Incas lies in a prison cell. It is a double cell. He is in one part, and in the other is a jaguar. He can see the jaguar only a few seconds every day, when the food for both prisoners is lowered to them through a trapdoor. The priest comes to believe that the spots on the jaguar are actually some form of writing: that the god of his religion has chosen this way of communicating with him, since he is the last priest of the temple. And as it turns out, he is exactly right.

I have always interpreted this situation as a kind of parable of the imaginative approach to experience. For whether we consciously recognize it or not, we are trying to *read* the universe, and discover meaning, discover consequence there, whether in the curious inscriptions on the hide of a jaguar, or in the course of empires and political destinies, or, as Ed White, in his vulnerable human body, must have looked for it among the animals of the Zodiac, floating weightlessly in their very country. Doing your thing can set you turning among the stars. It can also get you murdered in a slum. But if I could I would like to call forth the new man, the man of upthrust, with a philosophy of sun and steel and action, of weight-lifting and running and contemplation, of limericks (however bad), of audacity and the most stringent and exuberant self-discipline, for discipline makes true passion possible, and true passion is what we most lack.

That is really my key word, the possible. Possibility, and the openness to it, and the wit to recognize it and the daring to use it. In a poem which quite literally changed my life when it most needed changing, a poem I ran into by chance, John Davidson has a young man say, throwing off the Calvinistic constraints of his youth, and setting out from Western Scotland to London, "Men to know and women to love are waiting everywhere."

And so they are.

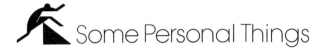

Some Personal Things

NIGHT HURDLING

In 1940 I was a senior in high school. My main sport was football, but my preference was really track. I was a big strong animal who could run fast, and I gloried in this fact. My conference, though I lived in Atlanta, was not the conference in which the big Atlanta high schools competed. I ran in the North Georgia Interscholastic Conference, or N.G.I.C., as it was popularly known. The high-hurdles event, which was my specialty, was often held on grass, up the middle of a football field. This was the case at the 1940 N.G.I.C. meet. We qualified in the afternoon, all of us trying hard but not so hard as to tire ourselves out for the night's final. In the trials I lost to a fine hurdler from Canton, Georgia, and then went out with him, soaked with shower water, and got a cheeseburger. I felt that I had not run well, that my start had been bad, that I had not been able to get a good grip on the turf with my spikes, that I had been too high over the hurdles, that my finish had been poor. But my conqueror had set a new N.G.I.C. record, and he should have.

When I suited up for the finals, though, I was ready. I felt that I had come to run. It was a cool night, and there were several hundred people in the stands, and, when they called the hurdles final, a great many people were clustered about the finish line, where the tape glimmered with ghostly promise for the winner. I ran in the next lane from the boy from Canton. We shook hands: a new friendship, a fierce rivalry, for I knew he would give no quarter, and I knew damn well that I wasn't planning to give any. We got down on the blocks.

Before us was a green sea of grass with faint line-stripes from spring practice across it. I concentrated on getting as much pressure on my legs as I could. I would try to get off well, though I was too big to hope for a really fast start. The gun cracked, and we were gone. I paid no attention to where anyone else was but concentrated on form and on picking up speed between hurdles. But I could dimly sense the Canton boy. At the fifth hurdle I could tell that we were dead even. The finish-line crowd was coming at us like a hurricane. I concentrated on staying low over the hurdles and made really good moves on the next three. I began to edge him by inches, and by the next two hurdles I thought that if I didn't hit the next two I'd make it. I also said to myself, as I remember, *don't* play it safe. Go low over the last stick, and then give it everything you've got up the final straight.

But I did hit the last hurdle. I hit it with the inner ankle of my left foot, tearing the flesh to the bone, as I found out later, and the injury left a scar which I still have. However, my frenzied momentum was such that I won by a yard, careening wildly into the crowd after the tape broke around my neck. I smashed into the spectators and bowled over a little boy, hitting straight into his nose with my knee. He lay on the smoky grass crying, his nose bleeding, and I came back, blowing like a wounded plow-horse, everybody congratulating me on a new N.G.I.C. record. But, unlike myself, I went to the boy, raised him up in my arms, wiped the blood from his nose, tried to comfort him, and kissed him. In memory, now, that was the best moment I ever had out of sports.

STARTING FROM BUCKHEAD
—A Home Address—

Some of you may know my family, and I am sure that you're amazed to see me turn out to be a writer. None of them has ever had the slightest interest in the arts, but as little interested as they were when I was growing up, none of them was as uninterested as I was. My main preoccupation was with sports. And though I was certainly an indifferent performer in the sports I liked best—football and track—I think that even at that early date I felt a dimension of movement, a kind of significance, in certain sports events that I don't think was ever noticed by my more successful competitors. The arc of the javelin, for example, mattered to me more than how far it went. And I liked the figure the broad-jumper made in the air more than anything else about the event: that is something truly beautiful to watch: the athlete in midair, with his arms raised, as Henry de Montherlant says, "As in a profound gesture of exaltation." In football, I had rather see the receiver of a forward pass wait for the ball than see him catch it and run with it. There was something in the quality of expectation that made the receiver graceful, just for an instant or two, and that was what I enjoyed watching. No wonder I spent most of the time on the bench! But I wasn't idle there; although I was collecting splinters, I was also collecting a set of rudimentary aesthetic responses.

Well, sports and girls: that was it for me, until the war. Sports, girls and motorcycles. All these were connected in rather a curious way. I was rather skinny as a boy, and I took up weight-lifting under the influence of an extraordinary person named Edward van Valkenberg, whom I have not seen since those days. He was a great reader of all kinds of poetry, mainly Robert Service and Kipling, and used to recite "The Cremation of Sam McGee" in between military presses, and that was the way I learned it, too. A friend of Ed Van's (as he was called) was a magnificent boy named Walter Armistead, whose enthusiasm for the swing music of the early 40's gave me my first notion of what genuine ecstasy might be. I never think of Blake's wonderful statement to the effect that "exuberance is beauty" without thinking of Walter, who was killed in an airplane crash about fifteen years ago, God rest his excitable soul.

Ed Van and Walter both had motorcycles, and I learned from them how to ride. I used to take off for a couple of days at a time, up through the mountainous country of North Georgia, where all my father's people came from.

After the motorcycle came the war. I won't dwell on that part except to say that I have written some poems about the war—particularly the air war. I will just say that because of my participation in warfare I have come, pretty much, to look at existence from the standpoint of a survivor: as someone who is alive only by the inexplicable miracle of chance. War interests me very much, as a kind of extreme and desperate symbol of the whole human condition. And ever since World War II I have always secretly believed that participation in combat links one with the soldiers of all times and all places. My brother Tom, for example, was in the Civil War—in fact, he still is. He is a Civil War relic hunter: that is to say, a *maniac*. And I'm not at all sure that my understanding of war—such as it is—does not come more deeply from going back with my brother into the war buried under the Georgia soil than the actual military actions I've been in.

At the time all this discovery of the Southern past was going on, I was working in Atlanta offices and trying to write poetry at night—and also, whenever I could, at the office. It is said by some that I wrote my first two books on company time, but that is not *strictly* true: there were at least three or four poems that I did on weekends and holidays. I remember one of my bosses enjoining me to "get the job done," and that is exactly what I was trying to do, except that it was a different job than the one he was talking about. But I liked business a lot, in some ways, much as I liked the service: because I otherwise wouldn't have known some of the people I found in both occupations. Oddly enough, most of these are people who have since got out of business, and gone into something . . . well, something else. Some are artists, some are writers; one is a minister.

Now this is nothing against business. Business is all right for some people; quite a lot of them. But it is no place for men and women who have an emotional commitment to another area. No real painter wants to be a Sunday painter, and no real poet wants to have his most passionate concern looked on as a hobby. But when you do work in offices and are trying to write—or to paint, or to act, or dance—you spend your off time with people who have the same interests—the same *real* interests—as you do. And it was under some such conditions that I began to get a sort of notion of what the artistic community is, because in one way or the other I formed my own. There were several people in Atlanta who were very good to me, and for me, and without whom I would never have survived as a writer. Dave and Anne Sanders, for example, gave me all I wanted to drink, and in those days I wanted a lot. My brother Tom's wife Pat believed in me as a writer when almost no one else did, including myself. There were the artists Jarvin Parks and Ed Ross and John Hardy, and there were Elsa Norris Dodd and George Beattie, and Judy Alexander and her gallery. There were the writers Jerry Horton and Paul Darcy Boles and Betsy Fancher. There was my old friend from Rice, Jim Young, a professor at Georgia Tech, the finest intellect I knew. There were Bess and Bill Finch who connected me with the dance, and with the concert musicians of Atlanta. They were my artistic community, and still are. For the artist does not exist in limbo: either in the limbo of outer space or the Sahara Desert, or in the limbo of Monday morning conferences on marketing. He exists because there is an atmosphere of value—that is, of *his* kind of value—into which he can enter, and in which he can live, move and create. Without this no artist can survive, and America is full of instances in which artists have perished for lack of it. I was lucky when I lived in Atlanta, for I found what I needed, and it saved me. There is no gratitude greater than the gratitude a man feels over a thing of this kind, for when he says "saved," he means literally that, and means to include his soul, the essential part of himself.

That brings me almost up to the present. But not quite, for I have not yet mentioned how I got back to North Georgia, about which I have written a good many poems, and which, next to Atlanta, I consider my symbolic home or fatherland, the landscape of the spirit. Nor have I mentioned the most important people in my whole stay in Atlanta, Al Braselton and Lewis King. It was through them that I went back to the northern part of the state, to the mountains and rivers, not on a motorcycle but in a canoe or on foot, talking philosophy, the metaphysics of the trout and the deer, the novels of Hemingway, and the twelve-string guitar of Leadbelly. These three-man trips to Tray Mountain and Brasstown Bald, to the Chattooga River and Noontootley Creek I now look on as unique mixtures of mental and physical excitement; I have had nothing like them since. They were full of the strangest things! Once, for example, when Lewis and I were getting ready to run a particularly beautiful and dangerous-looking river—I think it was part of the Toccoa—I was surprised to see Lewis take a hip flask out of his pocket and solemnly drink half of it. I had never seen him drink anything but champagne, and I asked him what this new wrinkle was all about. He turned to me and said, "Drink the rest of this, because the sensation of running the rapids when about half drunk is not to be missed." And by God, it was true! It was, and is.

Those are the main parts of this particularly odd Odyssey: how a decent enough and rather plodding young fellow from Buckhead ended up as a poet. And if I've left out the reading and studying and concentrated on the people, that's probably as it should be, for they are more important. And so if anybody asks you how Jim Dickey became a poet, starting from Buckhead, you can say that one day he got off the bench at North Fulton High School, but instead of going into the football game, he got on a red motorcycle belonging to Ed van Valkenberg and rode off into North Georgia. Tell whoever asks you, that Jim Dickey listened to a lot of jazz with Walter Armistead, that he took guitar lessons from Sam Worley because he couldn't wait any later than age forty to learn to play. Tell him that the man fought in a war in airplanes, reading Plato between missions, that he got a desperate education at Vanderbilt, worked in some ad agencies, drank whiskey with Dave Sanders, hunted deer unsuccessfully with Lewis King, shot some rapids with Al Braselton, looked at pictures with Jarvin Parks, and watched Bess Finch dance, and that he published, in the end, some poems based on these things.

And so, if you can imagine me, looking as I do now, as a skinny blond boy in an unstained football uniform, riding on a red Harley-Davidson through Fannin County, carrying with him a load of people—his particular artistic community: weight-lifters, archers, writers, drunkards, musicians, housewives, poets, painters, anarchists, tennis players, village atheists and business men—well, that'd be me. That'd be, as the hippies say, where it's at, coming from where it's been.

PLAY FOR VOICES

Log of a Stationary Navigator

Two young men from the local educational radio station, Luke Phillips and Michael Witkoski, asked me if I would help them make a tape for a program they had in mind, evidently much influenced by similar formats on the BBC Third Programme. We sat down with a recorder for an afternoon, and in a few weeks they came back with the following script, which with their permission I have edited and given a title. I left intact the long quotation from John Gardner, not only because it bears on what I am saying, but because I like it.—J.D.

SFX: *Crickets (sounding remarkably like radio transmission)*

Voice Over

DICKEY: The position of the observer on the earth such as myself, at my home at Lake Katherine, is such that the universe will disclose that position to him if he has the right key to it. The key is mathematical, but once understood, it does work, and it is infallible. It is built into the structure of reality at the deepest level.

Theme Music—5 to 10 sec. (Music under)

NARRATOR: For a poet, a poem is a destination—a place, and the success of any poet depends on how close he comes to the one true place that is the poem as it should be—not the suburb of the poem as it might be. To reach that place the poet must do more than think or feel or write. A poet must discover a course, find his path. He must chart a way through the worlds of life and of art, linking them together, making them cohere. Each poem is a risked voyage into the blank spaces of the map. For James Dickey, to be a poet is to be a navigator.

Music: Fingerpicking folk guitar—(Music under)

DICKEY: If you write poetry, or at least you have the attitude about it that I do, you're willing to gamble everything, on making it come off.

(Music up, then under)

NARRATOR: What James Dickey has called "a conspiracy of roots and stars" has placed him where he is: he writes books; he gives readings. At first he was nervous about this. He asked his wife if she thought he could do it.

DICKEY: She said, "Yes you can, if you can teach classes: just get up there and be yourself." Well, it sounded fine to me at first, and I said, "Yeah, that sounds like good advice to me, I guess." Be yourself. But which *one*? Which one? Anybody can find some sort of voice for himself—but the trouble is that sometimes you are under the mistaken impression that the current voice is the only possible one you can use, when the real function of the creative person is to get out there—or *in* there—and try to see how many different ones he can find. Monotony is the true difficulty with writers like Dylan Thomas. Dylan Thomas is in some ways the most original poet who's ever written in English, or maybe in any language. It's a wonderful sound that he has, but he has no other. It's all got to sound like vintage Dylan Thomas. Also, his subject matter is desperately narrow. Now somebody like Auden, who is extremely resourceful, does not have any one voice; or rather, he's got a lot of *variations* of the same voice, and he has tremendous range. His mind is a thousand times more various and more interesting and more interested in different things than Dylan Thomas'. Yet I prefer Dylan Thomas, myself; he's the kind of person I can really *go* with, all the way. I remember a review in the *New Yorker*, years ago, when two of the leading jazz pianists were Erroll Garner and George Shearing, both very good but very different from each other. And the reviewer said, I like 'em both; I respond to them in different ways, and I guess the only thing I can say about my response is that Erroll Garner moves you more, but Shearing gives you more to think about. That's the difference between Thomas and Auden, to take those two very influential and very good poets.

NARRATOR: The poet is the navigator who links thinking and feeling, concentration and instinct. To arrive at that unique place which is the poem, the poet must first comprehend this world, the world of life, and then leave it, journeying into another world, that of art and language. For this difficult voyage it is essential that the poet's navigational skills not falter, and that he always realize just where he is, even as he attempts to discover where he means to go. The poem is that realization. It both creates and affirms the fundamental order of things. In his book, *The King's Indian*, John Gardner, a friend of Dickey, and an extraordinary poet and novelist himself, reveals a haunting metaphor of this realization:

READER: *(over SFX of sea and ship's rigging)* "I was coming to be something of an astronomer. I could pretty well identify every glimmer or blink from the Andromedae to the Pegasi. I'd learned from the books about stars of varying magnitude, dark stars, twins, and the mysterious so-called wandering stars. My head was crammed to the beams with facts, and I carried them up a little higher with me every time I mounted the mast. There they ceased to be facts, became something more lively—singing particles in a sleepy-headed universe. I began to know things people don't know if they've never given up all private Identity to a shoreless sea or a forest extending, arch on arch, the breadth of fifteen mountains. I began to comprehend time and space not by mind or will but by a process more mystical, like the process by which old married couples understand each other, or trees in a valley keep minute track of the wanderings of birds and spiders. It began consciously enough, no doubt. I remember trying to make out exactly what time it was by the star's positions, and laboriously adjusting for the ship's changing locus. I never could seem to get a firm calculation, and I was stung by how cleverly Billy More could tip his red beard toward heaven and toss off, casual as a glove, our place and time. Then, one night, like a fellow coming out of a dream, I knew I too could do it. The whole universe moving around me, less like a clock than a huge, slow bird, the ship moving gentle and regular below me, my mind at the center of the gentle, seemingly random groping like the mind of God (I don't mean some judging, providential god but one who eternally rides and smiles)—the whole universe was my soul's extension, my ultimate temporal-spatial location, so that the roughly six cubic feet of air my fleshy inner shell displaced was as easy to locate in relation to the rest as the placement of my left eye in relation to my toenails. All this may seem purest gibberish to some. But it's a fact, as any crow can tell you, that the mind always knows where it is till it stops and thinks."

SFX: *(slowly fade ocean and ship sounds)*

DICKEY: I remember years ago when I first began to write and read a little German, which is a great language for poetry, in that the essence of poetry is concentration, and you get a lot of that in German because one word will take the meaning of three or four, five words in English. I came across the word *Einfühlungsvermögen* which means one, "one-feeling," or feeling *of*: feeling the same way as some other thing than you. "Empathy," in English, does not have quite the same meaning, because it doesn't make it seem as though you have the blood and nerves and essence of the other thing. Empathy just means that you're extremely sympathetic towards it; not the same thing as *being* it. And I remember also that not long after I discovered *Einfühlungsvermögen* I was reading Aldous Huxley's introduction to the letters of D. H. Lawrence, where he talks about the profound influence his friendship with Lawrence had. Huxley thought it was a put-on at first, that Lawrence should react to things in such an unusual and individual way, but he goes on to say that it wasn't long before he felt that he really *was* in the presence of someone who could tell him what it felt like to be a flower, or a tree, or a breaking wave, or the moon. This struck me as being very closely akin to my attitude towards things. It seems to me that a writer, at least one kind of writer, is very well served by being able to project himself into things that are foreign to him: that he have an encompassing and at the same time penetrating ability to feel what it must be like for something or somebody else. Novelists, of course, do this; think of the greatest novelists, with their enormous range, their ability to project themselves into any number of different kinds of people: men, women, children, social groups. But poets project in a different way than the novelists do. They don't require the expansion that the novel has, or the development of a personality or a situation over a period of time, or a number of pages. They go right to the heart, the essence of a situation, in just a few words. That's the quality of poetry I like best. I had rather read a few lines of Gerard Manley Hopkins' *Notebooks* than the whole of *War and Peace*.

The main thing for me is the act of writing itself. It's being immersed in the materials of the work that you're doing; getting *in* there with words—so deeply in there with them that possibilities open *out*, one after the other. There's a very bad poet named Kenneth Rexroth, who's a sort of elder statesman of the hippies and the beatniks, and I sometimes read through the books of his that I have around the house. He's usually uninteresting, but he said one thing in an otherwise undistinguished poem that I just thought was wonderfully good. He was talking about looking at frog spawn in a pool—minuscule life in a pool of water—and he says that "it's like looking into an inkspot and suddenly finding yourself looking out through the Milky Way." That kind of transformation is what poetry has for me. Once you've had that feeling about it, you can't take any other form of literature with equal seriousness, to save your life.

NARRATOR: Concentration and empathy for Dickey are essential. Literally so, for in his often-stated concept of poetry he targets in on capturing the *essence*, the indispensable quality of a situation or person or moment. This quality might be akin to what Aristotle called *quidditas*: the vital ingredient that makes something uniquely itself. Each poem has a different *quidditas*—each poem is a separate place. It is the challenge and joy of the poet to reach that place by piercing the levels of reality, capturing in words the essence. Placing the words on the page can be a physical struggle that involves much more than putting pen to paper or fingertips to typewriter keys . . .

DICKEY: A typewriter has to come into it eventually, because I like to see how the words look on the page, actually physically *look*, as though I had a blueprint. Eventually I type, but before that I use whatever's to hand: hands, feet, elbows, fingernails, pencils, paper, ink, ballpoints. Anything that will make a mark. I go at it "catch as catch can." It's a very physical approach to writing, I guess. Anyway, it's total.

SFX: *cut to (sound of typewriter w/ bell & return)*

NARRATOR: Words pattern on the page like ideograms of the I CHING: mysterious, complete, beautiful even in their form alone. Dickey examines their presence and display like a blueprint, anxiously searching for the one order that is right. The one order that makes all others unacceptable. The poem becomes a map of itself, and its structure has landmarks for the reader to recognize: repetition, rhyme, refrains . . .

DICKEY: I like refrains. In some of the early poetry that I wrote I would start out with the most difficult problem I could think of: to invent a rotating refrain, for example. But I saw, before I did more than one book's worth, that each of the pieces that I tried to write this way was getting to be more of a game than a poem, so I shied away from doing things that way. But it was a lot of fun. It's the kind of discipline a young poet should give himself. Part of writing, especially writing poetry, has a strong puzzle-interest, a game-interest. And the game is likely to turn up some pretty good stuff that wouldn't have occurred to you if you hadn't been playing the game.

NARRATOR: The game of poetry, serious yet endlessly joyful, is the one great game that brings into play all that James Dickey has known and seen and been and felt. His approach to writing is total: the whole man immersed in the voyage to the poem. All forms can be used: lyric, ode, sonnet, rhyme and sprung rhythm. Born and raised in the South he is heir to and part of the enduring tradition of the teller of tall tales, the yarn spinner, the ballad singer. He is close, always, to music. Himself an accomplished guitarist, he has recorded for the Library of Congress, and he has a great and abiding respect for those, like Woody Guthrie . . .

DICKEY: I think the best of Woody Guthrie is more than absolutely wonderful. He's an authentic genius, and I think that "This Land Is Your Land" ought to be the national anthem; it has far more to say to the masses of people than something like the "Star Spangled Banner," which is essentially sort of like a college fight song, and doesn't have the depth or appeal of "This Land Is Your Land."

NARRATOR: With his sextant James Dickey takes the position of the sun each day, re-affirming and defining his position in the place he has chosen as his home. The poetry, the stationary voyage, continues.

DICKEY: I now refer to Columbia, South Carolina, as the place where I was born—a second time. I like it here. It's the roots underground and also the stars overhead that conspire to put me here.

Here, I try to write as well as I can, according to whatever I can do at the time. But now I'm just a year short of sixty—which is getting on down the road—and I put my time in on the work I love most in the world. My wife and my children are outside me, in themselves, and there for me to love. But poetry is mine. My relationship to it is unique, or so I feel. And the longer I work with it, the more mysterious and difficult it gets; but on the other hand—to change persons—the more you do, the more you see you can do, and you want to get out there and try a lot of different ways. Some people, because of *Deliverance*, want me to write novels. And I'd like that, too. I've got a new one about half finished now. But my real gut commitment is not to the novel. I had rather try to find the apt word, or combination of words, to say a thing, than work out a narrative sequence. I am far more interested in metaphors themselves than I am in inventing imaginary situations between characters and dialogues between imaginary people. One part of my personality responds to doing these things—but not the deepest part. If you write a novel that's successful, and made into a movie, it gives your enemies a weapon against your poetry; that is, they say, "You should have been writing novels." They use the novel to beat the poetry with. But the least poem I've ever written is better than the whole of *Deliverance*. I like *Deliverance*, but I doubt if it'll last, and I do believe that the poems will. I'm quite willing to put everything on that assumption. If I'm wrong, I'm wrong; but I've been a gambler all my life.

NARRATOR: Like any good navigator, James Dickey has taken his soundings and read, squint-eyed and carefully, the wheeling stars.

His poems have come back, carefully ordered maps of the journey into those regions of the human spirit and the great world where few of us can venture ourselves, but which shape us, determine us, make us—in the ultimate sense—possible. The poems are more than a record of the journey—they *are* the journey.

DICKEY: I take the noon-position sight from the sun every day as a matter of homage to this particular locality. I want God to assure me, through the movements of the celestial bodies, that I really am here, at 34 degrees, no minutes and 2-tenths north and at 80 degrees, 57 minutes and 7-tenths west. This morning I was off about half a mile, but I'll get it back tomorrow.

BODY, BACKSTRETCH, AND THE OUTSIDE MAN

In the Depression, for a dollar you could get a whole handful, a double handful, of cars. These were lead, with maybe some tin, if that is possible; you wanted something that didn't sink like lead, but ran like it, fleeing Woolworth's. I never raced cars with drivers in them, lead or otherwise. At the wheel there must be air, invisibility, certainty, fantasy, possibility, ego, a new and old size of Self. Who is to say it was not the Soul that drove? Or all-souls: twelve of them? The family had a steep backyard driveway; I would line up six or eight cars behind a plank, see that the wheels were straight-on, switch the plank up and away and let gravity happen. Gravity was all right, but cement, though exciting at first, was too pitted and chaotic. Wrecks based on chance were in the end not only unsatisfactory but dull; there was no way of telling which of my Selves was the true champion, which his car, what color. I needed a channelling, a shaping of speed, a process of final confrontation. Knocking the ends and sides out of the drawers of an old dresser, laying the three bottoms end-to-end and using the other boards as rails, I made a closed track, propped on the steps of the back porch, and, after endless variations of slant, endless one-on-one matchups, got things down to the Big One: the pink racer and the gray lined up for the take-all money, and I remember the exact feeling of my heart dividing evenly: they both could not win, and a tie would not do. I no longer remember which—or who—won, but *I* won: what I won were pink and gray, themselves: the heart's own favorites, my lifetime totem tones.

Such was my introduction to speed, to ownership and partisanship, to bodily identification with the material world, to danger, uncertainty and ascendancy in their true colors. It led, then, to the first Soap Box Derby in Atlanta, where, again by fantasizing, I got my true body, size and all, and an inkling of what I needed to carry it through the world in masterful exhilaration. The Derby took place on a long hill on Northside Drive, no more than a mile from my house. In those days the boys really *did* design and build their cars, and at first I was intimidated. How could beings my own age—and some of them younger—have *conceived* of such arrangements of wood and cloth and metal, much less put them together? What was then called "streamlining" was only part of their appeal, but immediately the part I liked best. Car to car, the principles of air-flow were so differently embodied as to seem not to be seeking the same things from the same element. Some were pointed into gravity through a needle nose, some from a flattened, belligerent, low-browed stance. Some were carapaced, others upraised high on the largest allowable wheels; some were ribbed and rounded like zeppelins. One even took in air through an open prow, bent it around the driver and out a vent behind, a clear invitation to body-flow. Everything about the cars interested me in a new and vivid kind of physical, conspiratorial way: their numbers, the different means by which they took the air, their braking and steering systems, pulley-strung, intricate, diabolical. Enthralled, I wandered among them, totemizing, envying and loving.

The Derby took four days, as I remember, and was won by a countrified devil-fish, a manta-ray with short wings, its cowling made of canvas, clearly a triumph of design in all but the choice of materials; it came in flapping like a sail, setting a record on that suburban hill that stood for years, even against the onslaught of the Fathers, who, not being able to keep out, began to help the boys rig their cars and wound up having them manufactured in sheet-metal mills. But that first year, when the boys' cars *were* the boys' cars, opened up my capacity for experience as that canvas racer opened the turgid ozone of Northside Drive. No longer tiny and invisible but still retaining pink and gray as components of ritual magic, I learned that there were actual other bodies—fish, zeppelins, skimmering earth-shapes, air-boats on wheels—that would carry mine: that I could get into, control, maybe in-feeding the pure wind of speed around me, devil-fishing straight into such air, all-out. I had a new dimension of body, dream-like, called-forth, and it moved—at any speed—through the real world.

I was a third-rate athlete: a middling wingback in the fall and a fairly good hurdler in the spring. My best races were run, though, not by myself but by my chosen Self in the person of a Georgia Tech quarter-miler named Charlie Belcher, with whom I identified in all seasons. He was thin-boned, thin-skinned and gaunt, with jaw-muscles so prominent with determination that they suggested the bolt through the mandible of the Frankenstein monster as played by Boris Karloff, then lurching amongst us. Charlie did not lurch, but took off out of his holes in a manner whose savagery made you quail. Once in the backstretch he shifted—modulated—into a stride which was the most beautiful continued action I have ever seen the human form develop, or assume: the embodiment of an effortless preordination, a kind of floating. The 440 is a tough race, probably the toughest in track, and coming off the final turn Charlie had to bulldog his way in on will-power and those jaw-muscles; his finish was a fighting finish, and worthy of the Congressional Medal of Honor, but it was the backstretch run—or sharp-shinned swoop or intense float—that I lived for.

And—same- and other-bodied, nearing sixty—still live, wryly, secretly and involvedly. Beside any car I drive, building up speed, maintaining it, adding to it, in cities and suburbs but most especially on highways, over long flat straights—elongated versions of the backstretch of Grant Field Stadium—a ghostly Charlie Belcher, transparent with super-reality, is running, as much in the all-out float as he needs to be. Even at 160 miles an hour, barrelling out through the salt flats of Utah or the blow-sands of New Mexico in a four-barrel 427 Corvette Stingray Turbo, I see without turning my head that he is right beside me; he is controlling; he is floating; his passion is in his form, his style. I cannot gain; the more I accelerate the more he increases his intake of landscape, increases that perilous, flawless stride and ups his leg-speed. We move on, all-even, to wherever I'm going, and beyond, into the dream, still driving, still floating.

Two adventurers, hellbenders I grew up with, were dreamers of the day, though; those, as T. E. Lawrence says, who are not satisfied with fantasies, but act, so as to make them happen. Changed slightly, their names were Harmon Quigley and Jim Jackson, the first a handsome neurotic-looking boy of great abandon, and Jim a powerful tough who seemed much older than he must have been; in grammar school he played marbles with steelies, or ball-bearings, which should have told me something. They were car freaks, speed freaks in a sense pertaining only to locomotion, and it seemed almost inevitable that they should go onto the stock car circuit, just come down to our area out of the bootleggers' mountains to the north. The first official race was held at Lakewood Amusement Park in South Atlanta, and the winner, Lloyd Seay, a whiskey runner for "Fat" Hardy, was almost immediately murdered by his relatives and other partners in business. To my recollection neither Harmon nor Jim was in that race, but they were in others very soon after it; all through high school they raced and ran liquor, and added the last element to what had become, for me, an overpowering psychodrama of motorized Selfdom: illicitness. I have carried it and been sustained by it ever since, and arrested more than once, paying all fines gladly, given as tribute not to society but to Harmon Quigley and Jim Jackson, now turning gold in the golden years, honored citizens of Atlanta and Daytona Beach, but going with me always as the devil's own couriers of joy, burning the lawless air.

During the last of the young-time, from the age of 33 to 38, I worked in Atlanta in advertising, living on it and taking a private stand against it. Stand is not quite the word, though, because whatever it was I took was taken in a lime-green MG—the second-oldest model, just after the "classic"—and it was never standing when I could get in it. Over the low shape, like a stylized hump of earth, hung the spirits of pink and gray; when I turned on the ignition, Charlie Belcher settled into his holes and stared straight ahead into the wind he would create. I drove as much as I could; the rise in morale was particularly strong on the freeway going into Atlanta: something to sustain me through the day of King-Size Coke and the Tony Bennett Record Promotion, and all the way back down the other side of the divider when I was finished and going home to a drink, a family, and another night of writing poetry.

I got out of business, finally. I went to Europe and the MG sat on blocks, top down, cockpit cover on, waiting for whatever would be when I got back. When I did, I sold the house, left it immobile in the commercial world forever, put my wife and three-year-old son in the Italy-gutted Volks bus that served as heavy transport, belted my oldest boy, a wonderful conversationalist, into the MG with me, put my best longbow between us, plenty of sun-blocker on both faces and other exposed parts, and in new dark glasses took off for Oregon via Los Angeles.

But there was trouble. The MG kept heating up, and the brake-shoes, supposedly adjusted for the trip, wore down on the drums, state after state. I stopped in Birmingham, I stopped in Fort Smith, Arkansas, I stopped in Vega, Texas, and Albuquerque for consultation. Nobody found anything wrong. Then, just as we were dragging into Winslow, Arizona, there was a loud cracking noise forward, smoke poured up from the front wheels, and the brake pedal went all the way to the floor while the speed held. I was running through lanes of stores and toward an intersection whose lights were changing against me when I remembered Harmon Quigley, who had told me to gear down if you lose your brakes, and if you have to stop short, strip the box. Before I could strip the box, though, surrounded by more blue-black smoke than Satan when he fell or was pushed from the crystal battlements of Milton's heaven, we coasted to a standstill in a filling station that seemed fated to be there like the number a roulette ball stops on, or like Pandemonium. The demons of the station, who could draw no support from those of Albuquerque, Vega or Fort Smith, could not get out of this one, and grudgingly set to work on my brakes.

They worked for a solid week, and while my family wandered around town looking at kachina dolls, I took to going out to Winslow's chief tourist attraction, the ultimate botched Stillness, the enormous meteor crater said to be either the largest in the world or the second largest, depending on whether you side with American statistics or Siberian. Day after day, deprived of on-go and ego, I footed with confused intense feelings through the various levels of geologic time, the inner circumferences of the earnest hole, not thinking of Impact or millenia but trying to imagine Charlie Belcher blasting his high-strung form around those crumbling slants on centrifugal fury alone, like the motorcycle trick-riders at Lakewood Park during Fair Week around the walls of their thunderous, interior barrels, but the arena was wrong for Charlie; he could not adjust his stride to it. He needed the flat to run on, an endless backstretch, and he needed me in the pace-car.

He was sharp-shinned as a hawk. When I got the MG back, the first thing I saw, just out of Winslow, was a hawk—maybe sharp-shinned—on a fencepost. Loosed from Time, Charlie went right through it, and the hawk took off just as he did. I dug for out-of-town, my body and my son in-drinking the desert air five times itself in delight. Charlie Belcher's hair slicked-down on his hard, trim head, and there was a new bolt of determination through his jaw. I stepped down right-footed, uncompromising, and knew a lot of things that I had known, among them why men drive. Charlie was full into his float, piñon and sage flickering with him. I moved the needle higher; at seventy-five the car went pink and gray, all the way home: to homes behind, with us, and coming at us.

THE GRASS MOUNTAIN KID
—Family Camping Exposed—

There are, among other things in the world, cocktail bars. Either seated or standing, you feel quite at home in any of them, talking, laughing, drinking your liver away in mankind's great good science-created pleasure-dome with a million convenient locations. When night comes doesn't matter; it's dark in there anyway. You feel no wind, and see no moon. There are no insects, no animals, no birds, except in rare uneasy instances, a cockatoo or an aquarium of disillusioned fish. You could spend your life amongst such surroundings, and not have to worry about anything but the bill. You could spend your life there, and you're afraid you're going to have to.

Most likely far away, there is Nature, too, though, trembling with ecological ferment, stalked by industrialists like catamounts on bulldozers, whirling their chain-saws; Nature besieged by that variety of folk known optimistically as Developers. You feel guilty about not knowing it better before it's gone for good, and, somewhere on the third martini a mind-blowing and terrible idea comes straight out of the glass into your head. Camping. Worse still, *family* camping.

Seems like a good idea, there with the sad fish. For a few days, why not switch from the lounge to the tent? All that fresh air, as opposed to all this smoke. Get your family, buy some wilderness cooking equipment, and get the hell out. Out . . . but where *is* out? Where do you *go* camping, anyway? Well, you can start with an idea: the idea of mountains. You like mountains, at least in pictures, and you have some vague geographical notion of where there are some.

I must go on record as saying that I once did something like this, on some such impulse. The mountains happened to be in Oregon. After the fun—and it *was* fun, too, by the hokies—of buying the equipment, we went first to the Rogue River, for I also like rivers, however presented. We made the mistake of pitching our tent in a public campsite, for the sake of its "conveniences." The stay began depressingly. I went to the convenient bathroom with a flashlight. It turned out to be a deep whitewashed hole in the ground, and I could not resist shining the flashlight down into it. Doing nothing more than remembering what I saw is enough to turn me queasy, even today. The hideous view down that latrine gully of what literally must have been pounds of human excrement on those otherwise gleaming walls survives as one of the purer forms of horror that my particular mind possesses. I couldn't go to sleep in our diabolical new pyramidal tent for thinking of it, and it still wakes me unpleasantly in my more recent bouts of middle-aged insomnia, always at 4:30 in the morning.

So much for campsite camping. That was my last time. But it was really not all that bad, even so. We stayed at the site—but carefully avoiding the conveniences—another day, and at nightfall I climbed up on some rocks over the unearthly blue river. My God, I thought, there's nothing like *this* in a cocktail bar. There was the strange, river-sounding silence, and the moon was beginning to glow with major intensity. To that, I lost at least a little of my disgust with excremental whitewash, and felt that in some way I had entered an emotion far more important than the American's typical worship-fear of the body's off-scourings. I lay on the stone, my hat under my head for a pillow. The moon kept coming up, and took hold of my gut; below me, the Trout of the Last Light was circling in the first blue. I began to get the hang of something.

We went then, in our Volkswagen bus—a regular one, emphatically not a Camper—to a place near Alsea, on the west slope of the Cascades. We pitched our tent at Grass Mountain. It was the lonesomest spot I'd ever been in. There was nothing near us except the Unknown, as it took the form of bushes and trees. A partial road—logging road—ran to our camp and away from it. My wife had intended to cook something for us on her new wilderness homemaker's rig, but night came on too fast. My oldest son had intended to dig a toilet and put a decorous sheet around it, but dark got to us. We did manage to get the complicated tent erected, and the cots and sleeping bags at the ready. The other three slept on cots; I slept on the tent-floor, on an air-sack.

It was terrifying. I longed for campsite conveniences, and even more for a cocktail bar. We were deep in the strangeness of God. I reached up to touch my wife—after all, I was the titular head of the family—to afford some kind of reassurance, and she was not so much shaking as vibrating. This scared me—the old titular head—pretty badly. My biggest boy, then around twelve, who had formerly been of an ecstatic enthusiasm for the project, said, "Dad, why did you get us into something like this?" I then performed the most efficacious act I have ever perpetrated as a father. I reached up out of my sleeping bag and put my duck-feather-warmed hand on my son's face, and felt him relax with the only reassurance I was able to give him under the circumstances. I hope that when the time comes he will serve his own children so, and with a lot more frequency than I. All four of us shook into sleep.

Nothing happened to us: no bears, no evil men.

The next day looked like the first day of labor on Eden. Since the whole family piddled with archery, we had our gear with us. We strung the bows. I had a big, powerful Bear Kodiak, my wife had a bow just over the draw-weight for hunting in Oregon, Chris had about the same, and five-year-old Kevin had one appropriately named "Little John."

The terrain, perpetually water-logged and full of down timber and rotten wood, was strange to Southerners. "Don't you get us lost, you jackass," my wife said. "Don't worry about a thing," I answered. "They call me the Grass Mountain Kid." I knew, with my mind-boggling knowledge of the delicate art of primitive navigation, that if we stayed on the road, all we had to do was turn around and head down it the opposite way, and we'd be back at our camp. Yes indeed: at our home.

What happened then was wonderful. Every cocktail bar in the world blew away like chaff. We came around a bend, and to the left was a kind of cliff that opened on a huge, far-down field of conifers. Among the trees, spaced in a lovely, random arrangement, were deer. Dozens of them, all browsing, and then pausing to look around with delicate, dreaming alertness. I heard Little John rattle to the ground.

I turned and saw my youngest boy's hand over his mouth in wonderment, and I myself, in the manner of the young Wordsworth, felt that I had better hang onto a tree or I would take off straight up. *This* is the wilderness, I said to myself. This is what we came for, though we don't know what it is.

We went slowly back down the road, practicing the delicate art of the forest. A hunter had driven up. "Got him hanging?" he asked. "No," I replied. "But how about a morning shot of bourbon?" The cocktail bar had snuck up and blind-sided me.

That day we discovered, through the delight that was beginning to overshine our fear, the unmanmade world. And we also discovered that we lived in a blackberry patch. We picked a couple of quarts and took them back to our little suburban home in Portland. My wife made an epic pie with them, which we communally served to the faculty and students of Reed College, where I was then teaching. They had never had anything quite like it. The Hunter Home from the Hill was absurdly happy to say, "You know what these are? Blackberries. *Wild* blackberries. Picked 'em at a place near Alsea, on the west slope of the Cascades. Little hunting trip. Place they call Grass Mountain."

THE WILD HEART

The inner life of each of us—what is it? What is it made of? What is its value? Is it useful? Is it necessary? Is it, really, much of a life? We have, after all, such a nice external one, full of the soft seats of automobiles, thousands and thousands of things to buy, to eat, to be amused by. Yet the ego—a word one can hardly use any more without a derogatory connotation—is a thing that belongs to the very nature of man as wings to a bird or leaves to a tree. If it didn't we would have perished as a race long, long ago. There is really nothing suspect about it; the fault is only in how we regard it, how we acknowledge it, what we do with it. And yet we can't escape the notion, when we talk to other people, when we're by ourselves, that we are not really living at the center of this personal identity that we have: at the center of our being. In ordinary conversation, for example, when you look at another person's face you can tell perfectly well that he or she is not being what he wants to be, what he is, but what is most expedient, what he is supposed to appear as being, which includes a small measure, perhaps *very* small, of what he thinks *you* want him to be at that moment. And you are doing the same thing; so am I.

A lot of unhappiness in the world, it seems to me, comes from man's disregarding or misunderstanding the deepest purpose of his existence. He has somehow or other lost the sense of living life spontaneously, from the center of his being and his essential self, and so has lost the sense, the real sense, of the *consequence* of life, and often has the uneasy suspicion that he is a kind of living stuffed dummy. The most consistent question we ask about life, as we approach the thirties, the forties, the fifties; that question we most often ask ourselves, at five in the morning, already beginning to listen for the alarm clock, is: "Is *this* all life is? Isn't there something more, something better than this?"

Why should this be? Milton said, "The mind is its own place, and can make a hell of heaven, a heaven of hell." Why should ours so frequently make it a hell? How many of us have the sense of living all the time in Heaven, as William Blake did? Is it just the usual human fate, or what? For it's a simple fact of experience that sincere feelings overleap all barriers put up by the mind. And it's also probably true that there are certain similarities between the analogical working of the mind—the way it works when it is building its own sphere from its outer experience—and the means that God used when creating heaven and earth, though perhaps I oughtn't to claim quite so much as all that for the imagination. Yet whatever else the world we inherited is, it is indubitably a poetic one. And within this world I think it is most important to acknowledge our own reactions to its parts—our own comparisons of objects, our own symbol-making possibilities—not for whatever utility they may hold, or not for the clever things we can say at sherry parties, or even for the poems we can write, using them, but simply because they are things belonging to our own individual perspective on life, on experience, and as such are, really, quite literally who we are. One's inner life is made of inexplicables, and because they are inexplicables in terms of ordinary social parlance, we have the tendency—the compulsion—to set them at no account: as just being frivolous, valueless and even eccentric, and everyone knows how dangerous it is to be eccentric. What are some of these inexplicables? They vary, of course, with the psychological conditioning of the individual, and depend on his history, which is different from anyone else's. I have never been able to look at golf-sticks, for some reason or another, without a feeling of intense loathing. I have no earthly idea—or no conscious idea, anyway—of why this should be so; some of my best friends are golfers, though I have to admit that when they pick up the sticks a kind of vague atmosphere of evil comes over them that never happens, say, to tennis players or to archers. Now this is absurd enough, surely; yet nevertheless it is a true feeling, and it seems to me that it is something that I must inevitably recognize for me to understand who I am, even though this feeling doesn't get into practical action in any way; I wouldn't waylay a poor golfer, say, on the seventeenth hole, and murder him because of the strange, evil creature his golf sticks have made of him—though, incidentally, I am fairly convinced that no small share of the world's crimes are committed out of such inexplicable but very real motivations. Anyhow, though the social self may indeed perform a good service here, in keeping me from killing an innocent golfer—or at least innocent in the eyes of the law—I must, myself, be prepared to acknowledge my own feelings on the matter, and admit to myself the intrinsic evilness, where I am concerned, of golf clubs, whether I ever tell anybody else about it or not. It is in this world where, for no reason, or for the deepest, hidden reasons, golf clubs are evil and tennis racquets are good, where toadstools are somehow friendly, interesting objects and pinestraw is not, where granite is more beautiful than marble, that the wild heart lives: the untamable source of the emotions, submerged but never dead, rarely acknowledged, but the seat of almost all real happiness, nevertheless, and the place where the imagination has its being, and has its essential connection with what we are. Out of these unjudging responses, our real, mattering life is made. It is made, really, of what Wordsworth called "unknown modes of being," when we live and think and move as creatures essentially unknown, but interesting to ourselves. These are the modes of being to which the wild heart is accessible, and without which life—or what passes for it—becomes tame, ordinary, and finally insupportable. Without this quickening process, without the acknowledgment and promise of what is really felt, of what will be felt in the future, the dull hand of habit drives us all to the bottle, to violent pleasures, to guilt, to an artificial and temporary facsimile of what is our rightful due: a vivid and meaningful and aware existence.

My point here is that it is this "secret" or essential or sub-social self that poetry speaks to, and that all the arts at their best speak to and for: to the potentiality of the hidden and fundamental selves, speaking of not what is supposed to be felt or what it is of advantage to feel, but what *is*, ridiculously or solemnly, felt.

As we grow older, everything tends to lose its sense of consequence and interest and vitality, and grows tasteless, uninteresting; something only to be endured. It loses its sense of being *real*: everything is substanceless and illusory, and we begin to live, and even to *want* to live, in a kind of sleep-walking state, only enduring,

enduring, and now and then having a little bodily pleasure. Pleasure is really not pleasure any longer, but only a kind of drug. This is why, in many cases, only the most violent stimuli have much effect: sex, liquor, narcotics. The most extreme form and example of this is in Hollywood, where rich, beautiful, famous people are killing themselves and dying of thrill-seeking and boredom every year, almost every month: Those, as Pope says,

> Who purchase pain with all that joy can give
> And die of nothing but a rage to live.

But life, a serious, steady and enduring sense of the importance and interest of being alive, is not to be come by in such a manner. It exists only when a vivid apprehension exists in the beholder, and when he wants to live, not because he tells himself that he ought to want to, but simply because he does.

At the center of one's being, at that place where only *we* live, the mind is always quick and alive; it is always making comparisons, judging, rejecting whole-heartedly and accepting whole-heartedly. It can say, as in dreams, that rain sometimes looks as though it's falling upwards, that a cloud looks like a man and woman making love, that the edges of some leaves look like little saws (what would they saw?) and that water moves over rocks like a kind of heavy and another kind of light cloth, and that the sound of running water is always very beautiful and a little frightening, because there is something eternal about it, and because it has a kind of judging sound, like the sound in a sea-shell.

The important thing is that these ways—essentially imaginative ways—are how the world is given to each of us: the means by which we know it, and—in a sense—the ways in which we put the world together, make it cohere, make sense of it. It is important to recognize the claim of these primary judgments, the comparisons, and not be ashamed of them because they are ours, and have no official sanction or recognition in the social world in which we live. The "official" way of seeing and knowing is one great cause—perhaps *the* cause—of the deadening process that takes place in all of us except our children at a very early age, before they have had a chance to live with us very long. But even now, which of us hasn't wanted to answer, when we drive by red rose trees, or a low range of green hills, and someone else, maybe our wife, our husband or an older child has said, in our pathetic and touching and wholly inadequate kind of half-language, "Aren't they *beautiful*?" Which of us hasn't wanted to say, "Oh . . . they're better than *that*! They're . . . they're . . ." and then give up, most likely, and say limply, "Yes, they certainly *are* beautiful." But they *are* better than that; they're *different* from that; they are full of individual characteristics; we just don't, somehow, want to go to the trouble of saying in just what ways they are, and we *should* want to. I think there's a sense in which we're afraid of being rejected by others when we try to reveal ourselves to them; afraid of saying—of having said to us something like what is said in the most terrifying instance of non-understanding in all literature: in T. S. Eliot's "Love Song of J. Alfred Prufrock," when the poor, timid Boston aesthete tries to tell an "understanding woman" all about the meaning of his life, his secret thoughts, and so on, and she settles a pillow by her head and says in aggrieved tones, "That is not what I meant at all; that is not it, at all." Well, most of us yearn for communication, to share things with others, but it is not really an essential part of the process I am describing. I have gone far enough when I say that we ought simply to acknowledge these states at the center of being for themselves, for their own everlasting sake, and for our sake, simply because they are ours; simply because they are *us*.

The notion of inconsequence, of the unreality of things, that grows on us out of habit and the daily round, the triviality of the social context, the attempt to put up a front, to wear a mask, is, rightly seen, a kind of Purgatory, fully comparable to Dante's Purgatory, and to some parts of his Inferno. When we are children, we are given the sense of the consequence and vivid interest of the world, because it is new to us, but after that we must work for it. There is a poem, by Jules Supervielle, about this feeling of inconsequence which so-called "maturity" brings with it.

The Cloud

There was a time when the shadows,
In their true places,
Did not darken my fables.

My heart gave its light.

My eyes understood the chair of straw,
The table of wood,
And my hands did not dream
By the mistakes of ten fingers.

But now time falls apart
As under a thousand snows;
The more I come and go
The less sure I am of anything.

Hear me, Captain of my childhood,
Let's do as we did before:
Let's get back on board my first ship
Which crossed the sea when I was ten.

It took on no dream-like waters,
And smelled absolutely of tar:
Listen: it's only in my memory
That wood is still wood, and iron, hard.

For a long, long time, Captain,
Everything has been cloud to me, and I am dying of it.

What we need most of all, as individuals, is a renewed sense of that "intensified particularity" that the world gives us—that we give the world—enabling us to get all the way *into* life, into the world both as it is and as we make it: as it can be when we have achieved what Marianne Moore calls "the simplicity that is not the product of a simple mind but of a single eye." To do this is easy, and is also the hardest thing in the world. It is simple—and also exceedingly complex to see a white horse and a boy with perfect directness, without subterfuge:

> The youth walks up to the white horse, to put its halter on and the horse looks at him in silence.
> They are so silent they are in another world.

The author of these lines was D. H. Lawrence, known mainly

to the sensation-loving public for his much discussed novel, *Lady Chatterley's Lover*, which may be found, in pocket editions painfully underlined in black pencil, in a good many army barracks and dormitories of both sexes, in our worst and better colleges. But Lawrence was as different from your ordinary pornographer—your pornographer, like, say, the one who reads *Lady Chatterley* for its pornography—as God is from Satan. I have often been struck by Aldous Huxley's description of him, of Lawrence as "another kind of human being who showed us all, in the dreariness of living, that it is possible to be another and infinitely better kind":

> To be with Lawrence was a kind of adventure, a voyage of discovery into newness and otherness. For, being himself of different order, he inhabited a different universe from that of common men—a brighter and intenser world which freed you, while you were with him, of the drab one you lived in. He looked at things with the eyes, so it seemed, of a man who had been at the brink of death and to whom, as he emerges from darkness, the world reveals itself as unfathomable, beautiful and mysterious. For Lawrence, existence was one continuous convalescence; it was as though he were newly reborn from a mortal illness every day of his life. What these convalescent eyes saw his most casual speech would reveal. A walk with him through the country was a walk through that marvellously rich and significant landscape which is at once the background and the principal personage of all his novels. He seems to know, by personal experience, what it was like to be a tree or a daisy or a breaking wave or even the mysterious moon itself. He could get inside the skin of an animal and tell you in the most convincing detail how it felt and how, dimly, inhumanly, it thought. Of Black-eyed Susan, for example, his cow at his New Mexico ranch, he was never tired of speaking, nor was I ever tired of listening to his account of her character and her bovine philosophy.
>
> For an inhabitant of the safe metropolis of thought and feeling, to be with Lawrence was a most exciting experience; it was to find oneself transported from the

> world of received "fact" to the vivid and mysterious center of an extraordinary human consciousness.
>
> One of the great charms of Lawrence as a companion was that he could never be bored and so could never be boring. He was able to absorb himself completely in what he was doing at the moment; and he regarded no task as too humble for him to undertake, nor so trivial that it was not worth his while to do it well. He could cook, he could sew, he could darn a stocking and milk a cow, he was an efficient wood-cutter and a good hand at embroidery, fires always burned when he laid them and a floor, after Lawrence had scrubbed it, was thoroughly clean. Moreover, he possessed what is, for a highly strung and highly intelligent man, an even more remarkable accomplishment: he knew how to do nothing. He could just sit and be perfectly content, for he was, after all, in himself: a self whose importance he never doubted for an instant. And his contentment, while one remained in his company, was infectious.

There is that stillness, and of a particular man; there is the idea of Lawrence sitting quietly by himself, happy to be there. It is a good image, I think, when you realize that he is sitting at the very center of the uniqueness, mystery, beauty and immediacy of the world, of his own world; he is there so completely, in fact, that we others tend to note how very little we ourselves are willing to settle for; in living, how much there *is*, there really *is*, upon earth: how wild, inexplicable, marvellous and endless creation is, and in what vivid and self-discovering ways the mind can, if it wishes, come upon each of its parts, for the imagination is nothing more or less than the perception—or the personal creation—of individual meaning out of the essentially meaningless chaos—or the official or "public" meaning, which as far as we are *really* concerned is the same thing as meaningless—of the universe. It is making our kind of peace with the world, and in the end, if we are honest enough we will be perceptive enough, and will then conceive what will quite literally be the truth: that that kind of peace, the peace and sense we make of the world by means of the real affections and the real imagination, is what the Bible calls "the peace which passeth understanding."

And yet I have another ending, too: an ending from a novel by a writer I have never liked very much, W. Somerset Maugham. It is in *Of Human Bondage*, when the hero, the timid, crippled soul-searcher Philip Carey, comes home to his prosaic uncle, who has raised him and given him a little money to study art in Paris, which money Philip has squandered and for which he has nothing to show.

The uncle says:

> "Then your two years in Paris may be regarded as so much wasted time?"
>
> "I don't know about that. I had a very jolly two years, and I learned one or two useful things."
>
> "What?"
>
> Philip reflected for an instant, and his answer was not devoid of a gentle desire to annoy.
>
> "I learned to look at hands, which I'd never looked at before. And instead of just looking at houses and trees I learned to look at houses and trees against the sky. And I learned also that shadows are not black but colored."
>
> "I suppose you think you're very clever. I think your flippancy is quite inane."

But the young man is not inane, and not flippant.

COMPLICITY

"Woman is the promise that cannot be kept" said the poet Paul Claudel. But does she know that? She—her sexuality, her voice and eyes and skin and hair—is the promise that we men make to ourselves hour after hour every day, every day of our lives. If she is not the secret of the universe, then there is none. To us she appears in the clandestine and burning center of the mind as the form we most deeply desire and must create or die. There she is, dressed—or half-dressed—in her mysterious clothes, hair a little mussed, lips just moist *enough*. From going to and fro in the earth, and from walking up and down in it—the real earth, and not just the enchanted fragment of it that blazes in the longing mind to furnish her setting—she becomes a hidden archetype to the beholder rendered god-like by her presence: his possession and promise, soulless and soulful at the same time, receding, flashing up with terrible certainty at the most inopportune times that she then makes opportune. Behind her are real women, giving to the ideal the substance it requires from the lived world, and serving to make more powerful and imperious those all-powerful creatures of the depths of our being, the slaves of our needs who enslave us. We have seen her in actual beds, and seen her satisfactions taking place hiddenly, deep in the body, from their outward signs so powerful and intimate that we know, with awe and gratitude, that we could never attain anything of like consequence or even approach it. We leave her sleeping, and retire to the center of the mind, where she has taken a new dimension, another hairdo, another set of magic lingerie. We love her there in another one of her endless changes, and wonder when she will come true again, taking on the mortal and identifying flesh without which all ideals die, as a real woman, perhaps not yet encountered, unhooks her bra with the strange motion that only women have ever mastered, smiling with infinite complicity.

Talking It Out

IN TEXAS
An Interview by Paul Christensen

CHRISTENSEN: Your own career begins in earnest in the 1960s, a decade of almost frenzied experiment in poetry. What were the main directions of that poetry?

DICKEY: One of the main things that came out of the 1960s, I suppose, could be called confessional poetry, and would have to do with personal anecdotes, as in Lowell's family and his father's garbage cans with his initials on them or his trouble with his child or his feelings of guilt about his relationship with his wife or his periodic visits to the madhouse and his political opinions, and so on. The other main tendency is the opposite of this: it's the kind of thing that I try to do, which is essentially impersonal. It may have personal references in it, but the effect of the Lowell-type poetry is to close down the arena of the poem to one person's experience, that of the poet. If you're not interested in Lowell's father's garbage cans you are not interested in the poem that he is writing. I wanted something different, larger, more inclusive.

CHRISTENSEN: Are you saying that there would be nothing exemplary in the poem if it is this personal?

DICKEY: No; of course not. I'm saying only that Lawrence and Roethke don't close the reader down into a small personal situation; they open the world up to the reader. Roethke's *Words for the Wind* is something that you can participate in. He's not locked into the solipsistic world of a single person—the poem is in a sense causing you to, allowing you to, inviting you to participate in existence, which includes your own existence. This is the kind of thing that I try to do and I believe Roethke tried to do, that Lawrence did. I was thinking, for example, about a poem of Lawrence's where he refers to a fish as a grey monotonous soul in the water. Now the thing that makes that so good is the word "monotonous." There is something about a fish that *is* monotonous. Have you ever noticed that? Now, that's ingenious. I have never seen a fish after encountering that line of poetry without thinking, boy, that's right, that's right, and it's a real fish in real water, and yet my relationship to it, because of that line of poetry, is quite different from what it might ordinarily have been.

CHRISTENSEN: What about the word "soul" in that line?

DICKEY: That, I would even accept that, it's not bad. It doesn't *have* to be a soul, but it's *got* to be monotonous. The soul is not bad because there's something disembodied about a fish, since it's in another element than yours.

CHRISTENSEN: Beginning with *Into the Stone* and *Drowning With Others*, you have a voice that stands apart from the encounters of other people, whether it's initiations into death as in "The Lifeguard" or terrifying experiences or strange imaginings which you record as someone between the reader and the experiencer. But in later books you draw yourself closer and closer to the event until you become the one who encounters these other worlds, these other realms.

DICKEY: My major in college was philosophy; a quasi-philosophical article I did for the Great Books thing of the *Encyclopaedia Britannica* a few years ago was called "The Self as Agent," where I tried to show what is involved when you say "I" in a poem—"I" did this, or "I" have this opinion. What is the relationship between that "I" in the poem who is an agent of yours to the actual person, the poet himself? If I apply that to my own work I would say that almost nothing I have ever written about in which I used the first person pronoun, I ever actually *did*, or did in that way. There's not anything that I have ever written that's literally true. People talk about truth and the search for truth; I don't think that a poet is interested in finding the truth at all. Not in the slightest; he's interested in *making* it. The fish in the water doesn't know he's monotonous and neither does the human race, all except one person, and that is D. H. Lawrence. But now they do know, because he said it. That's an aspect of the truth that depends on a certain angle of perception and a certain linguistic way of embodying it in a poem.

CHRISTENSEN: So language creates truth?

DICKEY: Yes, but there are just as many truths as there are angles of perception. If you looked at the sun—you could say that it's shining, radiating, glowing, doing any number of things, which would all be more or less equally descriptive, but to the poet one would be more characteristic of his own perception of the sun than the other words would be.

CHRISTENSEN: But how does the poem convey to the reader that same sense of truth?

DICKEY: It doesn't, it gives him his own angle of vision—this is my feeling about it. The thing about poetry that's good, that I like the most, is this releasing factor, the releasing of the reader's mind. He may be in the same room, he may be 100 miles away, he may be ten or fifteen hundred years later into the future, but he receives. Poetry is a sort of ritual magic, essentially, and what the magic does is to release the reader's own imagination to him, make it available to him.

CHRISTENSEN: Not the poet's imagination?

DICKEY: No, that's impossible. The reader's imagination. If the poet is good enough, if he is persuasive enough, it's the reader himself who enters into the arena of the poem. And the poet gives that to him. And the more intensely and the more deeply he is able to give that to the reader, the better poet he is.

CHRISTENSEN: So art stimulates the internal process of the reader so that he is actually enjoying *himself*.

DICKEY: Yes; a person is eager to project himself into a situation:

eager. If he's extremely language-sensitive and has a great capacity for responsiveness, then he will get into a poem, a really good poem, very deeply, and it will be tremendously meaningful to him; if he's superficial, the poem will seem superficial or incomprehensible.

CHRISTENSEN: Many of your early poems were written in a strong anapestic meter, which is a very hard-thumping rhythm. How come?

DICKEY: It's got one quality that only a very obviously accented meter like that can have—it is rhythmically compelling, almost coercive, and I thought, as nearly as I can remember back twenty or so years, that that is in itself very much a plus factor, in some way, in some cases. Suppose you were able to get some valuable poetic insight into the meter; you would have this compellingness, this hypnotic effect which lots of poetry does not have. So I set out to see if I couldn't work it out on some such basis.

CHRISTENSEN: You kept this meter for the first couple of books.

DICKEY: Yes, because I wanted to see what I could make it do and the kind of subjects I could apply it to, and then I dropped it. I went on to something else.

CHRISTENSEN: But how do you compose a poem: Is it line by line or with a general structure in mind?

DICKEY: Well, I do it in different ways. When I first started I stuck with the narrative component as an armature, sort of a skeleton.

CHRISTENSEN: Did you ever write that up beforehand?

DICKEY: No, I never did that, because if you do that you lock the subject in too much. Chance is a very great element in my particular compositional *modus.* Chance—letting something come in and change the direction of the poem. It's a foolish writer who says no, because I started this other way, I'm going to have to stick to that. This is the Yvor Winters attitude toward writing, but the result is that you not only have got to stick with it; you're *stuck* with it.

CHRISTENSEN: It seems to me that chance is playing a larger and larger part in your work now.

DICKEY: Sure.

CHRISTENSEN: Especially in *The Zodiac.*

DICKEY: I like *The Zodiac*. It's so crazy. It is such an un-well-made piece of work.

CHRISTENSEN: You mean un-well-made in that you have forbidden yourself to make conclusions inside that poem?

DICKEY: I think that if I haven't done anything else in *The Zodiac* I have truly keyed-in on one of the most important things in the relationship of a person to his own poetry—and that is the combination of foolishness, daring and self-delusion that is necessary to make memorable poetry. In *The Zodiac* the guy's drunk all the time, and I try to get the admixture of drunken self-delusion and actual divinity, actual inspiration as it is, where you can't tell which is which.

CHRISTENSEN: Is this the Dionysian poet?

DICKEY: Yes, I suppose so, and I think *The Zodiac* does have that quality. I am convinced of it. A lot of it is maundering, a lot of it is foolish and self-delusionary, but the parts where he talks about taking triangular eyes to see heaven, and that sort of thing—that would not occur either to a sober man or a sane man. But it would occur to someone who is genuinely a poet.

CHRISTENSEN: It seems that your work began in a certain neatness and restraint, but as it progressed the language and form gave in to the experience more and more.

DICKEY: I'd like to think so.

CHRISTENSEN: Isn't this what the split line was all about? All those fragments spaced across the page?

DICKEY: Yes, with the split line I wanted to keep that memorability factor that the three-beat line has, to keep that compression where you would remember which words went with which to create an effect, but you would also be writing in a way that approximates the way in which the mind associates.

CHRISTENSEN: The way it clusters thought?

DICKEY: Yes, in clusters and bursts.

CHRISTENSEN: So, finally the placement of language itself begins to have a part in the poem?

DICKEY: Sure. In a poem like "Falling" or "May Day Sermon" I wanted to present the reader with solid and all but impenetrable walls—a wall of language in which you have these interstices of blank spaces at irregular places. It's a wall you can't get over, but you have to descend, climb down, in a way.

CHRISTENSEN: Now these openings in each of these long lines—you said somewhere that it was replacing punctuation, but it's much more than that, isn't it?

DICKEY: That's only one thing it does.

CHRISTENSEN: Isn't it also showing how the mind works—how it stumbles and hesitates and then plunges forward?

DICKEY: That's exactly right! I think *I* ought to be interviewing *you*! You have a very good grasp on exactly what I do mean.

CHRISTENSEN: But in more recent poems you have experimented with poems carefully centered on the page.

DICKEY: I didn't want to impose the split line on every poem. I wanted it to be unique just to a couple or three situations. These new poems, like some of the ones in *Strength of Fields*, employ a principle which I roughly refer to as "balance." The poem is balanced on the page, "trued up." My father was a rather good carpenter and that was a favorite term of his. I try to "true" things up, and give the poem a feel of hanging there, suspended: only precariously there.

CHRISTENSEN: Have you completed a kind of cycle in having expanded the poem to the breadth of the page and now trued it up to a natural symmetry?

DICKEY: Yes. I think it's incumbent on anybody who is a creative writer or especially a poet to push out always, push out the borders of what he can do. The trouble with most American writers is that they are afraid to make a mistake—they get a little inch that they can peddle pretty effectively and they just cultivate that inch forever. Whatever things could be said about me as a writer—anyone would have to admit that I have never been afraid to take a chance. I will throw away something that has been successful for me. I will throw away the anapestic rhythm, I will throw away the margin-to-margin organization, I will eventually throw away the balanced poem and go on to some other thing that I think would be interesting to try.

CHRISTENSEN: Much of your poetry strikes me as a criticism of the dullness and artificiality of the New South; one must go and replenish himself in the natural realm, in primitive things, to stay alive.

DICKEY: That's a formal structure for romanticism, I guess, but what else is there? That's what Lewis Medlock would say!

CHRISTENSEN: In poem after poem you are saying that one could die without rediscovering these things.

DICKEY: Sure. There's the whole question of what the Fugitives fought for: to keep the South an agrarian region, to resist the encroachment of industrialism is impossible, because the results of industrialism and mass production and the volume turnover system are so spectacularly transforming. When I go out in the woods, it's not something I'm familiar with in the sense that Thoreau would be, because of my confirmed amateurism and because I'm a suburban, not a rural, southerner. When I go out there and see that wilderness it has the quality of a vision, precisely *because* it is so unfamiliar. You are going out into something that's not going to last much longer. This is what Lewis says: we've got to try that river before they dam it up. It's going to go, it's all going to go: the whole natural world will be gone.

CHRISTENSEN: Is it accurate to say that it has been in the South that somehow the most primitive sense of being has been felt in our culture?

DICKEY: It took Mr. Faulkner seventeen books to get some kind of a provisional hold on the meaning of the South for him, and he is much more of a southerner than I am. But I was down in the Faulkner country last month and you can see that even now with the big university there and a lot of people around, it still retains the primitivism you mention: a sense of rootedness is very strong still, a basic thing, a feeling.

CHRISTENSEN: But it just seems to me that it's peculiar to the southern writer to try to find the most primal depths of existence—as though the gentility of its past was something he needed to penetrate, utterly.

DICKEY: I like to think so. I like to think that I deal in some way with the mysteriousness or the mystery of existence, which is both magical and terrifying and violent rather than reposeful. I like action. I'm not essentially a contemplative person. I like movement, I like bodily involvement with things.

CHRISTENSEN: Where do you go from here as a poet?

DICKEY: Unknown.

CHRISTENSEN: In *The Zodiac* you make a number of pronouncements through your protagonist which sound like a Poetics of your own. The necessity to draw something, some pattern, out of that chaos above and to believe it enough to continue to write. Am I off on that?

DICKEY: No, I don't think so. Another poet, I forget who it was, somebody I read years ago, had a wonderful phrase about the spread of stars overhead as "an eternal timorous design." One would be glad to impute a certain amount of uncertainty to God because we are raised believing in a mechanistic universe, a universe ruled by law and mathematics, the laws of physics and chemistry. But the idea that the whole thing as it was originally conceived was some sort of a hesitant uncertain kind of a scheme, is interesting to me. With physics and mathematics you see that there's a lot of evidence as to the *how* of the universe, the how of things, but absolutely none as to the *why*. This is what *The Zodiac* is about; it is trying to speculate about the why.

CHRISTENSEN: In some ways *The Zodiac* reminds me of the situation in "Eyebeaters."

DICKEY: Yes, I suppose it is in a way. In "The Eyebeaters" the poet is in an institution where these children tear off their bandages and strike their eyes because they get that spark from the nerve which is sort of the equivalent of seeing; it's all they'll ever have of seeing.

CHRISTENSEN: So these children are furiously beating their eyes for a vision, and your poet in *The Zodiac* is drinking to get this vision—does this suggest in some way that the impetus of the poetry you have been writing now has gone from the inexplicable mysteries that just simply enrich being to an effort in some way to wring sense out of the world?

DICKEY: Yes, but it's a sense that doesn't come out of the empirical evidence or the manipulation of scientific data. It's some sense that is deeply visceral and individual and emotional.

CHRISTENSEN: Like faith?

DICKEY: Well, I don't know, faith—that might be one solution, but even that's orthodox. At least most faiths are orthodox in some way, but I'm not interested in unorthodoxes. I remember something that D. H. Lawrence said. He's on to something important, and that's the relation of the individual intuitive existence with whatever *else* is out there: one's personal relation to it. He says, somewhere in one of his later books, that our main trouble is that we have lost the universe, that we have lost the cosmos, we have lost the sense of correlation with the cosmos. But he says that it is always, at any given moment, recoverable. I don't know if this is true or not. But I think that such is his persuasiveness, you *do* listen to Lawrence; you may not agree with him, but you listen to him. You should listen to him. He's maybe not a great novelist, and he's a very seriously flawed poet; if he has any significance it's as some sort of a moralist or a prophet. But he says this sense of intimacy with what is, with what was created by something other than men, or man, is always recoverable. This assumption—assertion—makes a profound impression on me. He said, start with the sun and everything will slowly, slowly happen. It will all come back to you, it will be given unto you. Now that's a powerful appeal, because the sun *is* up there. It is part of nature and it does shine and the rest of life is drawn from it. At least life on this planet is drawn from it. That's the *center* of things, if it has *that* much influence. The why of it is a mystery, but a mystery which exists. It is up there and it's part of what is, or at least of what is for us, but nobody will ever know why it's that way; there's no way to know. Lawrence would say it's better not to know. We don't need to know why it is, all we need to know is *that* it is.

CHRISTENSEN: So, in a way the sun is the source of a possible belief in something from which we have been cut off. So would you say that your poems are going through this kind of Lawrentian struggle? Is your character Ed Gentry going through such a struggle himself throughout *Deliverance*?

DICKEY: Well, I think maybe, but not overtly. He is like many people; he has a good job, he's a moderately intelligent fellow, but in him there is a current of a vague unrest. He realizes that something is missing from his life that might have been the most important thing in it. And there's no way for him to tap into this resource that may or may not be in his makeup, leading the usual life that he leads on a day-to-day basis. His life may be just going right on by, and the vital thing, the imperative thing, the individual thing, the soul, if you will, is never going to be discovered. That's essentially the situation of Ed Gentry. He wouldn't say that in so many words. Now Lewis, who is the guy who is so different from him, is a sort of a suburban superman who wants to realize himself, mentally and physically, but at the same time is haunted by dreams of atomic holocaust. He's gone into a lot of disciplines and he has mastered those disciplines, but there's something undiscovered in him too; he thinks he's going to find it in the wilderness, by taking chances, by risking his life, by getting off from civilization, inserting himself into dangerous situations like running the whitewater of those mountain rivers. He thinks that maybe that's the answer. But the idea of Lewis looking at the whole business as a game comes to a sort of a frightening apotheosis when Ed is climbing the cliff and is getting ready to pit himself with a bow and arrow against a man with a rifle; he sees that *he* is in the game. Lewis in some way, however weird, has been right about the meaning of the whole business and maybe that of existence itself, too.

CHRISTENSEN: But what was he delivered from in the experience?

DICKEY: The "deliverance" could have multiple meanings. The most obvious would be deliverance from the humdrumness of his existence. The other would be to move from being one kind of person to another kind of person: one with hidden powers. What I wanted in the whole sequence where he is climbing to the top of the cliff and begins to figure out a system of entrapment for the guy with the rifle was to show that this guy, who is a decent family fellow, has actually got the psychology of a born killer. He *likes* what he's doing, and as it turns out, his murder-ambush works just as he had set it up to work. *Deliverance* is about the energizing of qualities which otherwise would never have a chance to surface: that it takes extreme conditions to bring out. Matthew Arnold's phrase is "the buried life," the unlived life.

CHRISTENSEN: Does civilization in fact thrive on burying life?

DICKEY: I don't know if it does consciously, but that sort of burial is the result.

CHRISTENSEN: What poets like you do is go around examining what is buried?

DICKEY: Well, I suppose that's one of the functions that poets have. At least some of them. They try to dig through to that: the thing that's necessary, that's vital, that really *does* matter. Everything else is *Dreck*—you know, junk.

IN NORTH CAROLINA
Getting to the Gold with Terry Roberts

ROBERTS: It's not my first "official" question, but what's fatherhood like?

DICKEY: Terrific! You feel like you're standing in the main cycle of time and nature, part of the great chain of being. You have to be 59 to appreciate how great it really is.

ROBERTS: Around 1970-71, there were several books that came out which included your views on your own career. What path do you think you have followed as a writer?

DICKEY: A lot of different paths. One of them is film. I am working on a couple of movies now. I like the film medium very much, if you can get with people who are intelligent and creative about it and not just hacks. Hollywood has got its hacks as the literary profession has, but the good people there are truly good. Then, I have a novel I've been working on a long time. I've got a new book of poetry coming out in May, and all my previous work is being reissued in new formats. I have had to supervise these reissues, write new introductions, forewords, afterwords, and so on. That has been keeping me pretty busy. I have seven or eight books coming out now, some of them reissues and some brand new. I've just brought out the original screenplay of *Deliverance* with Southern Illinois University Press, with an afterword having to do with Hollywood's relationship to the writer. I've just contracted for a new book of more essays and miscellaneous writings and reviews and literary criticisms and journals. But all of this is a kind of spin-off from the main project, which is poetry. If you have enough of a grounding in poetry and have been at it as long as I have, you enjoy the spin-offs from it; they partake of the same quality as the poetry. But they don't demand the intensity that poetry does. Consequently, they don't result in the depression that poetry does when you can't get something to be the way you want it.

ROBERTS: How has your poetry changed?

DICKEY: I am working in new fields of imagery and subject matter.

ROBERTS: Did you intend to bring your new book out on your daughter's birthday?

DICKEY: It was planned after my daughter Bronwen was born on May 17th. My wife Deborah and I decided that it would be nice to bring out *Puella* on her first birthday. Arizona State is doing a "world premiere" of the book. I have never heard of a premiere of a book of poetry before, but they are doing a multi-media presentation of it on the publication date. So, I plan to go out for that.

ROBERTS: A lot of your early poetry was set in nature or somehow related to nature . . .

DICKEY: Well, nature is a very big place! I mean it's not just the usual pastoral version of pleasant hills and rivers and lakes. It covers everything there is, including the stars and the solar systems and galaxies; all that!

ROBERTS: Have you ever felt that you had become alienated or isolated from nature?

DICKEY: No, I don't think so. It's been my life-long labor to try to keep up contact with it. I am not in any sense a naturalist or someone who has a vested interest in it: someone like Thoreau, a first-rate amateur naturalist and biologist and zoologist. I don't claim to have any such intimate relationship with the natural world as Thoreau had, or Darwin had. I am a first-generation city man. Nature is sort of receding into the background of my past and my family. My father's family came from way up in the boondocks, in the northern Georgia hills, about 40 miles west of where we filmed *Deliverance*. Way up in the outback, an enclave of the mountains. His family moved to the city in the early part of the century or just before. I am the first generation of the suburban southerners, but my father's family's people are still up there in the hills, and I have always been proud of that and tried to draw on it in various ways. It's very funny about my family's ancestry. My mother's family were Confederates, but my father's family were Union sympathizers. They didn't believe the Union should be split up. Nobody ever bothered them up there, so they just didn't fight.

ROBERTS: Some years ago, you called yourself a poet of survival . . .

DICKEY: Well, I think survival enters into everybody's thinking these days. We live in the shadow of the bomb, and of several different kinds of germ warfare, and God knows what other kind of doomsday machines that people are thinking up while we are sitting here right now.

My values were formed by the service or military life, whereof my whole generation partook, as they say. I went into the service in 1942. I was at Clemson playing ball for Frank Howard, and everybody went into the service the winter of 1942-1943. Everybody went; *everybody*! Some were drafted, but most of us were volunteers. We knew we were going to get got anyway. I was overseas in the Pacific from the time I finished training till the end of the war, from New Guinea to the Philippines, and the rest of it, and we lived with life and death every day and every night. I suppose that if they hadn't dropped the bomb, none of us fellows would be alive. But they did drop it, and we did survive. We had our lives; then came the problem of living them.

ROBERTS: How do you think the war has affected your poetry?

DICKEY: I think it has given it a lot of impetus, maybe a sort of desperation or intensity. I certainly didn't want to live through those events just so I could get those qualities into poetry. They just happened to come into it willy-nilly.

ROBERTS: One more question about poetry in particular. A lot of your earlier poetry was concerned with this ability to communicate or to connect, perhaps instinctively or intuitively or magically—

DICKEY: I would certainly like to believe that it was concerned with such things. I would be very much beholden to whatever critic it was that said that about me. It depends on what you're talking about: connect. Connect with people, connect with nature, and then write about it or connect events or occurrences. Or just connect words themselves. Which do you mean?

ROBERTS: Are the new poems as concerned with nature?

DICKEY: The new poems? . . . The new book coming out in May is about women. My wife of 30 years died six years ago, and I remarried: a girl who was a student of mine, and at that time was a little less than half my age. We got a very good break this past year from mathematics, though. The press can no longer say I married someone less than half my age: as of last year, she became *exactly* half my age, and is now *not* less.

I got to thinking about the subject of young girls because I had married one, in my own late middle age. The marriage brought in a whole new set of possibilities to write about. I don't think there's a deeper part of nature than a woman. The blood of women is connected with the moon, the heavens, everything. They bear the very seed of meaning and existence. I wrote about the mysteriousness of coming of age, the stirring of the juices. Mainly, though, the feeling of fragility and mystery that there must be. And if it's not that way, I hope no female will tell me it's not.

ROBERTS: My next question is about age. Several of the writers you profess to admire particularly, Keats and Agee and Malcolm Lowry, all died fairly young. Being 59, what do you have now that you didn't have before as a writer?

DICKEY: A great deal of experience. Even more importantly, a great deal of thinking about it. And a great deal of writing, millions of words down, out of which I have gleaned certain rather shaky principles that I could not have got except by putting those years in on writing.

ROBERTS: And those principles . . .

DICKEY: You have to win those. You can't be put on to them by somebody else. You have to find out what's right for you, not what worked for another person. One of the great virtues of age is that you know what you're not *interested* in, and what could not *be* of any interest for you. I have several areas of that sort. Baseball is one of them: organized tedium. Ballet is another, for me. I cannot watch it without embarrassment.

ROBERTS: Can you say what those principles are . . .

DICKEY: If I write something down, I know that a given word has more potential for what I want than, say, this other word, whether the other one might do fine for somebody else's poem or not. The one I choose is right for me. Principles of selection: they are highly individual, and earned.

ROBERTS: I stumbled across something the other day, in *Sorties*, I believe. You said that you always must fight self-hatred or self-doubt. Has there ever been a point where you have been overcome by that?

DICKEY: Not *quite* overcome! I guess I would have committed suicide if I had been overcome by it. But one *does* self-hate, and I think that anybody who is trying to do anything in the Arts discovers that he does have to find some way to turn self-hatred into an asset instead of letting it be self-destructive: To compensate for the feeling in some way that is creative. To do something like John Keats, who was very short, did. He was only five feet tall, and that couldn't have failed to bug him. Napoleon was a very little guy, but he and Keats both found ways to make up for lack of size. All these weightlifters and body-builders have always interested me as cases of self-doubt and self-hatred so extreme that their overcompensation becomes grotesque. The artist, I think, is something like that; if he is truly an artist, he will make compensation for whatever it is that is causing him to experience self-hatred. He will make art out of it.

ROBERTS: What about writing essays and criticisms, and teaching? Is there any danger in all that of becoming too self-conscious?

DICKEY: There could be, but it's not inevitable. I like to teach. Teaching is a very good profession for me. It makes you get your own ideas straight. Shaw was right when he said, "If you ever want to learn a subject, teach it." You have to know a subject in order to show somebody else about it. I learned most of my formal grammar from having to teach it to students in engineering school. Engineering students want to know *why* the thing you tell them is so; what's the rule for it? And they don't take any easy answers. And that's a very good environment for a young teacher to be in.

ROBERTS: How does writing relate to all your academic activities?

DICKEY: I am able to teach people—or at least *some* people—to write because I am in the middle of the problem of writing, myself. I don't teach writing from the outside; I teach it from the inside. I am not imposing any rules on them. I'm showing them what's helped me and what's taken me a long time to come to, through many years of trial and error.

ROBERTS: Your having a new child, not being long a husband, is it fair to say that writing is the most important thing in James Dickey's life?

DICKEY: My family is the most important thing in my life, but outside of it, writing certainly is. It's what I have, and what I do. As the politicians would say, that's the ring I have thrown my hat into. I don't think I could acquire even a moderate degree of mastery in anything else, at this age. In other words, it's writing or nothing. I'll go with it, wherever it takes me.

ROBERTS: Do you have a schedule that you follow?

DICKEY: No, I try to keep two or three things going at once. My whole house is booby-trapped with typewriters. We have four, with a different project in each one of them. I am an active person; I don't like a sedentary life. The one thing I don't like about being a writer is that it forces you to be at least to some extent sedentary: to sit there and get the words down. But I try to keep moving as much as I can; I ramble through the house doing various other things. I stop by one typewriter and look at what's in it, and then most likely will sit down and start fooling with whatever is. If I get interested or even fascinated by it, I just type until I run out of the impulse to work on that thing. Then I go wandering off somewhere else during the day, see something else, and start in on *that* and work on it for a while. In a curious way, all the different projects—films, essays, novels, poetry—kind of cross-pollinate each other. You feel as though you have a tremendous resource working that way. You don't nail yourself into a box so that when that box is gone and shipped out you have to start all over again from square one. You always have something in some stage of composition; always something is coming along. Something is always getting finished; something is always getting started. I like that. It feels right to me.

ROBERTS: Is there any one type of writing that is most important to you?

DICKEY: Poetry is the most important, by far. I would junk everything else in a blink of an eye for poetry. That's the center of the creative wheel. If you hold that, then everything else that you want to do with writing, with words, will come. The discipline required in writing poetry is so infinitely much more difficult than anything else that other kinds of writing feel easy in comparison. It's as if you were an Olympic runner, and you practiced running with ten-pound weights on your shoes for six months, and then took them off. Then you could run!

ROBERTS: Of what you now have on paper, published, and what you have in your mind, is there any one poem that you think is the most important?

DICKEY: No, I would say the whole output could be treated as one big poem. I used to worry about not getting it all done. I was in the service twice, and I got held up by lots of different things. I raised a family, I worked in a business for six years, and it is very hard to compose poetry when you're nine to five in a very high-pressure business. I am a very slow worker, and the work built up little by little; finally I had one book, and years later I had another one. At last I thought "this stuff is really coming to me now. If I could just find the time to work on it. But I am traveling so much now, and I have to scramble so much to make a living that I am afraid I am going to get cut off before I've made my whole statement." I was afraid I'd be cut off from what I knew I could have done. I don't feel that any more. I could go any time now, and I would be willing to stand on what I have already done. I hope I won't have to, because there still is plenty I want to do. But if I had to I would go with what I have done.

ROBERTS: How about this novel? How long have you been with it? What do you hope it will be?

DICKEY: I really don't want to talk much about that. I have 400 or 500 pages of a draft, and I think it is good. It goes, but slowly.

ROBERTS: So, we are talking about 1,500 pages?

DICKEY: No; it won't be that long. I like to write long and then cut back. You can always take out, but you can't always put in. I like to put in everything while it's coming to me, and then look to see what I have.

ROBERTS: Did *Deliverance* go like that?

DICKEY: *Deliverance* was much easier to write than this current book. I came up with the whole plot of *Deliverance* in five minutes. It was eight or ten years before I brought it out, but that's misleading because it implies that I worked on *Deliverance* for eight or ten years, and nothing but. I did six other books at the same time, and these were more important to me than *Deliverance* was. I had no stake in the game as a novelist. I had never published any prose fiction; I had never even published a short story or written one. But the poetry was moving along well, so *Deliverance* was way down the ladder of priorities. I did work on it every now and then, and suddenly I saw that it was possible to finish the thing. And then somebody came along and offered me a contract for it. At that time I only had 90 pages written of a very rough draft, but Houghton Mifflin bought it anyhow and paid me a modest advance. I went on and finished it, and brought it out in '70, I guess it was. Immediately there was a movie contract, a paperback contract, it was in 30 languages, and much more bewildering complexity ensued.

ROBERTS: Are you happy with it now?

DICKEY: Yes, but I am tired of *Deliverance*. It's too much of a national institution, an industry or something. I can't even go on my favorite rivers. They're all full of people trying to exploit them.

ROBERTS: What are your favorite rivers?

DICKEY: The Chattooga, where we did *Deliverance*, is one of them. It's ruined now by people trying to cash in on it. All these river-running clubs and God knows what else. It's exactly what Lewis, the character that Burt Reynolds played in the movie, is afraid was going to happen. It's paradoxical, because I helped make it happen. It's just exactly what I didn't want to happen, any more than Lewis did or Burt Reynolds did, or any of the people who like that country up there. It's screwed up now. We did manage to get the Chattooga put on the wild and scenic rivers list. It was going to be dammed up, just like the river in the book, the Cahulawassee.

ROBERTS: You have a vast range of interests. There's canoeing . . .

DICKEY: I hope I can keep the physical part of things together. I had a huge operation about two years ago. I was not exactly at death's door, but I was immobilized in the hospital for a long time. The experience brought back the feeling of mortality that the war gave me and the rest of my generation. Human beings are very fragile. What I don't like about that feeling is that some of the human emotions that I esteem the most are daring and adventurousness, and if you're always worrying about your body you lose that feeling. That's bad. Especially for someone like myself who's essentially a gambling-type writer. I am not one of these play-it-safe people. I don't like making mistakes, but I do take gambles. There's no feeling of risk if you can't be wrong.

ROBERTS: Have you had anything that you felt in retrospect was a mistake?

DICKEY: Well, some things didn't come off as I thought they should. One of the worst feelings you can have when you read your earlier work is to look at a thing and say, "This is basically a very good idea, but I couldn't find the form for it. I didn't know enough then." That's one of the bad things. One of the good things is to look at your work and say "this is good. I wish I could find this vein again. I've lost it, but it produced this, and it's good."

ROBERTS: Archery, guitar, athletics, canoeing, all this; have you learned anything about writing from these things?

DICKEY: Plenty. They all go together, into the life itself. One of the main things in archery is that you wait till the shot is right. The whole question of timing in archery has found its own sort of way to get into lines of poetry. I am sure that in some way this happens.

ROBERTS: You're a better poet for having been an archer?

DICKEY: I think so. I am not all that great as an archer, but the two activities do have some overlap. The same thing is true in music. I fool around with the guitar a good bit, as much as I have time for. People talk about my ear, my rhythmic sense, and all that sort of thing. Sound is a very important part of poetry to me. If somebody were to ask me what the strongest influence on the rhythm of my poetry is, whether it's the English Prosodic tradition or the pulse of the folk guitar, I would say they are both important. I would even say that the guitar is more important. As far as I can determine, it is.

ROBERTS: Do you feel that you are particularly a Southerner?

DICKEY: Yes, I love the South. Some things about it I don't like, but I'm still a Southerner. I've returned to the South, from all over the place. Before I came to South Carolina I lived in Washington, D.C. Before that I lived in California. Before that, in Oregon. And before *that*, in Italy. I have been around and about a good deal. My experience has not been limited to the South, but, as I say, I am a Southerner. I will go with that.

ROBERTS: What do you think the South has given you?

DICKEY: The main thing is a sense of family: the integrity of the family unit. This doesn't mean just the immediate family, but includes the in-laws, the cousins and other people with the same blood. The sense of kinship is one of the things I like in Southern life. I also like the remnants of the old Southern tradition, as full of hot air as a lot of it is. There's still a lot in it that's good. I still believe in the things that Stonewall Jackson and Lee and those people felt were valuable: courage and dependability and other old-fashioned virtues that go all the way back to the Greeks. I still think they're virtues, and the sense of them has been strong in the South. There are a lot of crooked double-dealing people here, but the good human beings in the South have a degree of commitment to honesty and reliability that I have never seen in any other people.

ROBERTS: Do you think this sense is still there? Do you think your children and grandchildren will have it?

DICKEY: As far as I myself can give it to them they will. But under industrialism, much virtue has died out too. It may seem old-fashioned and square of me to say, but I think there's no substitute for those human qualities. I think that being brave is better than being cowardly. I think that being reliable is better than being irresponsible.

ROBERTS: Is there any poetry being written now that you think is particularly valuable?

DICKEY: Some of it is really good. I like force and depth in poetry. Not very many poets now have these qualities, but a few do. I think Robert Penn Warren is one of the better poets. If you know where to look, you can find some good ones. I don't see any world figures, though. I really don't know what's the matter with the poetic impulse in a cultural situation where an uninteresting professorial type like T. S. Eliot can become a virtual dictator of taste. His talent is quite slender. If all poetry were like his I would turn to something else.

ROBERTS: Is there anything you have read that has come to matter to you as much as Agee and Keats?

DICKEY: Agee, as fragmentary as he is, has got the right lick, as we say in the South. He's a man of enormous ability and talent. I think Walker Percy is very good, although he's now and then a bit whimsical for me. His other books are not as good as *The Moviegoer*. I like some of the Jewish writers: Saul Bellow is wonderful. I like a good many European writers, though I really don't read other languages fluently. But I like some of the European writers whom I have managed to connect with. I like Valéry. I like

Rilke and Hofmannsthal. In England, I don't look for a predominant influence after Eliot. Auden I respect and like, but he doesn't say as much to me as I wish he did. Too much head and not enough heart. Or guts, muscles, blood, whatever. Too relentlessly intelligent. I like somebody like Agee, who is just intelligent enough.

ROBERTS: One more question. I am going to do maybe an impolite thing and read you three or four lines that you wrote.

DICKEY: I don't think it's impolite. Go ahead.

ROBERTS: Over ten years ago, you wrote, "Will it ever be given to me to attain that large, free and essentially *simple* thing that I have wanted all my life? But at times I have sensed it and have been close. I wonder if this will ever be true again. Perhaps in death itself, perhaps not." This last question: from your present perspective, have you ever attained . . .

DICKEY: No, I don't think that will ever be given to me. Except I can get an approximation of it through infinite labor.

The idea that my statement seems to suggest is that I hope poetry will just come to me and I will sit down and reel off immortal verse, as Shakespeare may have done. Nobody knows what Shakespeare's working methods were, but he wrote an awful lot in just a few years, so he must have done it fast. We think about Shakespeare as one of these marvelous spirits who could just sit down and decide that Hamlet will say, "To be or not to be. That is the question." Just like that. Mozart would be a sort of an equivalent in the world of music. He used to be able to go out on a walk, and the music would just come to him. He could walk around the block or go down to the grocery, and write immortally while he was walking. He would just come in and transcribe, without any trouble. Everybody wants that ability, but I for one don't have it. I am a very slow worker. I dig down through layers of experience, as far down as I can get. For every word I keep, I throw away 100. But, when I've got that one it's the closest I can come to getting *the* word: at least for that place, *that* line in *that* poem. I work like a gold-miner refining low-grade ore: a lot of muck and dirt with a very little gold in it. Back-breaking labor! Infinite! But when this kind of worker gets what he's been after, he has the consolation of knowing that the substance he winds up with is as much real gold as it would be if he had just gone around picking up nuggets off the ground. It's still gold. The main thing is to get it, no matter how.

IN VIRGINIA
A conversation with Carolyn Kizer & James Boatwright

KIZER: Sometimes I have an uncomfortable feeling when I read articles by you and about you and the jacket blurbs on your books, some of which I suspect were written by you, about this persona that you're foisting off on the American public—you know, Dickey the great hero of the virility cult, great sportsman, gamesman, football player, ex-war ace—I mean all these things which are true but which seem to me not as relevant to you or your poetry as perhaps you'd like the rest of us to believe. I mean, how much of this is "con" and how much of it is real?

DICKEY: It would be hard to say. It wouldn't be true to say that I have no interest in people knowing about these things in regard to me. I do. But they are not in any sense any kind of substitute for anything that I have written. I was not published at the beginning, I suppose not now either, because of playing football at Clemson or basketball there or any other things that I have done. Those things have come up, and other people have noticed them and made something out of them. But this just happens to be the way my life ran. And this business about the virility cult: that's something that delights me! I'd love to believe it! If a Dickey virility cult grew up that would be fine with me! But this has nothing to do with what I'm trying to put down on a page.

KIZER: No, I realize that. But what I'm talking about, Jim, is whether you have deliberately tried to construct a persona to stand between you the poet and, I think, the extraordinarily sensitive human being, in the interests of protecting yourself from what's becoming a rather large following.

DICKEY: No, I don't think so. What you do deliberately and what you do inadvertently are sort of hard to distinguish between sometimes. America has always taken up its writers and made them cult figures of some kind or another. But I don't look on myself as a kind of poetical Hemingway.

KIZER: Oh, not at all. I realize you don't. But what I'm wondering is if you want the outside world to look on you that way to protect the sensitive you that doesn't want to be a cult figure.

DICKEY: I have never had any such conscious intention as that. American writers have always had to come up with some kind of strategy to protect their delicate inner workings, and so on: I realize that this is true. But I have never had any feeling that this is so in my case. If people want to pick up on these things and make something out of them it's very good for my ego. I'm delighted. But it's not a strategy which enables me to work when otherwise I wouldn't be able to work. Not at all. I don't look on myself as having a kind of schizophrenic existence or trying to come up with one. First an existence as a man and a guy who likes to do certain things, who likes to hunt animals and swim and do various other things of that sort and then another kind of shy, sensitive plant who writes poems and has to be protected by this other sort of Hemingway type. No, no. It's all just part of the same existence. I don't have any great feeling of distinction between doing one thing or another except as far as techniques are concerned. There's not a whole lot of difference to me between playing a guitar and shooting a bow. Just a difference of technique. Or writing a poem. It's a feeling of satisfaction that you get out of all three sort of equally. And they complement each other in a way. What you want to do is keep the self whole. I don't like this business of setting poetry off into a separate compartment that's got to have all this array and battery of protective devices to enable it to exist at all. I don't feel this. Maybe it would be necessary for other people but I have never felt any such necessity myself.

KIZER: I'll always remember the first time I met you when we bumped into each other in the Gotham Book Mart. I remember one of the first speeches you ever made to me. You thought writers in this country were far, far too self-protective. They were scared to work at ordinary jobs or scared to work in advertising agencies and the like.

They were always afraid of intellectual rape. I remember your saying to me then that you weren't the least bit afraid, and you thought writers would be a lot better off if they were tougher about things like that.

DICKEY: I sure do think so. I've always disliked this business of the writer, especially the poet, being a rare soul who is misunderstood by everybody around him and who takes to having all these very secret private rituals and so on. Rilke is an example of this. He is a very great poet but is also the kind of human being that I absolutely abhor.

KIZER: Well, we all know who the delicate little flower poets are—you know, people like Ben Jonson, and François Villon.

DICKEY: Oh, those are the delicate flowers that I like best.

BOATWRIGHT: What about the universities and the fact that universities take over poets? Will this inevitably make poetry that much more academic?

DICKEY: Well, it will in a way. Again it depends so much on the person. People talk about academic poets: these naive, simple-minded people like Kenneth Rexroth, always drawing lines of demarcation which have *less* than zero value. Over here are academic poets and over here are such and such poets. Virile beatnik poets, you know. That sort of thing.

KIZER: And the virile, beatnik poets who are talking about academic poets are always trying to get their jobs when they hear that one of them is sick or going to Europe, or something.

DICKEY: Well, quite a lot of the so-called beat poets are in universities and glad to be there.

KIZER: Exactly. But a lot of it, whether the academies are going to do anybody any harm or the business world or anything else, depends on how *formed* one is.

DICKEY: It depends on oneself and one's own resources. And also, it depends on how one takes one's own writing. I think one of the main difficulties in the life of the modern poet is getting time to work. It seems to me that one ought to be prepared to go quite a long way with any agency which gives one *that*. That's the simple and absolutely indispensable prerequisite for any writer: time to sit down and work out his problems on the page. This the university does provide. Now what it doesn't provide—and this is a much more intangible but also very necessary ingredient—is some kind of working arrangement whereby the writer can experience the world pretty much in the way he feels he needs to. This is where the university is sometimes difficult to reconcile with one's own ambitions and works. If you have a distinct taste for low life, as I do—the "wild side of life," as the old juke box tune has it—the university can be a pretty sticky situation. You're not supposed to be like that when you're teaching the young. But if there's something in your being that needs to *be* like that at certain times you ought to be able to do it. And this is where the university is a blockage.

KIZER: It seems to me, though, that one of the crucial things here is that we may have an instinct for variety—for living one kind of life one year and another kind the next. And the academy tends to. . . .

DICKEY: Well, it doesn't absolutely negate this or make it impossible but it surely makes it difficult—at times. This is when you do have to resort to a certain amount of subterfuge. If you want to go down in some low dive and get drunk, you don't do it as Professor X. You do it as a "guy." Then you put on your California-type dark glasses and . . . (I've never done this but I can imagine that it might be necessary.)

KIZER: I know various poets who've got into a lot of trouble because they didn't do it. But also, your academic career has been one which has invited a lot of changes. I mean, you've moved on from university to university, college to college.

DICKEY: I hit the universities like a thief. I have a horror of getting committed to one. And yet, eventually I want to settle down.

KIZER: But as Vachel Lindsay used to say, he had a horror of digging in. And I think this is what the academy encourages us to do.

DICKEY: It does. There's this kind of myth of stability and—what's the word?—"security" and "maturity." Any time I hear somebody say to somebody else that he is immature or that he should become mature my sympathies go out immediately to the one who is being told to be mature.

KIZER: Don't you think that on the whole poets tend to be rather emotionally retarded? It takes them a long time to grow up emotionally, if ever.

DICKEY: Well, again, I distrust myself. This business of growing up emotionally is so many times taken to mean simply conformity or feeling what one is supposed to feel as opposed to what one really does feel.

KIZER: I want to be good to other people, I want to be *that* mature, but I don't want the kind of stability, the kind of maturity, that we've been talking about.

DICKEY: I think the only good state of mind for a poet is the feeling of perpetual possibility. That something that happens today or might happen tomorrow is going to have a very powerful effect and a very great deal of value for you. If you know pretty much what's going to happen from day to day and you know the value or lack of value that it's had before, it's not likely to have any more than that tomorrow. It's this business of the unknown that seems to me to be the most fertile ground for the poet to live in. The thing that might happen that is totally unforeseen. Almost everything that I've ever written comes out of things that have happened to me by chance. There's got to be a way for the poet to open the world up to himself from the standpoint of there being an infinite number of chances, none of which he can predict, for him to move through and among.

BOATWRIGHT: You say poet. But since you talked about poetry as being a part of the whole man. . . .

DICKEY: No, I think the same thing would be true of any man. He doesn't have to be a poet. Or a poet *especially*. But a poet is not anything more or less than an intensified man anyway.

KIZER: But this means accepting a great deal of permanent insecurity, doesn't it?

DICKEY: Yes it does. But that seems to me a magnificently healthy environment for the soul or the spirit, or whatever you'd want to call it.

KIZER: I agree. But it's just exactly what most people aren't willing to accept.

DICKEY: That's right. But now this business of security. One of the things that I dislike most of all is to open up a magazine and see a long, sententious advertisement for an insurance company. The insurancc companies and their agents are the most subversive of all people on earth. They show off a nice looking old guy and nice looking old lady but the immediate feeling you have is well, they'd probably be having a good time if they weren't so old. It's like advertisements for glasses ostensibly showing that glasses don't make a pretty girl any less attractive or maybe they make her more attractive. But my feeling is that, gee, wouldn't she be pretty if she weren't wearing glasses.

KIZER: There is a girl in my office, a pretty blonde girl, who says, "You know, in twenty-three years I can retire from the federal government and I'm going to open a card shop in Pasadena." Now what could be more horrible?

DICKEY: There's a sad possibility that it might also be wonderful.

KIZER: But very remote.

DICKEY: It wouldn't be right for me or you.

KIZER: Of course security is an illusion. I mean, we're all going to die.

DICKEY: That's right. Now money is going to help you do some things. There's no doubt about it. I was not born rich. I don't like to be a poor person. But money is good only as it realizes more life for you and more possibilities. More intensification of experience, more variety and so on, instead of the dull kind of deadening treadmill of routine that so many people are on from the time they get into their teens until the time they die. I worked in business for five or six years and the thing that I detested about it was the deadening effect of it. And the fact that you are continually eaten up and your emotional strength depleted by problems which in reality you have not the slightest interest in.

KIZER: And which really don't exist, in our terms.

DICKEY: But on which you are dependent for your livelihood and the livelihood of your family and children. This is a savagely destructive way to live a human life. Savagely destructive and obscene, it seems to me.

KIZER: You always have talked and always will, I hope, about its being the whole person out of which poetry is written. And I wish you would say something about the body, about the physical aspect of this wholeness, because I think you're unique in this. Most poets are, you know, slobs. They're overweight or they have indoor pallor, they don't take care of themselves, they're covered with cigarette ash. But you do have some sense of your own body and of the necessity of taking care of it. And this has some relevance to the poetry too, does it not?

DICKEY: A very great deal. I suppose that I'm not overly stupid, although I run into, every day, people that are a lot smarter than I am. My work is almost entirely physical rather than intellectual or mental. There are many times when I am trying to write something that reason tells me to say in a certain way but it just doesn't *feel* right. It's something in the region of the solar plexus which tells me to say it this other way. There's no reason to say it the other way except that I just *like* it better. There's a very real connection of the whole physiological complex with what the poem is trying to say. I can feel it. It's instinctual with me and I would say largely visceral and muscular. There's a very real involvement of the musculature, such as it is, in the act. I like that. Terribly intellectual people like Auden and Eliot, essentially indoor men, probably would put this down as nonsense and they could easily prove me wrong. But I wouldn't go along with any such proof because I *know* and I know that I know. There is an old saying that the fox knows many things, but the hedgehog knows one *big* thing. I know one big thing. I think I do.

BOATWRIGHT: What's the connection between that and what you have said elsewhere about the uneducated or the self-educated poet? What's the connection between a poet's knowing something about poetry or tradition or history and his need to be physical, visceral?

DICKEY: I think it's a different kind of knowing. Again, I'm a little fearful about talking too much about this kind of thing. I can't intellectualize about this to any enlightening degree. I never have been able to do it for myself. And there's no reason to suppose that I would be able to do it for you, either. But again, all the different men that a man is split up into and which one must constantly try to bring into one's own kind of whole man who is really better than he is—you've got a lot of different sides that you do need to reconcile and yet they seem to exist coterminously, at your best moments, and in perfect accord. I've got a side that had rather do nothing than sit down and read long essays, critical essays, and argue with the author over every sentence. I enjoy that very much. But when I'm trying to write something, the best thing that I can do is to get into some kind of state in which no poem ever was written before: to believe that what I'm trying to do is the first attempt that has ever been made to say this. I'm awfully tired of the English poetic tradition and of the awful kind of dead hand that Eliot insists has to be clamped on the individual talent by the poetic tradition. I don't think any of that's necessary. You can use something from it every now and then for your own purposes, but the main emphasis to me is not tradition and the individual talent but tradition (small letters) and the individual talent (large letters), which may or may not have anything very much to do with the tradition. In fact, in some cases, in the ultimate case of the "new man," the new great poet, who I hope some day will arise, it will have nothing whatever to do with the tradition except insofar as the poet uses the English language.

KIZER: Well, perhaps you and I would say—we would have the emphasis put on tradition as it can assist the individual talent.

DICKEY: I agree. Or the tradition as being entirely irrelevant to the talent. It might be useful but it's not as Eliot says: a body of law that's got to be considered all the time. I don't believe that at all. I have read for years all these, well, translations when I didn't know the language, which I almost never did, but I've tried to come into conjunction in one way or another with Eskimo dance rituals and Bantu hunting songs and that sort of thing. And the revelations of those so-called folk as far as poetic imagery is considered are marvelously rich and evocative. They have nothing to do with Alexander Pope's use of the heroic couplet or Wordsworth's use of Milton's blank verse or any of that sort of thing. They never knew of the existence of it, to begin with. And yet those people are saying something out of a condition with which they are in a precarious and dangerous and sometimes desperate harmony, but always a harmony of some kind which, even when the environment destroys them, is some kind of harmony with the environment. I'm looking for some way to *relate* to things again and this is the reason I dislike so much these poets of alienation who feel humiliated by everything and who are endlessly examining their own motives. I'm looking for a way to respond with one hundred per cent of my humanity and not respond with ten per cent while ninety per cent stands back and says, Dickey you really are in love with your mother when you like this flower. I'm not putting down psychoanalysis or anything like that. I'm only trying to get some kind of way to give absolute, wholehearted response. Somebody (I think it was Yeats maybe) said that a man running at full speed has neither a brain nor a heart. I'm trying to get into the psychological state of the man running at full speed and see what he does have.

KIZER: Another thing that I resent, though, about the use that Auden and Eliot make of the word "tradition" is that it's such an exclusive, countryclub interpretation of the word "tradition." You just mentioned Eskimo culture, etc. I mean "tradition" is always Wasp tradition, isn't it? It's western European tradition. Whose tradition, and whose individual talent? It's a broader subject than they dream of in their philosophy.

DICKEY: I want to find some way in which it will be profitable to cut loose and go all out in some way, poetically, rather than constantly being under wraps and held back and hag-ridden by doubts. I want to find some way to commit absolutely and utterly to the poem that I'm trying to write. Now this may be romantic. Again, it can be disproved. I can disprove it myself and I will say that a good deal of what I am saying is nonsense. And yet there is a feeling I have that I want to try to do this and I will stake anything that I need to, up to my life, on being able to do it.

KIZER: I feel that a part of your detestation for this kind of fashionable masochism and *mea culpa* intellectualism that is all around us these days is simply because it's non-functional. It doesn't do anything for a poet or a creative person to go around beating his breast and wailing except to give him an assortment of hang-ups that he doesn't need.

DICKEY: Well, somebody may need 'em, but I don't need 'em.

BOATWRIGHT: You mentioned that the only tradition is the tradition of the English language. So you're not joining the group which talks about an American language as distinct from an English language.

DICKEY: I don't know that much about it. There obviously are differences but basically it's English with sub-varieties and variations which depend on our living over here and their living over there. But it's basically English, it's American-language English language, or the American version of the English language.

KIZER: Well, again it's rather irrelevant. You don't have to accept your mother at the expense of your grandmother. You can accept them both.

DICKEY: Local differences do matter. There are lots of magnificent Americanisms we have because we are Americans and our history has been what it has been. As well as a lot of magnificent Englishisms that they have because theirs has been as it has been.

BOATWRIGHT: But you don't feel that you've got to search out an American idiom?

DICKEY: No. Do you mean like Kenneth Fearing used to do, maybe?

A lot of slang and idiomatic things? No. In fact I sort of stay away from that. I wouldn't use it well, I know. There are certain things that I stay away from because I know that I have no ability to work in that genre. Satire is one.

BOATWRIGHT: I was going to ask you about that.

DICKEY: I haven't any desire or any ability to write satirical works. I can say mean things about people but I can't make them funny.

KIZER: Anyway, it's better to do it in private life.

BOATWRIGHT: I was struck in reading about the National Book Awards by the presence of two Southerners: there you were and there was Katherine Anne Porter, and then the piece in *Life* says that you are not a "Southern" poet. What do you feel about the Southern writer's being so obviously more important than he ought to be, if you consider the region, the number of people in the region, and so on?

DICKEY: I have one central feeling about the South and myself and that is the best thing that ever happened to me was to have been born a Southerner. First as a man and then as a writer. And yet I would not under any circumstances want to feel that I was limited in any way by being a Southerner, that I was expected, say, by other people to indulge in the kind of regional chauvinism that has sometimes been indulged in by Southern writers. One has a history which is intimately in one way or another bound up with the history of one's own people and one's own ancestors and people who live in the same region one does. The South has a tragic history, as everybody knows, but it has given me as a human being a set of values, some of which are deplorable, obviously, but also some of which are the best things that I have ever had as a human being. It's like in the E. M. Forster novel where Forster says of Mrs. Wilcox—"she let her ancestors help her." This is something that I feel very strongly. I have only run-of-the-mill ancestors but they knew that one was supposed to do certain things. Even the sense of evil, which is very strong with me, would not exist if I had no sense of what evil was. I got it through the family.

KIZER: I remember Mr. Ransom saying once that a sense of evil was absolutely *essential* to poetry.

DICKEY: I agree with that.

KIZER: And he said the trouble with somebody like Wordsworth was that he didn't have it. And that you've got to be wrestling with this all the time in poetry.

DICKEY: And somebody like Baudelaire capitulated to evil so much that it became a kind of Puritanism in itself.

KIZER: But in another sense he lost the other end of the dialectic.

DICKEY: That's right.

KIZER: You have to keep the tension between the two, as Stanley Kunitz says.

DICKEY: This is more or less, I think, the case. But again you don't keep it because it's going to produce valuable poems. This is an attitude that I just detest. These people who are saving themselves for posterity. My God, a poem is not anything but some words on a page. In the eternal battle between life and poetry or life and art, I'll take life. And if poetry were not a kind of means, in my case, of intensifying experience and of giving a kind of personal value to it I would not have any interest in it whatsoever.

KIZER: That's very interesting. Because I was going to begin this interview by saying that in some ways you're becoming to me a kind of Byronic figure and that's such a Byronic statement: if I have to choose between art and life I'll take life. I wonder if you've ever felt any sense of identity with Byron. . . .

DICKEY: As a matter of fact, he's the first poet I ever read except under duress. I don't like him very much as a poet, but . . .

KIZER: Well, that's irrelevant to what I'm concerned with.

DICKEY: But the figure of Byron, this is valuable to me. He is the example of the kind of man that I've always attached a particular kind of personal value to. The guy who is an enormous phony, but who makes the public take him on his own terms, the terms of his persona. And underneath it all is an extremely practical, hard-headed, and utterly honest person.

KIZER: It seems to me clear that Byron would have been a better poet if he had been a little less interested in the living Byron and a little more interested in the poetry that he was going to leave behind him. He really didn't give all that much of a damn, did he?

DICKEY: I'm not sure that's so. Byron never exhibited the slightest capacity to be a poet in any sense that I would think of as being a poet. He's an amusing social satirist who has a good many affinities with somebody like Auden in our time.

KIZER: I'm just interested in the Byron that wrote *Don Juan*.

DICKEY: Well, this is the social commentary.

KIZER: But don't you feel that he was trying harder?

DICKEY: Well, he was, but again that's a genre that doesn't attract me very much.

KIZER: But that's not where the parallels occur: the thing that we have said is that to him his life was more important than his art in the sense he made his art serve his life, and in the case of his relations with ladies sometimes it was quite useful to him in that way. Secondly, perhaps the only fault that I think of you as having as a poet is occasionally being rather self-indulgent. Sometimes the poems are longer, looser, and you're letting yourself out a bit more than I think . . . But perhaps one reason you're doing this, and that may be the reason Byron did it—you don't want to interrupt the flow, you want to get it out. Why, do you know?

DICKEY: Well, because in my own case (I can't speak for anybody else) when the impulse comes it brings with it almost everything that is necessary to the poem and also a lot of things that are not necessary to the poem. And sometimes it takes a while to figure out which is which. If you sort it out as you go along you're just as likely to cut out the good as you are the bad. In fact, *more* likely. You can always take out. But you can't always put in. At least *I* can't.

KIZER: Do you have much angst about the flow ceasing? I mean do you have a sense of having to write now while you're doing it well, having to write *now*. . . .

DICKEY: Well, a little of that. I thought you meant ceasing permanently.

KIZER: Oh no, no. I mean that you're riding a marvelous wave now of creativity. . . .

DICKEY: Oh yes. I want to go with that, such as it is.

KIZER: You're riding with it.

DICKEY: I'm always anxious to cast myself on that particular flood.

KIZER: I believe with Yeats that the sorting out can always take place later. We can go back and revise it when we're sixty.

DICKEY: But if you write it one line at a time and sort of choke up and if you're unable to go farther because this line is not very good . . .

KIZER: Or if a critical censorship takes place too soon . . .

DICKEY: Yes. If the critic is nagging you all the time you are not going to get anything out of your muse because she'll just flap away. I love the sense of the whole thing coming—good, bad and indifferent—everything coming and coming and coming. That's a marvelous feeling. That's the best part of writing poetry, to me. Because in this particular situation you have enough good things that you're getting down that you're having a marvelous exalted sense of absolute possibilities. You know, you think, Jesus, this came to me, this phrase, and if I can get a lot of other ones that are as good as this, this is going to be the greatest poem ever written! But at that stage of things the phrase is buried in the poem with a lot of things that are pretty good and some that are not good and some that are indifferent and some that are bad. But the eternal hope of a poet is that you seize on those good fragments and you say, boy, I'm going to make the whole thing like *that* phrase! So through the next successive stages you try to do that.

KIZER: But in the end of this rush and flow, and at the end of these phrases is death. Would you agree with or perhaps care to enlarge on something that Dick Hugo said once that I thought was very interesting? When somebody asked him what was the difference between poets and other people he said, well, he thought poets thought about death *all the time*.

DICKEY: Well, I know I do. But I wouldn't claim that as any exclusive prerogative.

KIZER: No, but I think it's amazing that most people don't. I mean the kind of things we were talking about, insurance company advertisements about old age, and security, and so on. This is the great unsaid thing. When you get there, my friend, you're going to be dead very soon.

DICKEY: I was reading something of John Fowles's—a tendentious book of aphorisms somebody sent me—but one thing interested me. He said, death is nothing without you and you are nothing without it. I know I'm nothing without it, but the notion that death is nothing without me is something that sort of interested me.

KIZER: We can use that. Do you have a sense of working against time and how urgent . . .

DICKEY: But that can be a very constricting thing. It can make you work on poems simply because time is growing less and you feel that you ought to be working on *some* poem. So you work on *some* poem. But for me there's got to be the sense of the absolute necessity of this particular thing that I'm trying to write. I don't want to be a professional poet in the sense of sitting down and doing something in verse every day. If I can't preserve the sense of personal excitement that I get from it, I have no interest in working on it.

KIZER: Don't you also feel in a curious way that death is further away in one's early forties than in one's late twenties?

DICKEY: Well, in a way.

KIZER: I mean death has retreated in my life.

DICKEY: You spoke about *angst* and there's a peculiar conjunction of kinds of angst in this particular situation, at least for me. The feeling that I have is that the better I'm working, the more aware of my own death I am. That when I've got a great flow going it would be doubly sad to lose it now. When I'm just slopping around the house, drinking, and not trying to write anything, not even answering correspondence, I say well, I've already done a lot of work, I've got five books of poems out, and I'll stand on this, and if I died now it would just do nothing but relieve me of a lot of boredom. But when I'm really working well, I don't want to die. There is a kind of conjunction between work and the way one feels about existence, I suppose. At least so it is with me.

KIZER: I would like to go back and pick up something else that we were talking about a while ago. It relates to the topic of death. And that is, of aging. You were talking about how, well perhaps dependent isn't the right word, *concerned* you are with physicality, with the physical in your poetry and of course also with sexuality. I sometimes have extreme anxiety about what I'm going to write about as I go on getting older because I feel this way about my poetry. That it's very dependent on physicality and sexuality; and if this goes what's going to take its place? What are your feelings about this?

DICKEY: I plan to go on in the sexuality field as long as I can.

KIZER: But biological processes are going to intervene. We can go through the Yeats bit and all that and have goat glands but I mean—inevitably it's going to catch up with us before we feel that we are finished with our working life, and then what?

DICKEY: Well, I don't know. . . . There's supposed to be a kind of serenity that sets in with old intellectual . . .

KIZER: That's not going to do much for poetry, Baby. I mean. . . .

DICKEY: I don't know. You take each age as it comes. If I could get some kind of transcendental serenity and magnificence of vision out of an absolutely sexless state I would want the utmost intensification of that, too.

KIZER: But Yeats got transcendental serenity out of goat glands. . . .

DICKEY: If somebody demonstrated to me that they would work, or if I had the money to pay for it. . . !

KIZER: The point is, you are peculiarly related to this whole subject. There are poets, the gamesmen, the game players, . . . sex doesn't matter much to them or, you know, the sort of polite lady poets who want you to know they went to Italy last summer, the place-droppers. I mean, this doesn't bother them . . .

DICKEY: I just happened to read in the newspaper something that John Masefield, of all people, said, who must be about three hundred years old: he's been poet laureate for at least two hundred! Somebody asked him how he felt about being old and he said, "How magnificent the vision grows at the end." For that reason, I would read anything he ever wrote.

BOATWRIGHT: What about the late poems of Lawrence where he speaks of the dark voyage?

DICKEY: Lawrence died as a comparatively young man. There must be another kind of way to die when you are very, very old. I have diabetes. As a matter of fact, when the doctor told me I had it I said is this going to shorten my life? And he said you should live out your expected time of sixty-eight years. But there ought to be something that corresponds in that period to sexuality or the old kind of "Chinese sage" serenity. There's something in the sixty-eight-year range of actuarial tables that ought to be good, too, and I intend to find out what it is.

KIZER: Well let *me* know. You may phone me collect, or cable. I think the Chinese did have something there. I think one of the things that they had, and it's very important to me, vis-à-vis you and other people who write poetry: it's friendship. And it's something that we have to hang on to very hard as poets and as people because it's something that's being bulldozed out of our life like trees and like buildings by this terrible trend toward homogeneity of everything.

And yet it is extraordinary poetry in which you sense this feeling that the relations, the non-sexual relations between people could be so desperately important.

DICKEY: I don't know much about Chinese poetry, but desperation seems to be singularly absent from what I have read of it. There's a lot of resigned sadness and so on . . . but desperation . . .

KIZER: No, desperation as a feeling doesn't exist, but friendship is an area of relationship that it seems to me Western life is losing. That an aspect of human relationship is atrophying in a funny kind of way. Sometimes I have a nightmare that nobody believes in falling in love anymore.

DICKEY: I like it a lot. I like falling in love. In fact, I do it all the time.

KIZER: I think it's terribly important.

DICKEY: It sure is to me.

KIZER: But do you ever have this feeling? That in America everybody is ceasing to believe in love, particularly in New York City?

DICKEY: Well, I'll tell you. There's a kind of dry rot of cynicism that I've been doing my best to avoid. If I can avoid that and avoid encouraging it in my children I would feel like I had done at least a little something. It's easy and frequently rather cheap to look cynically at almost anything, everything. As Robert Penn Warren says somewhere, when some learned fellow tells him that "Jesus in Gethsemane was only sweating from TB/*Timor mortis conturbat me!*" It's possible to look cynically on anything and everything. We belong to what I guess you could call, for want of a better term, the "aw, come off it" generation. But I don't want to come off it. I want to get on it.

KIZER: Right! But the point, again, and this is the thing that has always bored me about a lot of the talk of fashionable French intellectuals, the Simone de Beauvoir, Gide group: they've got it all figured out and they've got this cynical attitude towards everything. Madame de Beauvoir wrote in *The Mandarins* about the woman protagonist, like herself, serving her sixteen-year-old daughter and her lover breakfast in bed and thinking that's terribly cool, you know. I think it was an invasion of their privacy, among other things. But the thing I really hate about it is the implication that everything is acceptable, everything is mechanistic, none of it matters very much, it can all be reduced down to a biological level, a mechanical order, a boring mechanical order, and I can't bear any of this. . . .

DICKEY: I agree with you. All of human life, Carolyn, it seems to me, hinges on what you attach value to. It doesn't matter so much *why* you attach value to certain things or any analytical propensities of that sort. But if you see value in things and naturally gravitate towards those things and cultivate them and care for them and live in and about and with them you have the nearest thing that we human beings are ever going to get to a satisfactory life. It doesn't have to be satisfactory to anybody but you. I remember something I read in Patrice de la Tour du Pin's *La Somme de la Poesie*, part of which is a kind of a dialogue where this guy is a kind of cynical Parisian and he systematically goes around milking his glands with various women and sitting in the park reflecting on the futility of everything and the guy who's talking to him says, "Well, you talk about what a desert life is, and surely it is. But would it be so if you were not killing off everything in it?"

KIZER: Exactly, exactly. Being your own flame thrower and destroying everything in front of you. This is the thing that frightens me about fashionable New York and French intellectuals of a certain kind: that the beliefs which they hold about life are destructive to their own art. Therefore, obviously, on the simplest pragmatic level they ought to be thrown out. Because they don't work. They are miserable people and they produce art of a very limited range.

DICKEY: I don't want anybody telling me that the only fashionability as a writer is to be miserable. I've been miserable enough in my time. But it's like Roethke said somewhere toward the end of his life: "In spite of everything I seek to establish some kind of condition of joy." I am that way essentially myself, and I mean *essentially*. That may sound sententious, but it is something that I do very profoundly feel.

Joy, by God! I've had it only a few times but I'm willing to wait for it to come again. And nobody is going to tell me that it's square to put any faith in this sort of thing. It's the only thing that makes existence worth anything at all to me.

KIZER: As Ted said in a very late poem, the right thing happens to the happy man.

DICKEY: Right things *do* happen to the happy man.

KIZER: And we have to have that beautiful receptivity to . . .

DICKEY: Or the great phrase of Henry James—accessibility to experience: to go toward it, hoping that it's going to be good or great. The psychological state with which one greets what comes to one is of absolute importance. If one is determined to be cynical, nothing is going to be good. I'll tell you what I dislike so much: the people who, to give themselves a certain facile superiority, sort of agree with themselves and their compatriots in this opinion. The idea that *everything* is in some way sort of contemptible. Mary McCarthy is this way. If somebody has a nice looking hat on, if a girl or woman has a nice looking hat on at a party, to Mary McCarthy there is something contemptible about its being nice looking. Even if somebody is absolutely pure and good, terms one expects to hear from the nineteenth century, even this is a little bit square. It's naive and a little bit pitiful.

KIZER: Oh, absolutely. I've been called down by glossy intellectuals for using the word "good." In *any* sense. Whether it refers to food or morals. I mean, the term is just not acceptable because it offends their passion for relativism.

DICKEY: I don't want to put Mary McCarthy down. She's a very bright gal. But the single test of whether anybody is valuable to you as a writer is to ask yourself if that writer, Mary McCarthy or whoever else it might be, is anything that I'd want to be. Or has anything I'd want to have. I would rather have what Roethke has a hundred thousand times more than what Mary McCarthy has. I would rather have what James Agee had than a thousand Mary McCarthys. Now Mary McCarthy could use James Agee in a novel as a figure of the terribly earnest, over-emotional person who really is not aware of the way things really are. But that wouldn't matter to me.

BOATWRIGHT: Well, isn't there a real return to an acceptance of these square abstractions? The kind of abstractions that Hemingway's characters hated: duty and honor and courage and such words as that. What has returned is a willingness to admit the validity of words like *joy*.

DICKEY: I agree. What we want, again, is to achieve a kind of state in which we can function in the world, not only barely making it, the debits and the credits sort of balancing out so that we can just barely hang in there, but to burst through to some magnificent region of the human personality and the creative mind which will no longer have any debits but which will be all positive: which will be beyond anything that has been yet. I think, again, when we talk about tradition in poetry and all this, I think we've been hung up on a set of middling assumptions which do not have to exist. And once having been destroyed it will be seen as a set of the most trifling and inessential irrelevancies that could possibly have been. But if we can unite the joyous man and the absolutely uninhibited imagination we will have done something for our generation, I think.

IN *MADEMOISELLE*
Some of the Known

INTERVIEWER: I read recently that a Russian poet had once said that poetry is power.

DICKEY: Sounds more like a German poet. The reviewer, reviewing the book in which it was quoted, said poetry had always exerted a moral force, even if underground, in Russia, but that the statement was hardly true for the West, and specifically this country. It has *some* power. I don't know exactly what kind of power you mean . . . political, maybe.

INTERVIEWER: He was speaking about moral power, but political power is implied in that.

DICKEY: The big thing in the last 15-20 years in this country is to use the poetry platform and the so-called poetry reading as a pretext for getting up and making bohemian political speeches. I don't think that has done poetry any good at all. When I was reading with Yevtushenko a few nights ago, it was so propagandistic, so, it seemed to me, opportunistic, and so slapdash and so headliney that I went upstairs and watched the track meet. I got tired of listening to his rant about his various political opinions.

INTERVIEWER: In being with Yevtushenko, did you learn anything about Russian youth?

DICKEY: Not very much except that they sure listen to him every time he opens his mouth. Whether this is good or bad or whatever, I don't know.

INTERVIEWER: With regard to politics, however, didn't you once write speeches for Eugene McCarthy?

DICKEY: I couldn't make myself out to be anything that politically august. He had a great number of conferences about the speeches, but his was the final draft.

INTERVIEWER: What attracted you to doing that? It's a little atypical, isn't it?

DICKEY: When I went into the Poetry Chair at the Library of Congress he was the first one to come up there, the first of the lawmakers, the Senators, Congressmen, anything. He and Mark Hatfield were about the only ones that I knew at all well. McCarthy and I just had a very pleasant association. We liked each other and built up a very nice kind of a friendship out of it.

INTERVIEWER: So it was more personal than political?

DICKEY: Yes. I believed in what he was doing and wanted him to succeed in doing it. He might have been President, I think. I still think he could've if he hadn't backed off in some kind of way. He didn't come down hard enough; he didn't move decisively enough.

INTERVIEWER: When you were working with McCarthy, did "the pen is mightier than the sword" ever flash through your mind?

DICKEY: I suppose so. But I don't know whether it is or not.

INTERVIEWER: Can you think of a poet who has truly stretched language in the sense that you have spoken of stretching language?

DICKEY: There are many in the sense that I mean. Hart Crane is the first to come to mind. He did something absolutely new. Dylan Thomas is another one. That is, they remade the English language to their own specifications. They remade it and they used it for their own purposes and in ways that were peculiar and special to them. That's something like what I want to do, except it wouldn't be in the way of Hart Crane, or Dylan Thomas or John Berryman.

INTERVIEWER: But do you ever feel, given your intensity about poetry, that in working on your novels you are diverting too much. . . ?

DICKEY: Yes, yes. I do feel that very acutely, but in my operation, as I conceive it, poetry is sort of the center. That's the thing that holds everything else together, and everything else is an outgrowth of that in some way. Novels, screenplays, essays, even advertising when I used to work in that—everything spun off that central concern with writing poetry, and I intend to keep it that way.

INTERVIEWER: Does it all come out of an absolutely central rhythm that you yourself have, your own peculiar rhythm?

DICKEY: Yes. Writing poetry demands such an excessive and intense concentration on language and the uses of words and the placement of words and their relationship to each other and how they kind of shed light on each other or sometimes block each other out, that a discipline of that sort is going to make other kinds of writing seem comparatively easy. No writing for me is really easy. But all the other forms of it that I have ever tried are easy compared to poetry. That's the toughest.

INTERVIEWER: Yesterday I read this definition of a politician: "They're among the few people in America who still work, live by their wits, have no job security, endure brutal hours, and show great ingenuity even when they're thieves. They're the last people in America who go over Niagara Falls in a barrel—they take risks. Most of them have sufficient ambition to be extremely interesting; an evening spent with a politician is more entertaining than with just about anybody else." Do you think that's also a definition of a poet?

DICKEY: Some poets, yes. I'll tell you the best people that I've ever known, and also the worst, were all poets. The best and the worst. There are a lot of in-between ones too, of course, but poets, and this is true the better the poet is, are very intensified people, and they are usually highly intelligent. Some of them are too intelligent for their own good as poets, as writers. You've got to have a certain blindness in writing poetry so that you will follow without question an impulse, just to see what will happen to you. If you're cautious about it, if you think it might be foolish to try this thing out, that it might not work, you don't have that chance-takingness that poets should rely on. Some of the things that I've written that I like the best are ideas which if written out in prose or broached in conversation would simply be absurdities.

INTERVIEWER: Like what?

DICKEY: *The Sheep Child* and *Folksinger of the 30s* and some of those at about that time of writing. *Falling*, for example.

INTERVIEWER: When you were speaking of poets being among the best and worst of men, I remembered reading about a poetry collection. The reviewer, also a poet, completely obscured the reviewee by going into a description of poets which I found infuriating. She spoke of poets writing only for and being read only by other poets. She made them only slightly lower than the angels, an elite group scarcely made of flesh.

DICKEY: Well, I can see what she means because poets had no choice other than to become an elitist group because nobody outside their own circle paid any attention to them. That's not true anymore. Poetry books, at least some few of them, have very good sales, very good, I'd say.

INTERVIEWER: I think it's one thing to regard yourself as a member of an elitist group, but isn't it kind of another thing to regard yourself as elite?

DICKEY: I, myself, don't subscribe to that because although poets are in some ways extraordinary people and technicians, their strongest roots are in common humanity, in things that they do share with others, whether poets or not. And if they lose sight of that, they turn off into some blind alley. Someone talked about *Sorties* as being a very arrogant book. Why should anybody be interested in James Dickey's opinions on archery tackle? I thought that was rather unfair; I would be interested in reading anybody's journal, whether he was a well-known poet or writer, or whether he was a steamfitter or an Army captain.

INTERVIEWER: Isn't it also because you're deeply interested in how people actually work?

DICKEY: Yes, certainly, and their opinions. I love opinionated people. I can't bear people who don't have any particular relationships to anything or anybody, who're just kind of sliding through life sideways.

INTERVIEWER: Have you ever had a review that really hurt you? Maybe one or two that got a little too close to the jugular?

DICKEY: I don't care what people say about my work. They can take it or leave it—the work gets there, it's going to be there. But when they begin to use the work to make some kind of *ad hominem* judgment on me, it's very irritating. I don't think anybody, anything, that could be said about a person has not been said about me by somebody at some time in some journal. They do it for their own reasons, and so I don't care much. Reviews don't matter to me. The delighted, great, happy ones that just love me to death are not really much more pleasing to me than the ones that hate and revile me. It's all tangential to what I'm doing. My business is to create the stuff. That's what I'm interested in, not what gets said about it. I'll give you an example of the most recent of these *ad hominem* reviews. I think it's in the *Saturday Review*. There's a woman with an ax to grind about the masculine mystique and the *machismo* and so on of the American novel—*Deliverance*, according to her, is the latest example of this. She was very unhappy with me because the only things I said about women made them out as nothing but sexual objects and somebody that'd be kind of nice to have around the house and cook your meals. I'm concerned that there's a tendency for people to read, say, something like the scene in *Deliverance* with the studio girl and jump to the assumption that I endorse this attitude, which is not at all the case. It's an attempt to show a character and how he feels, not to tell the audience how I feel.

INTERVIEWER: You don't think it's possible for a writer to say something he doesn't know he's said?

DICKEY: Sure, and very desirable some of the time. But this lady in the *Saturday Review* goes on and on about what she takes to be the protagonist's callous attitude when he has intercourse with his wife and thinks about the studio girl while he's doing it. If she thinks *that's* rare, she doesn't know what goes on in the head, especially of men; I can't vouch for women! She deplores all of this and wants me to create a woman character with depth whom I really pay serious attention to—in the phrase that they always use, "as a real human being." But what she doesn't realize or doesn't mention anyway is that Ed, the narrator, rejects the vision of the studio girl at the end and acknowledges all of his wife's virtues that he has held too lightly: that he is shown believing in the reality of his wife and in her personality and character and has *rejected* the image of woman as sexual fantasy.

INTERVIEWER: In the film of *Deliverance*, are there things that you could say visually that you couldn't or would have found almost impossible to say verbally?

DICKEY: Yes, in some ways. The visual sweep of the Chattooga river itself, for example.

INTERVIEWER: Did you have any movie experience before?

DICKEY: I made a couple of documentaries when I was living in California, but I've never written a feature film before or had anything to do with one.

INTERVIEWER: Had you wanted to?

DICKEY: No. I'd heard so many horror stories of what happens to writers when they do this kind of work that I had rather, until this film came along, do my own work in my own corner instead of getting myself involved with directors and lighting technicians and the million personalities and problems in the world of making movies. I mean it's very frustrating. Everybody's got to be satisfied with his part of it, not only in itself but as it relates to the other parts. And it's just devilishly hard to get it right so that everybody's satisfied.

INTERVIEWER: In *Sorties*, when you were going over a book of Ben Nicholson's works, you wrote about decisions in working with forms, words. An artist said to me recently that it's much more difficult making decisions with words than with forms.

DICKEY: Well, it wouldn't be for me because words are kind of my thing, if I might be said to have one. I couldn't do any kind of interesting graphic work; I can't even write my name twice the same way.

INTERVIEWER: Why do you suppose poetry so often appeals specifically to the young?

DICKEY: When you are young and get interested in poetry, either deeply interested or just passingly interested, you fall into one of two categories of people. One class is interested in poetry itself. Those in it just love poetry, they read it all the time, and some of them try to write it. But the members of the other class like it because they have ulterior motives for liking it. They want to copy it out and send it to a girl or something. They associate it with something having to do with themselves and what they hope for. That type usually doesn't have a permanent interest in poetry whereas the people who really like it stay with it. In fact, when young I belonged to the second category myself. I identified with Byron. I liked his life and thought I understood it. It was very much of a personal self-aggrandizement on my part to read Byron and then quote him and talk about him. Byron is the perfect figure for that age. I still like to read about him. I just read a good biography of him—Leslie Marchand's.

INTERVIEWER: How long have you been teaching?

DICKEY: That's kind of hard to answer because I've been in and out of teaching over so many years. I taught a few months in 1950 and then was recalled into the Air Force. When I got out in 1953 I taught a couple of years, then I went to Europe for a while, then I came back and taught a little more, then I went into the advertising business for five or six years, and then went to Europe again, and taught again at one place and another. So I've been in and out.

INTERVIEWER: Have you found any changes among the young?

DICKEY: Yes, many. My main interest in them is the enormous upsurge of interest in writing there is in kids now. Militancy and social action are not nearly so important as they were a few years ago.

INTERVIEWER: Why do you think there's such an upsurge in writing?

DICKEY: I have a couple of private opinions, I don't know if they're true. But it would seem to me that people bombarded by advertisers and politicians and a constant stream of verbalization aimed at making them do something or not do it either consciously or unconsciously makes them gravitate back to a use of language which has no designs on them, where you can say something because you want to say it, because it means something to you personally, not because you want to get someone to do something by means of it. Poetry is just about the last repository of language, of depth language, where you try to offer something to another person, something of yourself, some insight that you've had, some phrase that you think is meaningful or life-quickening in some way.

INTERVIEWER: You can't do that as deeply or as well in a novel? Or in *Nightwood*. . . .

DICKEY: Well, no, because it doesn't have the concentration of language that poetry has. The means the novel has of doing this are not the means of poetry. But the ultimate thing about poetry is this enormous, reverberative and almost concussive concentration of a great deal of meaning in small space in language that is also rhythmic in some way.

INTERVIEWER: The novel tries to do it, though, in, let's say, the best of Virginia Woolf.

DICKEY: Yes, you can multiply a lot of instances. Melville, for example. Some of John Updike has this quality. But it is never as effective in prose. The best prose is not as good as the best poetry at doing this because it doesn't have the linear movement, the isolation of the image, and above all, the sense of a carrying rhythm that poetry has. If you read Yeats, for example, who's the great master of the utilization of the dynamics of language to say amazing things, you're just bowled over by the concentration and eloquence and power of what is being said and how it's being said.

INTERVIEWER: Have you finished the novel you've been working on?

DICKEY: No. I'm just getting it into shape where I can move on it, move toward it anyway.

INTERVIEWER: Do you think it will be your last novel?

DICKEY: I do think it will be, yes.

INTERVIEWER: So you can get back to poetry?

DICKEY: Well, I've been writing poetry right along with that, too. I like to work on other things at the same time.

INTERVIEWER: Is there anybody you would like to write about? Any writer or artist or guitar player?

DICKEY: I'd like to do an article on John Berryman: the kind of man he was, what made his life and what made him die. In this country we have a terrible mortality rate by suicide for poets. I've known at least two who killed themselves, maybe more.

INTERVIEWER: And why is that? Do you think it has something to do with intensity? And, possibly, with always having your nerves out? Skinless?

DICKEY: I do. There are poets whose lifestyles shape their work to such a degree that there's no way they can disassociate one from the other.

INTERVIEWER: How do you protect yourself?

DICKEY: I don't do it as well as I'd like to be able to, but I just concentrate on the work and not on the lifestyle. That's why I wish people would quit paying so much attention to me and to my interests—hunting and driving fast cars and that sort of thing.

INTERVIEWER: But you've created that interest.

DICKEY: Perhaps. I may have created that interest, but those are just things I do. I don't do them in order for people to write about them.

INTERVIEWER: True. But you're not precisely invisible.

DICKEY: No.

INTERVIEWER: You also said in *Sorties* and in other places too, "the main thing is to ride the flood tide."

DICKEY: Yes, I did. Just get yourself and your talent and go in and keep it moving and go where it takes you.

INTERVIEWER: Don't you find being a public figure, however, very difficult?

DICKEY: I certainly do, and if anything does me in it's going to be that!

INTERVIEWER: Why do you allow it?

DICKEY: A couple of reasons. One of them is perhaps a very naive one, and that is that it does, at least some of the time, some good for my craft and the people who practice it with devotion. In other words, it gets the word around about poetry, and it gets other people read too, and it gets the reading prices up at colleges. I will not see the American poets of my generation picked up cheap and given $50 for a reading of their poetry when the next week Al Capp will come in and be given $3,500 or Sammy Davis, Jr., $12,000, or Henry Kissinger, $20,000!

INTERVIEWER: You don't think it's ever doing something for your ego?

DICKEY: All that's ever been capable of being done either to or for my ego has already been done.

INTERVIEWER: Do you think anybody can really say that?

DICKEY: Perhaps not. I've been on public show for so many years that if a student in a girls' college comes up to me after the reading and throws her arms around my neck, I can guarantee you that it has nothing like the effect on me that it did when I was first starting out. I still like it, I can respond to it to some degree, but I don't go away from the incident saying, "Isn't that the very nicest thing that ever happened to me in my whole life?"

INTERVIEWER: Do you think you'll ever be able to say that again?

About anything?

DICKEY: Hard to tell. The toughest thing, as the poet grows older, or at least as this one does, is to keep the electrical kind of responsiveness to things and to people out of which poetry comes, must come. You tend to get insulated, depend too much on habit. Some of the things I did as a younger man—go up to a stranger in the street and tell him that I liked his hat, something like that—I couldn't do anymore. I would be too self-conscious. I figure that's something the young can get away with.

INTERVIEWER: Don't you think it goes beyond self-consciousness? You've had so much and known so much, have you ever feared someday losing the ability to respond—at least with the same intensity—because you've already responded so much?

DICKEY: Yes. I do fear it, but it hasn't happened yet.

INTERVIEWER: But I don't think you have to worry about "at the same intensity." There's a passage in *Sorties* in which you write about the word "pleasant" and how it becomes more important. It's absolutely true, but why be discouraged about it?

DICKEY: You get discouraged about it because you have a horror of yourself being one of the bland leading the bland. You know, the felt-slippered, middle-aged or old person surrounded by his dogs and cats and not responding, becoming a kind of connoisseur. Everything that I've ever done depends on a certain rawness of edge, and when you get insulated you lose that.

INTERVIEWER: How are you going to avoid it?

DICKEY: I don't know. I've been looking for ways. For a while, I thought drinking a lot of alcohol would make up the difference, but it doesn't. That's a diminishing return, that type of thing. What I would really like to do is go off in the woods somewhere and just take an awful lot of physical exercise and get the fat off my soul just like a boxer gets it off his body. Hemingway said that, and he was right.

INTERVIEWER: Both wildernesses—the physical one and the one inside your head?

DICKEY: Actually, I was talking about the real wilderness, what there is left of it. I know a valley in North Carolina which I can almost categorically guarantee that nobody but I and maybe two or three other people have ever seen. That's the place! I've got a suburban house I love. It's the only house I've ever owned. I've got all my stuff around it, you know, all my books . . . but I remember some lines of Robinson Jeffers which say, "In pleasant peace and security / How suddenly the soul in a man begins to die. / He shall look up above the stalled oxen / Envying the cruel falcon, / And dig under the straw for a stone / To bruise himself on." I need to find the stone to bruise myself on.

INTERVIEWER: Do you feel that people, as they grow older, grow too civilized inside?

DICKEY: Well, yes, but you can see the reason for that. You can't exist in society without making an awful lot of concessions, personal concessions. I've always been baffled by the word "freedom." What does it mean? "I'm free. I want to be free." I can see somebody who was in jail using the word with perfect legitimacy. But free, to be *free*! There's no such animal. I mean totally, anarchically free. There's no way to do it. You're bound by too many chains: your own flesh and your own needs for food and the rest of the things it takes. You're not free. You've got to make some concessions. You can't just drift around, as in Plato, a bodyless spirit.

INTERVIEWER: Do you know the line in that song "Me and Bobby McGee" that says: "Freedom's just another word for nothin' left to lose?"

DICKEY: Yes, that's good too. Finding your private ways in the public world: How to do it? Doing what you think you need to be doing and what you think you need to be thinking. There are lots and lots of personal stratagems—if you work in an office or anywhere else or if you're in school—to preserve and to extend your own identity.

There is nothing I would rather do, for example, than go in a student's room, where they have those mobiles made out of bits of wine bottles, you know, and a picture of Allen Ginsberg on the wall that they throw darts at—something like that—and a few records, some paperback books. The word "lifestyle" is very, very important now and it should be important and I hope it continues to be important. We're not such conformists in America as everybody thinks. Everybody is kicking and screaming to go the other way now, to be an individual, and that seems to me to be the best direction. Even if it takes the form of a lot of eccentricities, like the hippies. I like the hippies. They're gentle people. I think those outlandish clothes they wear are very colorful and nice. The only thing I would hold against them is the drug emphasis. But they are dead set against this business of being shoved into the gray flannel suit and the gray flannel image. They want to be themselves, even if they don't know who themselves are. They're looking, and I can't help thinking that's a good thing.

IN LOUISIANA*

A Conversation with William Heyen and Peter Marchant

I began the interview by asking him to read a poem that has been one of my favorites, "The Performance" (W.H.).

> The last time I saw Donald Armstrong
> He was staggering oddly off into the sun,
> Going down, of the Philippine Islands.
> I let my shovel fall, and put that hand
> Above my eyes, and moved some way to one side
> That his body might pass through the sun,
>
> And I saw how well he was not
> Standing there on his hands,
> On his spindle-shanked forearms balanced,
> Unbalanced, with his big feet looming and waving
> In the great, untrustworthy air
> He flew in each night, when it darkened.
>
> Dust fanned in scraped puffs from the earth
> Between his arms, and blood turned his face inside out,
> To demonstrate its suppleness
> Of veins, as he perfected his role.
> Next day, he toppled his head off
> On an island beach to the south,
>
> And the enemy's two-handed sword
> Did not fall from anyone's hands

*Edited from a transcription of a videotape produced by the Educational Communication Center on 12/4/1970 and sponsored by The Brockport Writers Forum, Department of English, State University of New York, College at Brockport, Brockport, New York.

At that miraculous sight,
As the head rolled over upon
Its wide-eyed face, and fell
Into the inadequate grave

He had dug for himself, under pressure.
Yet I put my flat hand to my eyebrows
Months later, to see him again
In the sun, when I learned how he died,
And imagined him, there,
Come, judged, before his small captors,

Doing all his lean tricks to amaze them—
The back somersault, the kip-up—
And at last, the stand on his hands,
Perfect, with his feet together,
His head down, evenly breathing,
As the sun poured up from the sea

And the headsman broke down
In a blaze of tears, in that light
Of the thin, long human frame
Upside down in its own strange joy,
And, if some other one had not told him,
Would have cut off the feet

Instead of the head,
And if Armstrong had not presently risen
In kingly, round-shouldered attendance,
And then knelt down in himself
Beside his hacked, glittering grave, having done
All things in this life that he could.

DICKEY: You asked me to read a poem called "The Performance," which I'm very happy to do. It's about the war, the Second World War, in the Pacific, where an American pilot named Donald Armstrong is beheaded by the Japanese. I remember him very well—he was my closest friend in the Philippines. The main thing I remember about him, besides the fact that he was a wonderful pilot, was that he was also an amateur gymnast. He used to do somersaults, flips, kip-ups and things in the squadron area. But he never could perfect his handstands. I guess this was because his center of gravity was so high—he was a very tall fellow. But he always used to be out there in the squadron area practicing his handstand. So, when he was beheaded, I thought about what I remembered of Don, and the image that I had in my mind was of the handstand. Years later I wrote this poem.

HEYEN: Mr. Dickey, I've admired "The Performance" for a long time and I'm happy to have heard it aloud. It seems to me that one of the things this poem does that makes it distinctively a Dickey poem is that it commits itself to an imaginative leap. I remember that in your book, *Self-Interviews*, you say that the most important capacity for a poet to have is the ability to commit himself to his own inventions. Would you elaborate on this?

DICKEY: Well, yes, I certainly do think the best ideas for poems that I have are usually the most far-fetched. I think that really the true creative act is to conceive, first, a thing, and then to find your way through the process of the administration of formal technique to making that strange vision live. I had a poem years ago where I tried to imagine what it would be like to die and then be reborn as a migratory sea bird. Now, on the surface of it, this is an absurd idea, but when you imagine yourself into the role of a person who has died from his human life and awakened on wings somewhere in the polar regions, then you get interested, you just wish it could be that way. And maybe it will be; I don't know.

HEYEN: And so many of the poems I admire, well, when I summarize their story-lines, their plots, they seem—on the surface—kind of absurd.

DICKEY: Yes, they *are* absurd.

HEYEN: Like in your poem from *Falling*, "The Sheep Child." It's funny, you know, that it's so convincing despite its point of view—a thing half child and half sheep speaks out from a jar of formaldehyde—but it's absolutely convincing during the course of the reading of the poem.

DICKEY: Well, that's the kind of thing I try to do. Of course, simple absurdity isn't going to guarantee anything, but it's that kind of chance-taking that may lead to something perfectly amazing that you want to try to hang onto if you can ever get the conception to begin with. Then you try to realize it in some way.

MARCHANT: You said something last night about the necessity for man to make some sort of connection with animals, with animal life. . . .

DICKEY: Yes. Though we can dominate some of the cosmos, in a sense we've lost it or we're losing it. It's not just the conservation issue which is, surely, in my opinion, the most important issue of our era, our civilization. It's not just that. It's the sense of being part of what Lovejoy called "the great chain of being." Randall Jarrell, one of my favorite critics and poets, was a great punster, and he said that we have substituted for the great chain of being "the great chain of buying," which is, maybe, something that's diametrically opposed, and will be the ruination of everything.

HEYEN: Where do you think we'll be when a man can no longer renew himself by getting in touch with the wilderness, the animal kingdom?

DICKEY: I don't know, Bill, but *my* chief terror is that they'll discover ways to keep me alive beyond my time, because I have a profound belief in living out my part of the cycle, as men have always done. Maybe I wouldn't mind having a few more years than people had in, say, Periclean Athens, or in the age of Shakespeare. I wouldn't mind having a few more years than that, but infinite time . . . no, no. It's better to die.

MARCHANT: You don't dread death?

DICKEY: No. I've been close to it so many times. I mean I don't want to die now—I want to see my youngest boy grow up and help him in any way I can. My oldest boy is already married—he just made a grandfather out of me; he's in the mainstream of his time now. But I'd like to see my little boy grow up and to help him, and I have so many things I'd like to write; but otherwise, other than that, I don't have the slightest fear of death. I just don't want to be incapacitated by some long, lingering humiliating disease, you know. Pain, and dying, are not good, but death itself is all right.

HEYEN: When I read about James Dickey it sounds as though he's been so many places and done so many things that he's lived three lives already. And this question occurs to me. I remember that when you reviewed Galway Kinnell's first book of poems you said that his progress as a poet might depend upon his life. What is the connection between life experience and poetry?

DICKEY: Some people seem to be able to distinguish, but . . . well, every poet is writing out of his experience, but the word *experience* is capable, of course, of an enormous latitude of definition. But with that fellow—whom, incidentally, I think a lot of—there seems to be an unusually close correspondence between his personal experiences and what he writes. This is true to some extent for any writer, of course, but it seems to be more true for him than for most. In my own work, you know, there are only a few poems that are factual representations of what actually occurred at a certain time and place. "The Performance" is based on what I remember of a pilot in my squadron, the 418th Night Fighter Squadron, but the business of having a vision of him being beheaded and doing flips and things beside his grave is just something that I made up.

MARCHANT: Were you writing poems through the war?

DICKEY: No. I got interested in poetry at that time, during the long ennui of the service. I'm the kind of person who can't be interested in a thing, really deeply interested in it, without wanting to see if he could do it himself. If I like guitar music, I want to get a guitar and play. It's a great factor in my own personal life; I mean the sense of participation in a thing. At no matter how humble a level: participator, not spectator. I love to see great basketball players, but I wouldn't love them so much if I didn't get out and try to shoot a few myself. Then I know how great those other ones are. At the

University of South Carolina we have a great basketball team, traditionally, year after year. And I go to every game, but I know better what those guys are doing because I go out in my yard and shoot baskets with my little boy. I appreciate the full measure of their accomplishment because I have participated. I have a vested interest, so to speak, in sports, because I'm able to do some things myself. That's important.

HEYEN: You have a poem called "The Bee" that I like a lot. In it there's kind of an homage paid to old coaches who give a middle-aged man the ability to jump out quickly enough to save his son from the traffic.

DICKEY: Yes, those old coaches. They've been misinterpreted in lots of ways; these days, with the "now generation," coaches are kind of looked on as proto-fascist figures, but I never had anything but the most intense gratitude to mine.

HEYEN: They wanted to chip away our excess stone, to bring that figure out, that man out.

DICKEY: Right. When all those old coaches who have hollered at you so much are dead, what you see, finally, is that all the chewing out they did was really an act of faith, because they believed that you could do the things they asked you to do; you could do better. You might not develop into a remarkable athlete, but it was always an act of faith when they chewed you out. It signified that they believed you were capable of being better.

MARCHANT: So, as a student you were probably more interested in athletics than in poetry?

DICKEY: Yes. At Clemson the only book I read was the play book, the football plays. I studied that. It was almost like a bible, you know. But it wasn't very hard to learn. It was a simple system—we ran the single wing. I played wingback. It would be, in the T formation, I suppose, flanker. But it was wingback in those days. In any case, it was a simple system to learn—just straight ahead brute force football, or as they said at Clemson, "three yards and a cloud of dirt." No, I wasn't reading much poetry in those days.

HEYEN: Does the current American fascination with a violent sport like football upset you at all?

DICKEY: No, no, I like it. I love to drink a beer on a Sunday afternoon and watch those great athletes. I think it's a privilege to watch somebody who does things that well. Football is so complex now, and there are so many good people pitted against each other.

HEYEN: And it could serve for the spectators as a kind of "moral equivalent of war," some kind of sublimation.

DICKEY: Yes indeed! That's one of the great phrases in American literature, for me, and William James is one of the great writers.

HEYEN: I thought I made that up.

DICKEY: You will, Bill, you will. The other one of James's that I think is great is when he says that alcohol is "the great exciter of the 'yes faculty.' "

HEYEN: Let's hear another Dickey poem. I was wondering if you'd read "The Heaven of Animals."

DICKEY: O. K. Again, to come back to experience, a word that we keep coming back to, I think that a creative writer, or maybe just a creative human being, really becomes creative when he realizes that experience is not limited to fact. Experience is everything—it includes fact—things that have happened to you. But it also includes things that you've heard about, that you've seen in movies, that you've read in newspapers, that you've fantasized about—all of that is experience, everything that ever impinges on the imagination, and is recallable, or even half recallable, or even subliminally recallable. All of that is experience, and when you throw the gate open that wide, then you begin to understand what the imagination is capable of doing. This poem, "The Heaven of Animals," comes from a Walt Disney movie that I saw called *African Lion*. I love those Disney animal movies. They're just so miraculously, marvelously vivid and interesting. *African Lion* was one of the better ones, and *White Wilderness*, where they had that wonderful twenty minute sequence on the life of the wolverine. I went to see that one so many times my children wouldn't even go with me any more! This poem came out of *African Lion* where they show a leopard fall from a tree onto the back of a wildebeest calf and drag it down and eat it—tears it to pieces. You think, gosh, Disney's getting pretty rough, you know, but all the time there's this unctuous voice of the announcer saying that this is all part of the great cycle of nature and that from this kill even the young of the vulture are fed. And sure enough, the camera pans up and the little vultures are getting theirs. Well, I thought that all this talk about the cycle of nature must be a tough thing to hear if you're the animal that's getting torn to pieces. I've always liked heavens and utopias, and I tried to invent a heaven for animals. St. Thomas Aquinas says animals have no souls, and therefore they're perishable, not like us wonderful human beings. But this always seemed grossly unfair to me. So, if you're a poet you try to imagine a heaven of animals. But it wouldn't really be a heaven if the animal was deprived of his nature. I mean the killer must still be able to kill, and the hunted should still be hunted.

Here they are. The soft eyes open.
If they have lived in a wood
It is a wood.
If they have lived on plains
It is grass rolling
Under their feet forever.

Having no souls, they have come,
Anyway, beyond their knowing.
Their instincts wholly bloom
And they rise.
The soft eyes open.

To match them, the landscape flowers,
Outdoing, desperately
Outdoing what is required:
The richest wood,
The deepest field.

For some of these,
It could not be the place

It is, without blood.
These hunt, as they have done
But with claws and teeth grown perfect,

More deadly than they can believe.
They stalk more silently,
And crouch on the limbs of trees,
And their descent
Upon the bright backs of their prey

May take years
In a sovereign floating of joy.
And those that are hunted
Know this as their life,
Their reward: to walk

Under such trees in full knowledge
Of what is in glory above them,
And to feel no fear,
But acceptance, compliance.
Fulfilling themselves without pain

At the cycle's center,
They tremble, they walk
Under the tree,
They fall, they are torn,
They rise, they walk again.

HEYEN: That's quite a poem. It strikes me as perfect, inevitable, true to its own invention. Did it come hard? Your poems go through a great many revisions, don't they?

DICKEY: Oh, yes.

HEYEN: I wonder: I was reading Paul Carroll's essay on this poem and he was saying that you'd focused on just particular animal qualities and activities, and I was wondering if "The Heaven of Animals" was ever much longer than it is now. What do you remember about this poem?

DICKEY: Well, I wrote and rewrote this one for a number of weeks. I finished it, as a matter of fact, in an American advertising office and I had my secretary type it up. I realize that this is heresy. I suppose I should have written it in some sort of isolated retreat, but I didn't. And my secretary didn't know what it was about—"what is this," she asked, "some kind of religious poem? Are you going to send it to a religious magazine?" I said, "No, I suppose in a way it's a religious poem, but I'm going to send it to the *New Yorker*." And they brought it out, and now I laugh when I remember that exchange in the corridor of one of these sterile business houses about this poem which, for better or worse, is some kind of mystical vision of creation.

There's not much else I can tell you. No, this one was not longer, though most of my poems are cut down from six, seven, eight times longer than they are originally. I like to write long.

HEYEN: "The Heaven of Animals" is from your second book, *Drowning With Others*. What kind of change from *Into the Stone* did you begin to feel with your second book?

DICKEY: Most of the poems of *Into the Stone* are in variations of a dactylic or anapestic rhythm—depending on where you start to count—whether you think of it as a rising or a falling rhythm. Most of the poems, not "The Performance," were in those rhythms. I moved over from that into more of a three-beat organization which was less heavily rhythmical. I never have gone back to what I did in that first book, though I read the things that I did there and have the distinct sensation that I did just enough of that and not too much. It can get to be a vice, writing overly rhythmical poems. But I do have what Richard Wilbur once called a "thump-loving American ear," and I recognize the danger, too well, of writing too many thump-loving poems. You know, one can read poets like Yeats and Theodore Roethke and Shakespeare and all those wonderful folk who gave us great literature, but I also have a marvelous, lovely feeling for bad poetry. I read an awful lot of it and doubtless I write some too. But I love Kipling, and even poets like Robert Service. I can read a lot of that, recognizing every minute how awful it is, but also liking it, enjoying it.

A bunch of the boys were whooping it up in the Malamute saloon:
The kid that handles the music-box was hitting a jag-time tune;
Back of the bar, in a solo game, sat Dangerous Dan McGrew,
And watching his luck was his light-o'-love, the lady that's known as Lou.

When out of the night, which was fifty below, and into the din and the glare,
There stumbled a miner fresh from the creeks, dog-dirty, and loaded for bear.
He looked like a man with a foot in the grave and scarcely the strength of a louse,
Yet he tilted a poke of dust on the bar, and he called for drinks on the house.

Boy, it's just such fun, it's just lots of fun.

HEYEN: You're going to spark a Service revival.

DICKEY: That's all right. There have been worse.

MARCHANT: Which poets were you reading during the war?

DICKEY: Oh, I read everybody I could find. One of the greatest moments of my life was when the war was finished and the great Okinawa hurricane of October the 9th, 1945, hit and blew away practically the whole island, and it wrecked the service library down at ISCOM, Island Command—we were already getting to the acronym stage then—and there were books scattered around, full of coral guck and mud, and they were just for the asking, because nobody would ever know who came and picked them up. I picked a collected Yeats out of the coral slime, and a copy of *Understanding Poetry* by Brooks and Warren, and, oddly enough, a book by J. B. Priestley called *Midnight on the Desert*.

MARCHANT: And then you began writing after the war?

DICKEY: Well, I was writing a little bit during the war. I think I really started as a writer by writing long, erotic letters to girls, from the islands, from the foxholes and tents of New Guinea and the Philippines. I think I was really born as a writer when I looked at a letter that I'd written this girl, and I *didn't* say Gee, this will have the desired effect if I ever return to the States. I looked at what I'd put on the page of this letter and I didn't say that. Instead, I thought *Jesus*, that ain't bad! That is, I got interested in the thing itself rather than in any kind of ulterior motive, and I think it all started out with as simple a thing as that, simple as it is.

HEYEN: In 1964 you published a no-holds-barred collection of criticism, *The Suspect in Poetry*. Would you talk about two of the kinds of poetry that seemed to you then to be suspect? I mean, on the one hand a kind of poetry that you see to be too elegant and fastidious, and then, the Beat poets. And then there are the confessionals. I know this is a terribly broad question.

DICKEY: Beat poets and hippies are in there trying—God knows, nobody can shut them up—but I look for memorable language, and if I don't find memorable language, and I find a lot of self-aggrandizing pretentiousness, I react violently against it. Their stuff is mostly an effort to be imaginative by unimaginative people. And poems about drugs. I think there could be terrific poems written about drugs, but not those poems, not the ones I've been reading. I wrote an introduction to an anthology of new poets, but, aside from just a few of the poets represented in the book, I found much of the same sort of unimaginative, self-assertive sort of thing.

Again, the confessionals, the so-called confessional poets, my objection to them, to Anne Sexton and Sylvia Plath and even to a good deal of Lowell, is not that they're confessional (that's fine), but that they're not confessional enough. They're slickly confessional. There's nothing I detest worse in poetry than glib talk about one's personal agony, about being in insane asylums and so on. Ted Roethke had more of a mental problem than Lowell and Sexton and Sylvia Plath and anybody else you would want to mention, but he was able to transcend that, and at the the end to come in to some sort of condition of joy. Sylvia Plath and some of the others are brilliant whiners, and one gets tired of that prolonged whine. It's valid and even moving to a certain extent, but that's not all there is. One must eventually move out into something far larger than one's personal scab-picking.

HEYEN: I can't quite put my mind's finger on the question I want to ask you now, but let me try. It has to do with the undercurrent of what you've been saying. It seems to me that again and again what I sense in your poetry and in your criticism is an emphasis on the humanism, or the morality or larger concerns of poetry. But that's not it, exactly. You wrote about Matthew Arnold's poem "Dover Beach" this: "The implication is that if love, morality, constancy, and the other traditional Western virtues are not maintained without supernatural sanction, there is nothing." I mean there's a sense—I want to say something like this: behind your poems there's the idea that what the poet has to reach for is not necessarily affirmation, but, yes, a kind of affirming of values.

DICKEY: Yes. I just read a very brilliant, wrong-headed, and fascinating book by Robert Ardrey called *The Social Contract* where he calls man a cosmic accident. In college I got interested in astrophysics because a subject as big as the universe, to put it literally, is interesting to me. As Edwin Arlington Robinson says in one of his letters, the world is a hell of a place, but the universe is a fine thing. I don't know about worship. I've been called a religious writer. My own point of view is pretty much D. H. Lawrence's. He said that he was a profoundly religious man who didn't happen to believe in God. But whoever or whatever force it was that created the universe, that caused it to be, whether blind force or determinism or the God of the Old Testament or chance, the rain of matter upon matter, as Democritus thought, is worthy of worship, even if it's indifferent to worship. I believe that whatever the originating agency was, it doesn't have any cognizance of men, or our conditions, troubles, whatsoever.

HEYEN: Yes, and you've angled in on what was on my mind. . . .

Well, I've been watching my watch, worried. I want us to have some time to talk about *Deliverance*, but I wonder if you'd read one more poem first.

DICKEY: Sure.

HEYEN: Would you read "Sled Burial, Dream Ceremony"? We walked over here this morning . . .

MARCHANT: In a snow storm . . .

HEYEN: Yes, Peter and I thought this would be an appropriate poem.

DICKEY: We've been talking so much about death, and I used to be much given to writing about death. Here I tried to fathom what it was, what death is, essentially. I finally decided that it's being in the ultimate strange place, the thing that's most completely different from what you're accustomed to. This is about a Southerner who dies. Death to a Southerner is to be in a place where it snows all the time, where people go fishing through the ice, where men wear scarves around their heads against the chill wind, where there are such things as sleds for transportation. That's the ultimate strange place for a Southerner.

While the south rains, the north
Is snowing, and the dead southerner
Is taken there. He lies with the top of his casket
Open, his hair combed, the particles in the air
Changing to other things. The train stops

In a small furry village, and men in flap-eared caps
And others with women's scarves tied around their heads
And business hats over those, unload him,
And one of them reaches inside the coffin and places
The southerner's hand at the center

Of his dead breast. They load him onto a sled,
An old-fashioned sled with high-curled runners,
Drawn by horses with bells, and begin
To walk out of town, past dull red barns
Inching closer to the road as it snows

Harder, past an army of gunny-sacked bushes,
Past horses with flakes in the hollows of their sway-backs,
Past round faces drawn by children
On kitchen windows, all shedding basic-shaped tears.
The coffin top still is wide open;

His dead eyes stare through his lids,
Not fooled that the snow is cotton. The woods fall
Slowly off all of them, until they are walking
Between rigid little houses of ice-fishers
On a plain which is a great plain of water

Until the last rabbit track fails, and they are
At the center. They take axes, shovels, mattocks,
Dig the snow away, and saw the ice in the form
Of his coffin, lifting the slab like a door
Without hinges. The snow creaks under the sled

As they unload him like hay, holding his weight by ropes.
Sensing an unwanted freedom, a fish
Slides by, under the hole leading up through the snow
To nothing, and is gone. The coffin's shadow
Is white, and they stand there, gunny-sacked bushes,

Summoned from village sleep into someone else's dream
Of death, and let him down, still seeing the flakes in the air
At the place they are born of pure shadow
Like his dead eyelids, rocking for a moment like a boat
On utter foreignness, before he fills and sails down.

MARCHANT: That's an intriguing poem. . . . The very strange place, and a kind of death for the Southerner, to make a kind of transition to *Deliverance*, might be a world without wilderness.

DICKEY: Yes, it would be. Really, that's the motivating force behind the novel. That's what causes these four, or at least three of these ill-prepared suburban Southern businessmen to go up into the mountains and try to run down a river, all this suggested to them by the fanatical leader of the party, Lewis Medlock. We all feel shamefaced about the vanishing of the wilderness, and we do feel that it is incumbent on us to get out there and see a little of it before it's all gone. That's really the motivation for the trip that forms most of the narrative of *Deliverance*. We should, fellows, really we ought to see the wilderness before it's gone forever—take pictures of it with expensive cameras. Ha!

MARCHANT: How did the novel develop?

DICKEY: Well, mostly very slowly. I was living in Italy when I first got the idea. As nearly as I can recollect—this was in 1962—I was lying in bed in Positano, on the Amalfi Coast, where we were living at the time, and the basic plot came to me and I knew, in five minutes, everything that was going to happen in the book. But it was eight years later before I published it. It took me a long time to work it out the way I thought it should be. I usually generate ideas for poetry relatively easily, but not for anything that's amenable to fictional treatment. I think this is one of the only two or three fictional ideas I've had in my entire life. God knows when I'll get another.

MARCHANT: And do you find yourself a bit astonished to be a best-seller, both in America and England, with *Deliverance*?

DICKEY: Well, yes. It's very gratifying. You know, I saw an old Robert Taylor movie on television the other day where he was a Roman conqueror—Deborah Kerr was in it, and Buddy Baer—and he was going in triumph through the streets of Rome with all these captives in chains, and part of the ceremony, evidently, is to have a little man go along behind the chariot of the conqueror intoning "Thou art only a man. This too shall pass away." It's very nice to have all this attention paid to the novel, and the money is certainly not unwelcome, but I'm not foolish enough to believe that this is anything more than transitory.

MARCHANT: When you were writing it did it ever occur to you that it might be a movie?

DICKEY: Well, no, I just concentrated on writing it. It occurred to me every now and then that I'd like to see it done as a movie, but it surely was not conceived with that as an eventuality. I mean it would have been nice, I thought, but the main thing is to try to get it down on the page. It's not something like this fearful, this awful best-selling book *Love Story* which was conceived as a movie and then written as a novel. I like the word, and the image. The film image, that's a different thing. But my business is words, and that kind of magical property that they have of calling up images in the mind. That's my business, and that's what I have to attend to, and not worry about these other things that might eventually happen as a result.

HEYEN: Are you working on the screenplay right now?

DICKEY: It's already done.

HEYEN: What kinds of difficulties are there in moving from the novel to the film script?

DICKEY: The main technical difficulty is that a good deal of *Deliverance*—the center section of it—has to do with how Ed Gentry, the narrator, tries to second-guess this hillbilly that he thinks is trying to ambush them. So much of that goes on in his mind, and I had to try to find some kind of visual equivalent to transfer his thought processes to the screen so that it would be understandable to the audience as to why he does what he does when he climbs up the cliff. And I did that by developing a long conversation between Gentry and Bobby Trippe. Before Gentry starts he says "Now this is what I'm going to do, this is the way I've got it figured." So he just tells Bobby, instead of thinking about it as he's climbing up out of the gorge as he does in the novel. But aside from that it wasn't very difficult, and it was very interesting. In fact, I put some things into the film version that I wish I'd thought of in time to put them into the novel.

HEYEN: For me it's a terribly tense scene after he gets to the top. You've managed a great deal of suspense because in an earlier scene Gentry spooks and misses a shot at a deer, so I find myself wondering if he'll miss the hillbilly. . . . And the two hillbillies seem to me to be wonderfully realized. They're in a climactic scene, certainly, but not in much of the novel. Are they based on people you've known, their kind of pure evil?

DICKEY: They're based on acquaintances of my father; I remember some people like that. There's some kind of absolutism about country people. As Lewis says in the novel, there's almost no hill family, or "crackers" as we call them at home, that doesn't have at least one relative in prison. As Lewis says, some of them are in for running liquor and other things, but most of them are in for murder. Up in those Georgia hill counties, life and death are very basic gut-type things, and if somebody does something that violates your code, you *kill* him, and you don't think twice about it. But to come back to those two characters in *Deliverance*, I think the foremost fear of our time, especially with the growing crime rate, is of being set upon by malicious strangers, who would just as soon kill you as look at you. In fact, a lot of them would *rather*, you know. It's this being set upon by malicious strangers that's the focus of the novel.

MARCHANT: Your characters, all but one, take the law into their own hands because they're afraid the law won't be on their side.

DICKEY: It wouldn't be, either.

MARCHANT: Like Lewis' killing . . . so, as a writer are you really agreeing with the decisions your characters make?

DICKEY: I would have done the same thing they did, probably.

MARCHANT: You wouldn't have gone to the sheriff?

DICKEY: No, no, I wouldn't. Drew, the decent fellow of the bunch, wants to keep within the system, the moral and legal code of his time and place and country. Lewis doesn't want to. He thinks that these are essentially artificial and would work against them. If you murder a hillbilly, no matter what he was doing to you or a member of your party, if you shoot him in the *back* with an arrow, as Lewis does, you'd just better think twice before you commit yourself to being tried, up in those mountain communities that are inbred to the point of imbecility and albinoism, where everybody is everybody's kin. Lewis is right, you know. I would have felt exactly as Ed does.

MARCHANT: But the sheriff in the end seems to know very well what's gone on.

DICKEY: I don't think he knows *very* well, but he suspects. . . . Are you talking about Deputy Queen, the one who thinks they should be detained, or the one who lets them go?

MARCHANT: The one who lets them go.

DICKEY: Yes, the reader is meant to think that he probably knows that something happened. Ed says as he's leaving, "I hope Deputy Queen finds his brother-in-law." He says, "Oh, no, don't worry about him, he'll come in drunk. He's a mean guy anyway, and old Queen's sister'd be better off without him. So would everybody else." You are meant to suppose that Benson or whatever his name is has been pretty troublesome in the locality and Sheriff Bullard is sort of glad to get rid of him.

HEYEN: I was thinking that as you were writing the novel you must have developed a tremendous admiration for Ed, finally. He proves to be the strongest one, he proves to be the hero, and he's also the most sensitive one, I think.

DICKEY: Yes, I like Ed, you do get to like him, but I didn't want to paint him so that the reaction to him is overwhelmingly in his favor. He's got a lot of things wrong with him. But one of the things I wanted to do in *Deliverance* was to show the energizing of certain capacities in men which ordinarily do not have a chance to surface. I remember you spoke of John Berryman when he was at Brockport. I remember that he told me or wrote me—at least I credit this statement to him—that in this country a man can live his whole life without knowing whether he's a coward or not. And I think it's important to know.

MARCHANT: I had a mixture of feelings when I came to the end of the novel. I was so relieved to get out of that community and back to the suburbs, but I felt sad—the middle-aged tenderfeet gathering around that calm, civilized lake—and this is probably exactly the way you wanted me to feel.

DICKEY: It is.

IN NEW YORK

Craft Interview with *The New York Quarterly*

NYQ: *Deliverance* got us to thinking about the poet's writing novels—

DICKEY: Almost every poet feels like it's incumbent on him to try to write at least one. That was my situation.

NYQ: When did it start?

DICKEY: *Deliverance*? Or do you mean poets generally?

NYQ: Poets generally.

DICKEY: If you take enough time to try to write poetry, and you're serious about it, you build up considerable linguistic skill. The poor human creature, the poet, cannot help thinking that, in a culture that rewards written things as it does the works of certain novelists, it might be possible for him to subsidize his poetry-writing out of the proceeds of a successful novel. For example, Karl Shapiro just has a new book called *Edsel*, and I think this is one evidence of the tendency I'm describing. Hart Crane, in a letter somewhere, when somebody asks him why he doesn't write fiction, says, I've just never been able to think of anything with a plot. Neither have I, except *Deliverance*. It just seemed to work out.

NYQ: Was there any shift in adapting to a different form?

DICKEY: Not much; it was fascinating. What I missed at first was what I had depended on as a resource for a long time: the poetic line. You don't have that in prose; you have the sentence and the paragraph. But you don't have the rhythmical continuity of the line. And I missed that for a while. But then you get interested in the other resources, the prose resources, and what the paragraph can do, for example. You carry your poetic, your word-choice ability into that, instead of into the line.

NYQ: Now if we can go over to some other roles a poet has, aside from pure poetry—his working as critic, or as teacher. As critic, you said: "I am for the individual's reaction, whatever extraneous material it includes, and against all critical officialdom." (Preface, *Babel to Byzantium*) This was '65, '66—do you still feel the same way?

DICKEY: Exactly. There are some things in *Babel To Byzantium* that I was absolutely and dead a hundred percent, 180 degrees wrong about, but that wouldn't be one of them—yes, I do feel exactly like that. I was wrong about some of the poets I talked about. I've changed around about a good many of them.

NYQ: Is it something new that a critic is able to be so much more open about something like that now?

DICKEY: I think it is. And I think that *Babel To Byzantium* had something to do with this. At least I hope it did.

NYQ: Yes. We couldn't imagine certain critics in the post-war period making such a statement.

DICKEY: No. You have, of course, a literary critic like Yvor Winters, for example, and you know that this fellow feels that he cannot afford to be caught contradicting himself. That's too rigid. I think you should have different opinions at different times. The whole thing should be open and fluid, and not locked into some strait-jacket of a self-imposed critical system.

NYQ: The function of criticism has changed, because—

DICKEY: I hope it has.

NYQ: —because that was a pretty dogmatic and tight attitude.

DICKEY: It used to be more so than it is now.

NYQ: Now criticism seems to be more trying to—what? See into the poetry?

DICKEY: Why is it a critic can't say about a book or a poet, "I loved it last week; this week I dislike it"? Or, "I disliked it last week, but I'm crazy about it now." You know? Of course you can't have any system that way, but there's something about the human mind that insists on being dogmatic and systematic. I think it's a terrible mistake.

NYQ: We don't seem to have any people now who are trying for any kind of *definition* of poetry.

DICKEY: No.

NYQ: What poetry is.

DICKEY: No. Nobody will ever know what it is.

NYQ: You also mentioned, in that Preface, Auden's idea of a "censor."

DICKEY: Yes.

NYQ: Which you describe as—

DICKEY: But *he* changes, too.

NYQ: Yeah?

DICKEY: I don't mean Auden, but the censor.

NYQ: Along with the censor, you develop this idea: "the faculty or in-dwelling being which determines what shall and what shall not come into a poem, and which has the final say as to how the admitted material shall be used." You said that was derived from—Coleridge?

DICKEY: Or someone. Or not from someone.

NYQ: Is this—

DICKEY: It's what Coleridge calls the "architectonic" faculty.

NYQ: Is this something that can be taught? Or trained, or conditioned?

DICKEY: It can be trained to some extent, and conditioned to a large extent. But taught? I'm not sure about that. I'm a college professor, as so many of my generation are, and I work with students every day of my life, and I've never been able to decide that.

NYQ: No?

DICKEY: I think there are some sensibilities that a teacher of creative writing of a certain kind can be extremely good for. There are also certain ones that you can be death and destruction for, even though you're doing the best you can. You can turn out to be the worst possible influence they could ever have come onto. You know? And I've been both ways, lots of times. The teacher really isn't God, all he has is his own opinion—and as I say, opinions change.

NYQ: The younger generation now are teachers—

DICKEY: But I've been an awful lot of other things besides a teacher. I was an Air Force career man, I was a professional guitar instructor, I've been an awful lot of different kinds of things. But as Hemingway said somewhere, "The main problem for an American writer, or indeed for any writer, is to find a way to survive and get his work done." The University, for me, worked out badly at first. It works out badly at the lower levels, for the writer. But at the upper levels, where they let you have your way, it's good. But as a teacher of freshman English, controlled by the syllabus, supervised all the time—that's humiliating, and that's why I got out.

NYQ: This business of poetry workshops is, historically, a fairly modern thing. What do you feel is the value for a young person in going into a workshop to study under a known poet? Did you, looking back now on workshop experiences you may have had, feel they were very formative for you?

DICKEY: I never was in one. I've taught them, but I've never been in one. I have a feeling it would have been bad for me.

NYQ: Bad for you? Did you ever have the experience of a formal structure of criticism by your peers?

DICKEY: No, none at all. I developed completely in the dark, and very haphazardly.

NYQ: Do you feel there's too much emphasis now on group criticism?

DICKEY: Yes I do. I do workshop work, but I do it because so many people are doing it badly and destructively.

NYQ: We'd like to shift now to an article you wrote in 1965, called "Barnstorming for Poetry." That article described the poet as public reader, and we're curious to know how much you feel that experience may have had a subtle effect on the work you're doing now.

DICKEY: None.

NYQ: None at all.

DICKEY: None. I write an awful lot of poetry that's not suitable for public readings, and I don't write anything just to be able to get up there and read it.

NYQ: Do you feel the word placement in the poetic line has been at all altered by oral reading?

DICKEY: No.

NYQ: You imply there are a lot of traps in the economics of poetry readings.

DICKEY: Plenty.

NYQ: And in the frenetic pace which some poets might not be up to sustaining.

DICKEY: Well, it's killed a lot of them.

NYQ: And altered their style.

DICKEY: Yes.

NYQ: To what extent do poetry readings actually complement the center of a poet's concern?

DICKEY: Well, I've never really taken the time to think about that.

NYQ: You never feel nervous.

DICKEY: I tell you, yes I do feel—did you say menaced?

NYQ: Nervous. But menaced also.

DICKEY: Menaced, yes!

NYQ: At times you feel you might be getting—

DICKEY: Yes!

NYQ: —a little further away—

DICKEY: Yes!

NYQ: —from writing poetry.

DICKEY: Yes, I do, because it's fatally easy to fall into this business of doing nothing but going around giving readings.

NYQ: And then—

DICKEY: Because after you've gotten up to a certain level, like Lowell and Berryman maybe and a few others, where you can get these enormous fees, you not only figure that you really don't have to write any poetry any more, you figure that it's better if you don't.

NYQ: Yes?

DICKEY: Because the reputation that brings in this dough is already there, and if you write more stuff, you're just giving somebody a chance to bust you.

NYQ: Hemingway had that problem . . .

DICKEY: Sure he did.

NYQ: You have to keep the images straight, and see yourself basically as poet.

DICKEY: The only thing that's going to save you is the basic love of the thing itself: poetry. All this publicity, the dough, the women—especially them—are fatally easy to come by.

NYQ: Yes.

DICKEY: And a certain type of person is going to settle for that. I won't. I won't do that.

NYQ: If we can shift a bit. You use a phrase, a concept you call "presentational immediacy"—

DICKEY: That's a phrase of Whitehead's.

NYQ: Well, you describe it as "a compulsiveness in the presentation of the matter of the poem that would cause the reader to forget literary judgments entirely and simply experience." Does this have to do with the oral presentation of the poem?

DICKEY: No, I don't mean it in that sense. In fact, I'm using it in a different sense from Whitehead. No, I don't mean the presentation, say, from a reading platform. I mean, for words to come together into some kind of magical conjunction that will make the reader enter into a real experience of his own—*not* the poet's. I don't really believe what literary critics have believed from the beginning of time: that poetry is an attempt of the poet to create or recreate his own experience and to pass it on. I don't believe in that. I believe it's an awakening of the sensibilities of someone else, the stranger. Now if I said the word "tree," you and I would not see the same tree, would we?

NYQ: We're not sure.

DICKEY: What would you see—just as an experiment, what tree would you see?

NYQ: A very gnarled old oak tree that's been blasted by lightning.

DICKEY: I'd see a pine tree!

NYQ: Yes.

DICKEY: So if I use the word *tree* in a poem, this would be something that would bring out your gnarled oak tree to you, you know, when that wouldn't have been what *I* had in mind at all. It's an awakening of the sensibility of someone else. It's giving *his* experience to *him*. It's revitalizing his experience, rather than trying to pass yours on to him. You see what I mean?

NYQ: Yes. "Presentational immediacy," then, would be in the composition. It would also carry over into the performance, into the reading of it. You mentioned, about 1965, you said, "Of late my interest has been mainly in the conclusionless poem, the open or ungeneralizing poem, the un-well-made poem."

DICKEY: Now you know I didn't know what the hell I was talking about! It sounded good at the time! Well, I think what I did mean in that—the open, conclusionless poem—was that I was brought up on poetry that came essentially out of criticism. I was educated in the era of the New Criticism, and the neat poem with the smashing ending.

NYQ: Yes.

DICKEY: I think maybe we can do something else now. You know, you have to keep moving around. There's a certain type of poet who was young in the '40's, James Merrill was one, Wilbur was one, Anthony Hecht was one—fine writers, fine poets—but they got sold on that neat kind of poetic construction, and it turns out that the only work they've ever done that's good, that's remarkable, is what they've done to transcend what they were initially so good at.

NYQ: *NYQ* began as a reaction against a lot of what you were talking about: the University periodicals, quarterlies which were too entrenched. But we were talking about "presentational immediacy."

DICKEY: I've got to make a Whitehead reader out of you! If *you* can understand him, please tell *me*! He's the most difficult philosopher I've ever read.

NYQ: What about Heidegger?

DICKEY: Oh, but Whitehead's got so much more to him than Heidegger. When you read Whitehead, you know there's something going on up there, if you could just rise up to it. You just feel about Heidegger and his *dasein* and all of that business, that it's just philosophical jargon. I like philosophy, and try to read it when I can. At Vanderbilt I had a good professor, a disciple of Wittgenstein, named Christopher Salmon, who was an Englishman, and a very, very good teacher. I also took as much astronomy as I could.

NYQ: Great.

DICKEY: I didn't really get well into English until I went into graduate school.

NYQ: Was that on the conviction that you did not want to be exclusively in the English literature department?

DICKEY: Probably. I didn't want the kind of officialdom that that entails. At Vanderbilt I had the best teacher, the two best, the three best teachers I ever had. Old Salmon was one, who died this hideous, agonizing, humiliating death of cancer, rectal cancer. He was one of the three best, and another one was Monroe Spears—I don't know whether you know his work—he's an American literary critic, an 18th-century scholar. And the other one was my astronomy professor. His name was Carl Seifert. He was killed in an automobile accident, a couple of years after I left there. But he opened me up to the magic of the universe. He's the only person that I have ever encountered who had *feelings* about the universe. Most of us, you know, just take it for granted.

NYQ: Did you continue an interest in astrophysics?

DICKEY: Not as much as I wish I could. I always feel like I could get it back. I don't know if I could get the math back, but I could get some of it back. I used to do a lot of spectroscopy work, analyzing calcium lines.

NYQ: Could we look at an example now of "presentational immediacy"? There's an image in "The Lifeguard," two lines:

> Beneath me is nothing but brightness
> Like the ghost of a snowfield in summer.

Is this the beginning of what you would call "magical conjunction"?

DICKEY: Well, I would like to think so. A moonlit lake would be like a disappeared snowfield. You know how pure a field of snow is, not even a track on it, nothing to disturb its purity—that's what I tried to get, anyway. The ghost—it's disappeared, it's gone, it's not a lake, the snow's all gone, in summer, it's all melted—but if it were there, if it existed, it would look like this.

NYQ: Is there anything in its absence?

DICKEY: I hope so.

NYQ: Can we look at another image, in "The Movement of Fish," in these eight lines:

> Yet suddenly his frame shakes,
>
> Convulses the whole ocean
> Under the trivial, quivering
> Surface, and he is
> Hundreds of feet away,
> Still picking up speed, still shooting
>
> Through half-gold,
> Going nowhere. Nothing sees him . . .

This reads like onomatopoeia, as if you had actually recreated the sudden disappearance of the fish.

DICKEY: Yeah, you've seen fish do things like that; you don't know what's scared 'em, they just jump and they run like hell. There's nothing bothering 'em . . .

NYQ: So much of that seems to work through what you've done with the placement of the lines, that suddenly the fish is gone.

DICKEY: He is; *long* gone.

NYQ: Could we look at another image, this one from "The May Day Sermon," just a part of a line, the one describing the young man starting the motorcycle, and it's divided into units:

> . . . he stands up   stomps   catches   roars

Here the space units work in recreating the physical act of starting the motorcycle. Is this an example of what you couldn't do when you went over into prose, you couldn't try to recreate the river using unit phrases?

DICKEY: No, it wouldn't work. You know, I see that split line stuff that I've done, I'm not doing it any more, but I see it in almost every book of poetry that I pick up in bookstores. It's sometimes very effective, it's just like any other device, it's good when it's used rightly, and it's bad when it's used wrongly.

NYQ: Do you feel that about any theory of placement, like breath line or variable foot?

DICKEY: Well, it also has to be used with tact and intelligence. To get back to Coleridge, to get back to what we call the architectonic quality, you've got to know when to do it, and how to do it, and when not to do it.

NYQ: How long did the composition of "The May Day Sermon" take?

DICKEY: Years and years.

NYQ: "The May Day Sermon" doesn't seem cinematic, because it's so telescoped—there are so many images working at the same time. There's the sermon to the women, and the whipping of the girl, and the previous action of the sex with the motorcyclist—there are these several realities going on at the same time, it doesn't seem like it could be cut down to one plane for cinema.

DICKEY: If anything could be said good about that poem the best thing that I would like to have said about it is that in it, especially toward the end, there is an authentic frenzy.

NYQ: You seem to be a part of all of it.

DICKEY: Yeah, and the fog and the motorcycle. I'd love to *do* something like that, I'd like to be the guy on the motorcycle, I'd like to be the girl and the father, I'd like to be the chickens and the snake—

NYQ: The poem seems to be like Jeffers' "Apology for Bad Dreams," in that it begins with such a strong image; in the Apology it's the whipping of the horse—

DICKEY: Which is tied up by the nose or something like that—

NYQ: —but the Jeffers poem is more on a lineal plane, like he gives you the image, and then he gives you the meditation on the image, and then he gives you the statement.

DICKEY: You know, he's very underrated, isn't he? Jeffers. I'll tell you why I think so; I think he's one of the few American poets we've ever had who had an authentic sense of grandeur. Beside Jeffers, the poets that are paid so much attention to now are just so many scab-pickers, you know? They concentrate on their little hang-ups, and bitch about them. Those things exist, of course—but those gigantic schools of fish and those flights of birds, they also exist, in Jeffers' imagery! Marvelous *big* imagery, galaxies, oceans. They exist, too.

NYQ: Jeffers was writing out of a locale, a region, and you're also writing out of a specific locale and region. Is this some new kind of regionalism, different from Sandburg's and Frost's?

DICKEY: I don't know—people say so, but I don't really know. The fact of being a Southerner, as far as that conditions you as a writer, or conditions *me* as a writer, is simply an accident. I don't have anything doctrinaire to feel about it. I do not, for example, as the people who taught me did, as Donald Davidson and Allen Tate—people who were agrarians and had a political stance based on being Southerners, and a poetic stance, and sociological stance—I don't have anything like their orientation. I'm not like that. My Southernness or my regionalism or whatever you choose to call it is simply an accident. Now Wendell Berry is a fine poet, but he's much more of a Southerner than I am and attached to a locale. We need somebody like him, who really is rooted in the land and believes in it and lives on it and loves it and writes about it. Wendell Berry is the kind of writer that Jesse Stuart should have been, you know. But we need him, because the land is disappearing, and we're not going to do anything from now on except live in places like New York, those huge metropolises of chromium and glass.

NYQ: You once wrote: "To be a white Southerner in the mid-20th Century is to realize the full bafflement and complexity of the human condition."

DICKEY: It is; it still is.

NYQ: So that it becomes less a hard regionalism than an existential predicament.

DICKEY: Yes, that's essentially what it is. You cannot transcend your origins, no matter how much lip-service you give to political ideas. You cannot, no matter what.

NYQ: And the poet is—

DICKEY: He's a creature of gut reaction, he has to be. Your background is not my background. You might not feel what I feel. But with all the business now about race, and so on, Black Pride and Black Power and all of those things: the Blacks should have them. No man wants to feel helpless. Every man should have his pride.

NYQ: What about Black poetry?

DICKEY: I wish some really good Black poet would come along, but I haven't found him.

NYQ: Do you feel that political statements, or social statements, are concerns which are not the immediate business of the poet?

DICKEY: I think you must be eternally wary of poetry that has newspaper value, topical value, don't you think? Great poetry has been written, as we all know, out of the heat of public occasions, like Yeats' poetry, "Easter 1916," and those things. But the tendency now, with Robert Bly and some of these people like him, and Ginsberg, who's really not a poet at all, is simply to use poetry as an occasion for making speeches, which is a terrible, terrible mistake. People who go to those readings, and who seek out these authors on that basis, really don't care anything about poetry. If you go to a reading by Ginsberg, one of these awful group readings, and so on, you hear all this applause, say, where he works in material about Bobby Seale and the Chicago trial and the political conventions and that sort of business, and the audience applauds wildly. They're not applauding the guy's poetry, they're applauding themselves for holding the current fashionable social and political opinions that this guy gets up and tells 'em about. That has nothing to do with poetry.

NYQ: We'd like to get into some very practical aspects of being a poet. We gather your work takes gestation time before you actually start writing it down.

DICKEY: Yes; if I have one principle, rule of thumb, I guess you could say, as a writer, it's to work on something a long, long time. And try it a lot of different ways.

NYQ: Is this labor in actual drafts or worksheets?

DICKEY: One after the other. I tell you what you can do, and it might be interesting for you to do. Washington University Press has some of my papers, and they've got these huge stacks of three, four, five hundred pages of work on a single poem, and you could see what I did from that.

NYQ: A poem like "The May Day Sermon," we imagine, would have gone through a tremendous amount—

DICKEY: Two or three hundred drafts. And that's typing it out laboriously time after time.

NYQ: Most of your work is done at the typewriter?

DICKEY: Yes.

NYQ: How much work is done in longhand or pencil?

DICKEY: I do it any way. I attack the problem any way I can, but always end up with it undergoing the "trial by typewriter," as I call it.

NYQ: On your travels, you spend so much time on the road, do you carry a notebook?

DICKEY: I do, I don't use it very much, though. I also carry one of those tape things.

NYQ: Do you compose into the tape?

DICKEY: No, I do other kinds of writing on the tape. I have a new book out I did that way. It's called *Sorties*, which is a lot of journal entries and things taken off of tapes and also some new essays.

NYQ: What about dry periods, when you just are not able to get going?

DICKEY: No, there's never one of those. I've got so many ideas, I've got stacks of ideas and new projects and so on, enough for twenty lifetimes! Most of them will never be written. There's a sense in which you assign priorities: the poem that I just can't keep my hands off, that's the one I do.

NYQ: You never experience any blockage—

DICKEY: No, no, it's the opposite, I just don't have the time, enough *time*.

NYQ: We can finish, if you like.

DICKEY: Well, let's end up with one thing that I would like to make in a statement, a very simple and a childish and a naive kind of a statement. What you have to realize when you write poetry, or if you love poetry, is that poetry is just naturally the greatest thing that ever was in the whole universe. If you love it, there's just no substitute for it. I mean, you read a great line, or somebody's great poem, well, it's just *there*! I also believe that after all the ages and all the centuries and all the languages, that we've just arrived at the beginning of what poetry is capable of. All of the great poets: the Greek poets, the Latins, the Chinese, the French, German, Spanish, English—they have only hinted at what could exist as far as poems and poetry are concerned. I don't know how to get this new kind of sound, or this new kind of use in language, but I am convinced that it can be done by somebody, maybe not by me, but by somebody. I feel about myself as a "writer" like John the Baptist did, when he said, "I prepare the way for one who is greater than I." Yeah, but look who it was!

AT HOME: THE VOICES OF JAMES DICKEY

With Bruce Joel Hillman in *Writer's Yearbook*

WYB: You have said that you don't agree with T. S. Eliot's theory that the work and its creator are separate. Does this imply that your work leads us to you personally?

DICKEY: Well, in a way it does. There should be an aura of a distinct human personality which hovers around the words in some way. Maybe this is an illusion, but it is one of the basic illusions of art. Everyone has his own personal idea of Shakespeare, as he does of Jesus Christ.

WYB: So a careful reading of your work would give us a good idea of what you are like as man?

DICKEY: I think so. But it's important that it be different for different people. There should be for everybody some feeling that you're talking to an actual person instead of reading poems that have been arranged by a computer. You can read the poetry of Robert Lowell and tell exactly what he's like: very nervous, sort of uncertain, but a man with very violent emotions, and all torn-up and divided within himself—all this from the *way* he writes, aside from his choice of subject matter. You can tell a great deal from how a writer writes. You can tell almost as much about what he is trying to hide, maybe, as what he actually does get out. But the sense of the man, the enduring part of him, is in the poem.

WYB: So your enduring quality. . . .

DICKEY: Well, every poet hopes there is going to be something that will be enduring, but it has to be in the words. It is not like an actor or a movie star. So much of the actor's personality, someone like Burt Reynolds, is in the fact that he *is* a movie star, that he's around *right now*. The actor's lot is very time-bound. The poet's situation is somewhat analogous to that, but not exactly. Words are a different sort of medium. They are extremely private in that when you read a poem, you're forming your own inner vision of what the poem gives you to form a vision about. In a movie, everything is right there in front of you. The poem gives you something that by means of the poem you give yourself. If I say river and you call an image of a river to mind, your river and mine would not be the same, probably not even the same color.

WYB: It's interesting that you mentioned Robert Lowell. *The Atlantic* called you two the only major poets working in English today and. . . .

DICKEY: Somebody else said that; *we* most certainly didn't. I really don't like those pieces where they compare you to some other writer. There really is no competition among poets, at least not between the poems. There may be a bit of ego competition among the poets, because they're human, but poetry really should not be a competitive thing. After all, Robert Lowell and I are not running in the Olympic games against each other. We're trying to say something that is unique to us. He says things his way and I mine. People go to either poet for what may be in it for them, the readers. And that is the unique experience of a poem, which can come only from one person or the other, as the case may be. You bring to it what you have.

WYB: Are you disciplined?

DICKEY: In some ways, yes. Not so much in the day-to-day routine of living, and I believe that chance is very strong in any poet's writing. Even a mistake of some sort will lead to something that's maybe not a mistake, or at least not as much of a mistake.

As far as working on things in a sort of determined way for a long time, that I do. I will not let a subject go until I have got it as close to what I think it ought to be as is humanly possible. I work by successive drafts. You never finish a poem; you abandon it. You should work hard to get as close as you can, not to some idea of perfection you had before the poem was begun, but an idea of perfection that develops as you work and work on the poem. It's different and usually better than what you had originally conceived.

I use the same approach on all works, whether poetry or prose: I tacitly assume that the first 50 ways I try it are going to be wrong. Yet, the essential thing is to make it seem inevitable, to take all the sense of labor out of it. I very much believe in the principle of superabundance and the attendant principle of cutting back.

I write out of subjects. Some poets urge you to give the initiative to words, to go where words take you. I generally will work out of situations and bring the words to that situation, instead of working from the words outward to the situation.

I am experience-oriented, rather than word-oriented. Or rather, I have been up until now. I'm sort of interested in trying the other way, to see what there might be in that.

WYB: Are you working at that now?

DICKEY: Yes, some. The new book has at least partly the other approach to it.

WYB: That would be *Puella*?

DICKEY: Yeah, it's *Puella* now. It began as *Flowering*, when I thought I was going to be working with an artist on it, then changed to *Deborah Puella*, and now *Puella*. It's unusual, not at all like the other books. In it, I undertook a difficult, but fascinating, task, which was to write a series of 19 poems about a young girl moving from childhood through the gateway into womanhood, to try to catch the changes in her life, her thinking, the things she does. I can't really *imagine* what a boy would feel like in that time of life, because I *know* it too well. Here I have to imagine the world of a young girl. To a poet, at least for my kind of poet, that's much better: to have to create the effect entirely from imagination.

Some people occasionally say, "Why don't you write more poems like those in *Buckdancer's Choice*?" I don't want to write like that. All the poems I wanted to write that were like I wanted to write when I wrote *Buckdancer's Choice* are *in Buckdancer's Choice*. Self-imitation is not right for me. I would rather make some mistakes than be repetitive. If I can't take a chance on what I write, do something different, well, then writing has no interest for me at all.

WYB: You have said, "Failure is the most creative thing about the poetic process, if you learn what to do with it." How do you turn it from disadvantage to advantage?

DICKEY: Well, this will only happen after you've been writing—and failing—for a good long time. Then you develop a kind of critical sense about what you write. You can tell when something is good, but it would be just as good in somebody else's work too. You want to hold out for those things only *you* can say. You satisfy these two criteria: one, something that only you could say, and two, that you judge is good *even* though it's something only you could say. These are rare times when you get something like that, but you can tell. You know it when you think to yourself, "Did I say that?" And then the other part of your brain answers, "Yes, I did. And nobody else could have." That's when you know you're on to something.

WYB: I have heard you say that you believe in a poet writing a great deal and publishing a comparatively small fragment of it. . . .

DICKEY: Yes, I believe in that very much. The main thing is to write a lot to keep yourself immersed in the subject of poetry, to stay deep in its creative possibilities.

WYB: How much unpublished Jim Dickey material is there?

DICKEY: Oh, God, hundreds of items! One of the university libraries wanted to look at my papers, my correspondence. My literary executor was showing them through the files, and there are 20 or 25 full boxes of unpublished manuscripts. I had saved them all because I thought I would eventually go back through them and be able to use the ideas for other things. But now I know I can't do that. The new stuff is coming in at such a great rate that I don't need to go back to the old stuff. I wish I could; I wish there was that much time. I had some ideas that I flubbed very badly, and I might not do so badly on them now, maybe. But I've got new things that are always coming in and I've got to give the best of them a chance.

WYB: How do you choose that which you're going to publish?

DICKEY: I publish the things that seem to me to have solved some of the problems I set for myself, or which have a particular distinctiveness about them. I ask myself if I can truthfully say I had initially a good idea for a poem, and that I did fairly well by it. So many times I end up thinking, "I never found the form for this one. This was initially a good concept, but I was not able to realize it." That happens a good deal to me. But you can't know what will eventually work out until you try. And you should try a lot, and very hard, and very long.

WYB: You say the process goes on all the time, even in sleep. That you never have any layoff periods . . .

DICKEY: This is true.

WYB: . . . and that you are "one of those slow, plodding, searching writers."

DICKEY: Amen. I think the tragedy of my poetic generation is that people are willing to let stuff go and be published simply because there are people who can and will publish it. The bookstores are flooded with forgettable books that are good, but not good enough. They just don't make it around the bend into the area of being good, or memorable, or with luck, even unforgettable. Many are called good books, but few really are.

WYB: You told me that when you were asked to read "The Strength of Fields" at Jimmy Carter's inauguration, you considered it an obligation to use it as a forum for promoting poetry, the "neglected art," and that it would have been an act of cowardice not to take the opportunity.

DICKEY: I still think so.

WYB: Do you feel a continuing obligation to promote poetry?

DICKEY: In some sense, yes. Of course, it is the discipline I live by, and to a certain extent for, and naturally I have an interest in what happens to it. Poetry is, I think, the highest medium that mankind has ever come up with. It's language itself, which is a miraculous medium which makes everything else that man has ever done possible.

WYB: You have said you came to poetry because it is your "essential nature" to be a poet. Yet, you didn't write your first poem until you were 24, and didn't publish your first volume until you were 37. Are you saying you were born a poet, but took 24 years to realize it?

DICKEY: There may be something to that. I think that if you have to have a definition of a poet, then a poet is someone for whom words have a maximum of significance.

WYB: You have written just about every kind of writing there is—poetry, advertising, novels, screenplays. . . .

DICKEY: I guess so, including a little music. I haven't written any outright journalism, though; that is, I don't believe I've *reported* anything.

WYB: Although you did cover the Apollo moonshot for *Life* magazine. . . .

DICKEY: I did, that's true, but I did it in verse.

WYB: Perhaps that's just another kind of journalism, adapted to your own *way* of reporting.

DICKEY: Maybe it is. I'd like to think it is because some of my best friends think that journalism, including the interview, is the great art form of our time. Norman Mailer does, and so does George Plimpton, and they are both superb at it, as is Tom Wolfe.

WYB: You have called poets "more human" than other people. . . .

DICKEY: Well, maybe; but they are more attuned to the connections between language and things, existence and experience. Words have the capacity for these people to change reality, to deepen it, to make it more meaningful and perhaps mysterious. For the poet, composition is the making of a spell of some sort.

WYB: Can you be a part-time poet?

DICKEY: Yes, I think so. Of course, the composition of poetry is different for different people. Myself, I couldn't be anything but a fulltime poet. But someone—Max Beerbohm, I believe—said the difficult thing about being a poet is finding what to do with the other 23½ hours in the day.

But that isn't the way it is with me. Sitting and staring at a manuscript in the same place and in the same physical position is not right for me. I need to have something in the typewriter that I have gotten down in white heat, and then leave it for a while and go on to something else before going back to it. It is amazing how quickly you can then see what to do with it: this should come out, you shouldn't encourage that to happen in this poem, but it would be OK to try out a little bit in this direction. It's kind of a shakedown process.

WYB: Which is why you keep three and four typewriters with three and four projects scattered around the house?

DICKEY: Yeah, sure. Because in some weird way the projects will tend to help each other. The best artists I've known wouldn't work on just one canvas at a time, either. They'd have four or five right in line in their studios.

WYB: You make a lot of connections between the visual arts and poetry, not to mention your collaborations with artists like *Jericho*. Is there some relation here for you?

DICKEY: Well, no, except that painters are makers of visual images, and poets make mental ones. I like images; I love pictures. I am very visually oriented. But I would be a very good blind man, too, because the tactile sense is very strong in me. Hearing is also important, but on the other hand, I have no sense of smell at all. None. So I am a blind man in my nose.

WYB: So do you avoid sense-of-smell images in your work?

DICKEY: I can't have any. If I tried, I'd have to guess.

WYB: In *Self-Interviews*, you wrote that you have only one criterion for what will eventually become the subject of a poem: something that keeps recurring for no apparent reason. Do you mean your poems sort of filter up from the subconsciousness into conscious thought?

DICKEY: Yeah, I think so. You drop something, say an incident that will eventually become a poem or a novel, either deliberately or undeliberately into what Henry James calls "the deep well of unconscious cerebration." And later on, you bring it back up and it has undergone a metamorphosis. The unconscious has worked on it in some way, transformed it.

WYB: Is that work, part of the writing strategy?

DICKEY: I think it is. It's not a conscious part. It's very much an unconscious part. I can remember many things in my work that were that way, and they came out as different from what the actual experience was. It's a commentary, sort of. Like the war poems, some of them based on actual incidents. A long poem of mine, "The Firebombing," for instance, is not based on any one mission I flew. It is a composite of several different ones, plus a lot of invention that seemed to go with the other stuff.

WYB: Does that sort of process lead to a lot of 3 a.m. wake-ups to get something down?

DICKEY: Yes, it does. I do that often. If it wouldn't wake my wife I would use a recorder where I could talk out the essential things. But I don't usually sit up all night. One of the essential ingredients for a writer, particularly a writer like myself, is to keep the energy-level fairly high. My first orientation into adult life was athletics, and there is a lot that can be learned from sports. Especially about pacing yourself.

WYB: To relate to that, you have said that when something looks close to being finished, you're capable of 17-hour stretches at the typewriter.

DICKEY: Yes; then I want to go full-blast on that and nothing else. When I see, or think I see, the well-known light at the end of the tunnel, I want to *get* there. Even so, when I think I've got there I sit for a while and chances are I'll fiddle and fool with it some more. But if the essential of it is down, that's a great, great feeling: if you think it's got the qualities of being good all the way through. If you see that with luck, and a lot more work, you can get the thing where no word can be changed without diminishing the piece: when you see you have a situation like that, you want to push.

WYB: Did you push hard to finish *Puella*?

DICKEY: Yes, to finish it. To finish strong. You know, finishing is a very important part of the race, sometimes almost more important than winning. To finish; to finish strong and on your feet.

WYB: You have mentioned that you're pacing yourself better these days. . . .

DICKEY: Yes, I'm always falling back on that notion of pacing, which I used to feel was not so important as I do now. I'm almost sixty. If you haven't learned to pace yourself in a creative way by that time, you never will.

Also, another element ends up being part of the scene—drinking. When you go hard and constantly, liquor is going to enter into your efforts to keep things going. It is a good short-range stimulant, but it's death and damnation if you apply it as medicine. Your body cannot stand up under constantly going all-out, and you're wearing out physically, and you're getting older and trying to hold it all together with alcohol. James Agee was a great all-night talker and drinker, and that's what killed him at the age of 45. I used to drink a lot, and I enjoyed it enormously. And if I had it to do over again and I didn't injure my health, I would do it again—or twice as much. But it begins to get to the point where there *is* harm, and you can tell. But when you get to that point, you're usually in too deep to get out of it easily. And so, when I saw that was likely to happen in my case, I left it. I don't drink anything now but an occasional beer.

WYB: So it's only fairly recently that you have been so taken with the idea of pacing yourself.

DICKEY: Yes, and I'm getting more down on the page. That's where my immortality is going to lie, if anywhere: in what I've put down, not what I've said at some bull session or cocktail party. Besides, I love to write. Writing is an obsession with me. I have a plain and simple fascination with words. There are so many combinations of possibilities! I love the sound of words. The English language is the greatest medium for communication in-depth or in any other way that has ever been devised. It is the perfect language for poetry; you couldn't get a better one. It's got many great advantages and only one or two disadvantages.

WYB: And what would those be?

DICKEY: The main disadvantage is that it's rhyme-poor compared to something like French or Italian. But if you don't write rhyming poetry, that's no disadvantage. And even if you do write rhymed verse, there are poets who feel, like Auden, stimulated and challenged because of the paucity of rhymes in English. Auden thinks that's a source of strength to the formal poet.

WYB: Do you use tools of the trade, say like rhyming dictionaries?

DICKEY: I'm sparing in the use of such things, although a thesaurus is a different matter entirely. I also will read through dictionaries for fun, particularly that huge thing that comes with a magnifying glass attached because the entries are so small: the O.E.D. That's one of the best gifts I ever received. Reading a dictionary, or just perusing it, locks you into words. To be immersed in the element—words—is extremely important for a poet.

I am an inveterate notebook keeper because being one is good practice. But I also read a great deal and I am very interested in interviews with poets as a good way to gain insight. This is kind of the age of the interview and nobody likes to give out interviews more than poets do. Consequently, there are hundreds of interviews with poets on this side of the Atlantic and in England and elsewhere. Some surprising things come out.

I also advise poets to become great readers of newspapers. Every issue is full of items of much bizarre interest. This is the sort of thing which engages my attention for a potential poem: I read once, years ago, about this guy in the 19th century who had just been married and had a son. He was exploring Upper Siberia where they found that mammoth in the glacier. Now, this is almost too pat to be true, but it is true. Well, he fell into a crevasse and his body was left in glacier ice. Years later, at 36, the son was exploring the same area and found the father. He, too, like the mammoth, was preserved. You have this curious situation of the son getting the father out of the ice, and the father is 15 years younger than the son is. He looks younger; he *is* younger! Now that would make for a good idea for a poem.

WYB: You have said that you have a horror of backsliding, of not being as good in whatever you're doing this year as you were last year.

DICKEY: Yes, I've thought about that, and you can never really tell. And when you've published as much as I have, and you get to be about my age, there are going to be people who want you to do what they are familiar with. They inevitably say, "He's slipping, he's not as good as he used to be," or "His early work was much better," and so on. But I really don't care about being as good as, or not as good as, or better than. That is not my primary consideration. My primary consideration is to *change*. I dare not use the word *grow*; there may or may not be growth involved, but to change. To still keep that openness, that chance taking-ness as part of the work. Not to be afraid to make a mistake, even if it's a long and costly mistake.

The whole tragedy of the American poets of my generation is that they were afraid to change, most of them. Lowell did it to some extent. Roethke did it, but even he was beginning to repeat himself badly at the end. What I want is to be willing to fail, rather than stagnate. That's what keeps poetry exciting for me. Not only to do something that nobody else has done before, but to do something which *I* haven't done before. There are so many selves in everybody, and just to explore and exploit one is *wrong*, dead wrong, for the creative person. He must get more selves to speak up in different voices.

Commencements and Other Tentatives

COMPUTERIZED RAPE AND THE VALE OF SOUL-MAKING

University of South Carolina Commencement, 1 June 1968

As graduation addresses go, this one will be so short that I might even feel justified in calling it, not a speech but an anti-speech, or, using the even more popular prefix, a non-speech.

It is directed into a particular and peculiar kind of limbo, the never-never land between university graduation and a full entry into the work that one fancies one wishes to spend the rest of one's life doing.

But I had better change that. The choice has been made a great deal earlier than the moment of getting the diploma, the moment of entering into the new job, for the job is a direct result of the education that leads to it. So, within a certain range of possibilities, it is not so much the job that one chooses to take, but the job that one *must* take.

For we are nothing if not specialists. That is the secret of our success. That is why we can transplant hearts and explore—and eventually exploit—the bottom of the sea, and set up bombing platforms in space. That is why we can release the energy of blind matter and utilize the radiance of the sun in ways that the sun never dreamed of.

But we are also an age of discontented specialists. I will not recount the evidences of our discontent; I will simply refer you to the newspapers. Any newspaper on any day, or any time of day.

We creatures of the twentieth century are, for better or worse, two things: specialists, and, as a result of our specialization, prisoners and beneficiaries of a kind of half-benevolent, half-indifferent economic concentration camp. We are all committed to it, and we are all victimized and rewarded by it. We live and die within its walls because, for us, that is all there is. Even the attempts to escape or drop out of it, to flee from it in hippie beads, by means of bohemian communes, drugs, or by any other means, are still made possible by the system itself, and could not exist without it. What we call civil violence—and non-violence—are enacted against its background. Rebellion would have no context without it.

Though various kinds of modifications in the science-dominated economic system we live in will be tried, the system will never change basically of itself, so long as its results are as spectacular and profitable as they have always been: that is, so long as it *works*, and continues to create and dominate its own environment: so long as it keeps us alive and reasonably well-fed, keeps us busy and amused; so long as it *keeps* us.

So we are specialists. Some of you will be—no; some of you already *are* scientists. Some are businessmen: those scientists of the smile and the handshake, the territory and the credit card. Some will be artists of one kind or other, and some—a few, perhaps, according to their lights—will be criminals. I myself—an ignorant man, almost a poet, as Santayana said of himself—am also a specialist: a specialist of sensibility and of words, a specialist of incantations and spell-casting, which is to say, a failed magician.

How did all this come to be? It came to be because a tradition evolved, and when it reached us, we inherited it. It came to be because our ethic and our religion died, and we were left with nothing but money. We were left, as Mark Schorer says, "with a life that is motivated solely by economic need, and a life that is measured at last by those creature comforts that, if we gain them, allow us one final breath in which to praise the Lord."

My generation fought World War II, and some were also in the Korean, or first hot cold war. What did we want? Why did we fight? Did we believe in something new coming of it, as anyone who is prepared to shed his blood and give his life feels he is entitled to do? Or did it seem only a matter of necessity? If so, of *what* necessity? And, since we won, why did we not hand on to the newer generations, such as yourselves, whatever . . . whatever it was the new generation tells us, twenty-five years later, we should have been fighting for?

Part of the answer to this is that the structure of any particular society does not change that abruptly *ever*, except in violent revolution or military defeat. In victory it does not change. Those who won are only too happy to recover and return to things as they were.

Another reason, however, lies in the continuity of tradition, watched over by the vested interests of the society. When T. E. Lawrence wrote the first draft of his *Seven Pillars of Wisdom*, an account of his part in the Arab Revolt of World War I, he spoke bitterly but with resignation of this. Lawrence had hoped for the creation of a united Arab state, but at the peace table this idea was overturned—or, as Lawrence and Winston Churchill thought, betrayed. Speaking of the desert war and its aftermath, Lawrence wrote (and I may be misquoting a word or two here, for I am quoting strictly from memory):

> We sacrificed everything in those whirling campaigns, and spared nothing of ourselves. But when victory was achieved, the old men took from us the triumph that was ours. Youth could win, but had not learned to keep, and was pitiably weak against age. We stammered that we had fought for a new heaven and a new earth, and they took from us the victory we had shed our blood for, and made it into a likeness of the world they knew. Doubtless, when we are their age, we shall serve our children so.

But is there nothing else but this? Is there nothing but the idealism of youth betrayed, generation after generation, by the caution and the entrenched power of the old? In our case—or more specifically, in *your* case—is there nothing but the passing on of a man-killing competitiveness and a specialization that yields more and more material and physical benefits—comfort and health, not necessarily in that order—and fewer and fewer reasons for them? Modern medicine, for example, can save your life. But can medicine—even psychiatry—make it *worth* saving? After all, you don't want to "learn to live with it"—the phony panacea of medicine men: you want your life to matter: you want to be whole. And if this is not possible physically, you certainly want it to be true spiritually.

Ultimately then, life—any individual life—is a question of values: of the values that the individual either accepts from an outside source or engenders within himself, from whatever means. And values, in turn, are a question of . . . of the self. And the self is a function—if a poet may borrow for a moment a mathematical term he has no right to use—the self is a function of what I should like to call the "range of response."

Wherever we are, the potential range of response is always very great, and includes not only a response to what is there in front of us but in addition all the associations, memories, images, fantasies and trains of thought that it evokes: that it evokes in us alone: *alone*. These associations are things that have to do with the self, or with what used to be called, in the days before scientific terminology laid such a *complete* hold on us, the soul.

John Keats, who is for me one of the great human presences in the whole of history, wrote in a letter:

> The common cognomen of this world among the misguided and superstitious is a "vale of tears," from which we are supposed to be redeemed by a certain arbitrary interposition of God and taken to Heaven. What a little circumscribed straitened notion! Call the world if you please a vale of Soul-making. There may be intelligences or sparks of divinity in millions, but they are not souls till they acquire identities, till each one is personally itself. The world is . . . a system of spirit-creation. Do you not see how necessary a world of pains and troubles is to School an intelligence and make it a Soul? Man . . . is formed by circumstance—and what are these but the touchstones of his heart? And what are the touchstones but the provings of his heart? And what are the provings of his heart but the fortifiers or the alterers of his nature? And what is his altered nature but his soul?

Keats is arguing in favor of a valid emotional life: for *real* rather than stereotyped reactions, for a willing and outgoing sensibility, for a greater accessibility to experience, for a greater range of response. He is arguing in favor of a large and vivid—and also a deep—

participation in a wider and wider circle of *kinds* of experience, for variety and whatever we can learn from it. And he is against, as *we* should be, a desultory non-participation in a narrow, stultifying and prisoner-like activity that reduces the potential richness of human existence to a useful conditioned reflex. Men working in factories have thought and written like lords of the world, lords of the Word, and rich playboys with nothing but money, time and women have killed themselves out of enforced sterility and inconsequence.

I am not holding a brief for adversity as "ennobling," or anything of that specious sort. But I *am* saying that the only thing that can save us from the state of affluent "invincible apathy" we are drifting toward is a new awareness of what inner resources actually *do* lie within the minds of any individual human being: that each of us has, or can have, not only because of what he is—already is—but because of what he may, by means of these inner resources, become.

For the tragedy of modern man, the tragedy of his productive specialization, is not so much the environment he has created by means of it, but is what might be called the rape of his sensibility: the dreadful mental and physical laziness that has descended on him: that he feels entitled to. Our vaunted leisure is in reality a terrible kind of psychic laziness, an unspeakable sloth of the spirit that kills off everything—the aliveness of sensibility and the capacity to respond deeply and fully—that the leisure ought to guarantee, and the individual ought to hold out for as his birthright and his due.

For, as Keats says, the self—or the soul—does not exist until we create it; does not exist *unless* we create it. The materials from which we create it matter—matter greatly, of course. But these can be found anywhere that we find ourselves. It can be found on the west-coast docks of Eric Hoffer as well as in the bull-ring of Hemingway. It can be found in the biology labs of New Orleans as well as in the revolutionary China of Malraux.

We don't see enough, respond enough, feel enough. The next time you happen to look up and see a bird in a wind trying to land on a telephone wire, look—really *look*—at that bird; you haven't seen him yet.

André Gide, the French novelist, moralist, immoralist and philosopher, was always profoundly concerned by the "incompleteness" of man. He believed that man is whatever he will eventually make of himself: his possibilities are limited only by his unfortunate eagerness to accept ready-made definitions.

And yet, as Gide also believed, "man is inexhaustible." So, I myself believe, is the individual man, so long as he lasts. In his inexhaustibility lies his salvation, but he must *use* it. And therein lies the true and creative nature of twentieth century revolt. For it is no good to throw out the window penicillin and plastic arteries, the turbo-jet, the cyclotron and the computer. Getting rid of these things will not give us back our wholeness. They are possible parts of it. It is no good to retreat, infant-like, into a sucking on the teat of chemical fantasies, no good to cop out on drugs, no good to indulge in a pious "rejection" of what you don't have the guts to change. The truly productive revolt is the revolt within the individual sensibility, in the refusal to allow the "new environment," which is only an intensification of the old environment, to stultify the creative responsiveness of the single human being, who is me, who is you, who is anybody alive enough to stand up and see lightning and hear thunder—though, come to think of it, even *these* conditions are not prerequisites. What we need is an enormous new openness. We need to admit that there is no category of things to which one must respond in an official way. There are philosophies of nihilism and of the most repellent human attitudes which may yield profound human insights; much of twentieth century literature, for example, is based on these. We must at all costs end the *officialdom of response* thrust continually upon us by the mass media, by society, by the world we live in.

For what matters finally is just the "accessibility to experience" of which Henry James spoke, almost a century ago. We must realize that to any and all of us, the whole range of response and feeling possible to us as human beings, is *always* possible, at any time and at any place, if it truly rises and we don't suppress it in the name of some vastly inferior ideal: some notion engendered by the suburbs or the Kiwanis Club or the American Legion or the Baptist Church.

Sympathy increases with receptiveness. Enthusiasm increases as awareness grows sharper and deeper.

As I said earlier, the external world will be what it is. What can change is not it, but us. We can both enter more deeply than we do into those activities we have chosen to undertake—our particular specialties—and at the same time we can refuse to be limited by them; we can transcend them; we can perch with the bird on the wire. What can change is not the environment, the world men have made by their specialities, but men. And with *that* change, we really *may* change the world. As Ezra Pound said, "The oak does not grow for the purpose or with the intention of being built into ships and tables, yet a wise nation will take care to preserve the forests. It is the oak's business to grow good oak."

GUILT AS BLACKMAIL
—Remarks on Some Qualities of Life—
Wesleyan College Commencement, 1971

"How can you possibly stand there and eat that ice-cream cone when children are being firebombed in Viet Nam?" We are guilty: you are guilty, I am guilty, America is guilty, the world is guilty. And there are plenty of people to tell us so. You might have sacrificed all your life to send your son to medical school. You might belong to the board of directors of the SPCA. You might never have done an unkind act in your life, said an unkind word, thought an unkind thought. No matter; you are guilty. So am I. So is America. So is the world. We are guilty partly because the human race is in deep trouble, and we are part of the human race. But that is not the whole story. Whether we are good people or bad—and most of us are somewhere in between—we belong to what I call the Age of the Moral Put-down: or, even better, The Age of Moral Blackmail. This is especially noticeable among intellectuals, though in one form or other, it runs through all levels of society. We are constantly being told that we are indeed our brother's keeper. And the keeper not only of our brother, but his family, his nation, his earth. And of course that is true. Men make their fate, and must live by their decisions, no matter what the consequences of these may turn out to be. I have no quarrel with that assumption; none at all. But what I do object to is the permeating poison of the guilt *climate.* I object to moral blackmail: I object to the person who tries to coerce me into agreeing with his political views by threatening to call me a fascist if I do not.

Dostoyevsky once said that he could find no peace as long as a single child was dying of typhoid fever. That is a noble statement; I never read it without being profoundly moved. It could only have been spoken by a sensitive, saintly man. But it is asking too much of the human condition. It is, in its way, a contributing factor in making for this climate of guilt that I am trying to describe. It is so because it assumes the possibility of perfection in human affairs. It assumes that if there were no disease—at least no typhoid fever—men would be free of terror, and, yes, free of guilt: of belonging to a race of beings whose children sometimes die in terrible suffering. I myself profoundly wish that typhoid fever and all other diseases could be eradicated forever. My own brother died of meningitis, and my mother and father and the rest of the family have felt the loss in anguishing ways ever since. He died before I was born, and even so I have never ceased to feel his absence. But this does not mean that because of his death I have never felt joy, exaltation, caprice, foolish fun: it does not mean that I have never enjoyed eating an ice-cream cone. And it does not mean that because the mysterious, perhaps unfathomable way in which the universe is put together is what it is, including the senseless and hideous death of my brother, I must bear the universal guilt of being a part of the universe in which such senseless and brutal and incomprehensible things occur. I think that it would have been better for Dostoyevsky to have eaten a few ice-cream cones every now and then, instead of gambling and drinking all the time! My point here is this: that if we wait for perfection—medical perfection, political perfection, perfection of international policy, perfection of any and all kinds touching upon human affairs—we have doomed ourselves and our emotional lives irrevocably. Those perfections are not forthcoming. We must find our joys, our exaltation, among the conditions where we find ourselves, no matter what these may be.

I issue no call for "the new complacency." I believe that we should do our best to right the wrongs that very obviously exist, in America and in the world. I believe we should conquer cancer and, if possible, all other diseases. I believe we should even do our best to conquer death itself, which, I am told, is now at least theoretically possible, and may eventually be practically possible. I agree with Jean-Paul Sartre that man should act, and he *must* act, and his culture and his personal life should reflect their most inventive and humane side, if any of us is going to survive at all. These things we all know. I want all of us to live forever, to love each other, to have a true human community.

But we're not going to have that without some kind of knowledge of limits, some acceptance of what we really can do, and an equal acceptance of what lies beyond us, and what is manifestly impossible to us. When I was a boy, I remember hearing it said that Thomas Edison remarked that if he had devoted his life to it, he could have established communication with the world of spirits, the world of the dead. Now, that is fascinating; I have been enthralled by this idea all my life. According to his idea, if Edison had not invented the electric light bulb and the record-player, but had concentrated all his energies on this other project, I might have been able to speak to my dead brother! And yet, one knows—or *thinks*, perhaps I should say—that such a thing is not possible. More than anything else, we need to set possible goals. The French writer Albert Camus, as eloquent an essayist as we have had in our benighted century, says, at the end of his book on the spirit of rebellion called *L'Homme Revolté:*

> In this noon of thought, the rebel disclaims divinity in order to share in the struggles and destiny of all men. We shall choose Ithaca, the fruitful land, frugal and audacious thought, lucid action, the generosity of the man who understands. In the light, the earth remains our first and last love. Our brothers are breathing under the same sky; justice is a living thing. Now is born that strange joy which helps one live and die, and which we shall never again renounce to a later time. On the sorrowing earth it is the unresting thorn, the bitter food, the harsh wind off the sea, the ancient dawn forever renewed. With this joy, through long struggle, we shall remake the soul of our time, and a Europe [and I would say America here] which will exclude nothing. Not even that phantom Nietzche who, for twelve years after his downfall, was continually invoked by the West as the ruined image of its loftiest knowledge and its nihilism; nor the prophet of justice without mercy who rests, by mistake, in the unbelievers' plot in Highgate Cemetery; nor the deified mummy of the man of action in his glass coffin; nor any part of what the intelligence and energy of Europe have ceaselessly furnished to the pride of a contemptible period. All may indeed live again, side by side with the martyrs of 1905, but on condition that they shall

> understand how they correct one another, and that a limit, under the sun, shall curb them all. Each tells the other that he is not God; this is the end of romanticism. At this moment when each of us must fit an arrow to his bow and enter the lists anew, to reconquer, within history and in spite of it, that which he owns already, the thin yield of his fields, the brief love of this earth, at this moment when at last a man is born, it is time to forsake our age and its adolescent rages. The bow bends; the wood complains. At the moment of supreme tension, there will leap into flight an unswerving arrow, a shaft that is inflexible and free.

So let us not ask the impossible of ourselves, and turn on our neighbor because the impossible is beyond anyone's power to achieve. I believe very much in social action. But I will not have the few moments of joy in the only life I will ever have contaminated by people who profess to find me guilty of the ills of the world, of creating the problem of racial discrimination, of firebombing children in Asia. Margaret Mead, the anthropologist, said last week in a debate with James Baldwin that she will work to right wrongs, but will not suffer guilt for acts she did not commit and thoughts she did not think. In reference to the dropping of the atomic bomb on Hiroshima, she says, "I am absolutely certain that if I had been asked I would have said not to drop it. I have no doubt, and therefore I have no guilt . . . I don't say because I'm an American I share the guilt of what America did when I didn't know it was doing it."

Nevertheless the world is full of people who are quite willing to poison your life, take away your moments of abandonment and joy, and gut you emotionally with the knife of *their* assumption of *your* guilt. And that is a wrong thing for us to be doing to each other. The last thing we need at this point in our history is to set on each other and attempt to show, privately, but more like publicly, how much more moral I am than you are. This practice, no less than many other of our ills, is a product of the ego: of essentially weak people who think that if they put you down in this manner, then they are of necessity up. It is, in fact, in itself one of the most immoral kinds of action possible, and it is a strange and in some ways amusing paradox that all this poses as morality.

We have enormous energies in this country, but we must see the situation among us for what it is, or they will be lost, and the real good that we could do together will be dissipated. Let us see the age of moral blackmail for exactly what it is. And let us keep our individual joy and our moments of release and abandon, which have nothing whatever to do with firebombing. What we want more than anything else is a sense of our personal worth, and it is only the weak and cowardly who attempt to get a synthetic form of this from imposing a sense of guilt in others. Thomas Wolfe says, in a slightly different context, but in words which might very well have been written for this particular occasion:

> Such is the nature of the struggle to which henceforth our lives must be devoted. Out of the billion forms of America, out of the savage violence and the dense complexity of all its swarming life; from the unique and single substance of this land and life of ours, must we draw the power and energy of our own life, the articulation of our speech, the substance of our art.
>
> For here it seems to me in hard and honest ways like these we may find the tongue, the language, and the conscience that as men and artists we have got to have. Here, too, perhaps, must we who have no more than what we have, who know no more than what we know, who are no more than what we are, find our America. Here, at this present hour and moment of my life, I seek for mine.

And we should all seek for ours, each in his own way. It is a lonely thing, this being a human being. The private world and the public world intersect in some places—in a lot of places. But some part of our lives must be *absolutely* private, and should not be contaminated by what happens in the public world. Otherwise we are lost; our lives have gone for nothing: we have had no moments of assurance and delight. We have not been able to find that "separation from the world" that Van Gennep talks about: "that separation from the world, that penetration to some source of power, and the life-enhancing return."

And we must have that. The climate of guilt, the age of moral blackmail, make it harder and harder to attain. But we must hold out for it no matter what. Not complacency, but the thing that is implicit in the smile of Jay Gatsby, which seems to bespeak some secret knowledge of "the promises of life." That will create us as a people, but we can't achieve it by making hangdogs of each other.

There is plenty wrong, but ruining each other's private life is not going to cure it, but only make us sicker. I would like my own joy and my own privacy, even if I, like you, belong to the generation

that lost
The world and took the moon.

HORSEMEAT AND THE NEW MIND
York University, Toronto, 30 November 1967

W. H. Auden says that he likes to write things—poems or articles or speeches—for specific commissions. I am not sure that I do, and when President Ross asked me to come up here and talk about the University and the New Literature, I was a little hesitant, because I don't really know what *the* new literature is, or even what *the* University is. Nevertheless, I got interested in the subject, as writers will tend to do: interested, that is, in developing my own very fragmentary and biased notions about some of the writing that is going on now, and about the relationship that this may have, or come to have, to the new kind of student who is emerging in North America, and to the institutions where he is studying.

What I would assume about the university at the very beginning is that it still believes at least to some extent in the nineteenth century, or Arnoldian, notion of the university as offering goods that are both imponderable and operative: that is, human goods beyond the merely technical or mechanically specialized or those concerned with earning a living or "getting on in the world." Someone once told me at a cocktail party about a doctor and a minister at *another* cocktail party. The doctor was apparently a thoroughgoing believer in the new scientific orthodoxy, and in the course of their conversation, had occasion to remark to the minister that, should the necessity arise, he could save the minister's life. "Ah," the minister is said to have replied, "but you can't make it worth saving." Now, it is in this particular realm, the realm of personal values, of insights and responses, that literature, new or old, operates. And it seems to me also that the students in universities now are more aware of this than they have ever been in my time.

From my observations, such as they are, students are more interested than formerly in things we would roughly group under aesthetic or philosophical headings—that is, as subjects that *mat-*

ter—than in purely technical subjects, which fascinate only a relatively small number of college students, though I suspect that many more are engaged in these subjects through the coercion of their society. At any rate, the Berkeley riots and the others like it indicate, more than they indicate anything else, a genuine horror of the mechanical, computerized world we are building for ourselves. People, particularly the young people, have a genuine and abiding terror of losing themselves, even if they haven't a very clear idea of what these selves are. In the strange, half-articulate and rather touching idiom of the hippies, the student of today wants "to do his thing."

The new literature has a great deal to say about people of the age of most of the hippies. Some of it is funny, some tragic and some merely horrible. The projection of a *type* of character is slowly emerging from this writing. No longer is the hero—or maybe we should say protagonist—the *engagée* man of Sartre's and Camus' novels, or the "metaphysical adventurer" of Malraux's, or the doomed specialist of war or bullfighting, sticking to his code, as in Hemingway. Now, the protagonist of the novel—and of a good deal of poetry, such as Robert Lowell's or Philip Larkin's—is bewildered. There are many examples of this I could cite, but I would like to use an excerpt from Walker Percy's wonderful novel, *The Moviegoer*, to stand for the rest, partly because I like it, but mostly because it is more original than most of the writing we encounter these days. The speaker is Jack Bolling, a young fellow who lives in New Orleans and suffers from—and also glories in—a condition he refers to as his "invincible apathy."

> My aunt is convinced I have a "flair for research." This is not true. If I had a flair for research, I would be doing research. Actually I'm not very smart. My grades were average. My mother and my aunt think I'm smart because I am quiet and absent-minded—and because my father and grandfather were smart. They think I was meant to do research because I am not fit to do anything else—I am a genius whom ordinary professions can't satisfy. I tried research one summer. I got interested in the role of the acid-base balance in the formation of renal calculi; really, it's

quite an interesting problem. I had a hunch you might get pigs to form oxalate stones by manipulating the pH of the blood, and maybe even to dissolve them. A friend of mine, a boy from Pittsburgh named Harry Stern, and I read up the literature and presented the problem to Minor. He was enthusiastic, gave us everything we wanted and turned us loose for the summer. But then a peculiar thing happened. I became extraordinarily affected by the summer afternoons in the laboratory. The August sunlight came streaming in the great dusty fanlights and lay in yellow bars across the room. The old building ticked and creaked in the heat. Outside we could hear the cries of summer students playing touch football. In the course of an afternoon the yellow sunlight moved across old group pictures of the biology faculty. I became bewitched by the presence of the building; for minutes at a stretch I sat on the floor and watched the motes rise and fall in the sunlight. I called Harry's attention to the presence but he shrugged and went on with his work. He was absolutely unaffected by the singularities of time and place. His abode was anywhere. It was all the same to him whether he catherized a pig at four o'clock in the afternoon in New Orleans or at midnight in Transylvania. He was actually like one of those scientists in the movies who don't care about anything but the problem in their heads—now here is a fellow who does have a "flair for research" and will be heard from. Yet I do not envy him. I would not change places with him if he discovered the cause and cure of cancer. For he is no more aware of the mystery which surrounds him than a fish is aware of the water it swims in. He could do research for a thousand years and never have an inkling of it. By the middle of August I could not see what difference it made whether the pigs got kidney stones or not (they didn't, incidentally), compared to the mystery of those summer afternoons. I asked Harry if he would excuse me. He was glad enough to, since I was not much use to him sitting on the floor. I moved down to the Quarter where I spent the rest of the vacation in quest of the spirit of summer and in the company of an attractive and confused girl from Bennington who fancied herself a poet.

When I think of my own time in the University—Vanderbilt University, in fact—I remember a number of incidents very much like this, though with me it was astronomy rather than biology. And now, twenty years after the fact, I like to fancy a university that could include, and in the head of one student according to his need, both the kidney stones of pigs and the "spirit of summer." It is traditional for young people to look to the University for the answer—*the* answer. For young people believe that there *is* one, or at least there is one for *them*. And when they find it they can then do "their thing." I have always disliked, on the other hand, the notion of the university as a place which compels the student to mutilate or ignore one part of himself in order to develop another to the point of a fanatical and in many cases not a very fulfilling kind of specialization. All this has been said before, of course, but it is necessary, I think, to draw these lines firmly again before there is much of a chance of relating the new literature to the University, either an ideal one or any real one.

But let me read you something about another aspect of the new literature's protagonist. This time he is not a New Orleans southerner searching for the "spirit of summer" in his "invincible apathy," but an ex-basketball star who is now selling potato peelers, has a wife and the other desperate encumbrances of modern life. This is from *Rabbit, Run*, by John Updike. Harry, called Rabbit, has just come home from his selling job. His wife is

> watching a group of children called Mouseketeers perform a musical number in which Darlene is a flower girl in Paris and Cubby is a cop and that smirky squeaky tall kid is a romantic artist. He and Darlene and Cubby and Karen (dressed as an old French lady whom Cubby as a cop helps across the street) dance.
>
> Then the commercial shows the seven segments of a Tootsie Roll coming out of the wrapper and turning into the seven letters of "Tootsie." They, too, dance and sing. Still singing, they climb back into the wrapper. It echoes like an echo chamber. Son of a bitch: cute. He's seen it fifty times, and this time it turns his stomach. His heart is still throbbing; his throat feels narrow.

> Janice asks, "Harry, do you have a cigarette? I'm out."
>
> "Huh? On the way home I threw my pack into a garbage can. I'm giving it up." He wonders how anybody could think of smoking, with his stomach on edge the way it is.
>
> Janice looks at him at last. "You threw it into a garbage can! Holy Mo. You don't drink, now you don't smoke. What are you doing, becoming a saint?"
>
> "Shh."
>
> The big Mouseketeer has appeared, Jimmy, an older man who wears circular black ears. Rabbit watches him attentively; he respects him. He expects to learn something from him helpful in his own line of work, which is demonstrating a kitchen gadget in several five-and-dime stores around Brewer. He's had the job for four weeks. "Proverbs, proverbs, they're so true," Jimmy sings, strumming his Mouseguitar, "proverbs tell us what to do; proverbs help us all to *bee*—better—Mouseke-teers."
>
> Jimmy sets aside his smile and guitar and says straight out through the glass, "Know Thyself, a wise old Greek once said. Know Thyself. Now what does this mean, boys and girls? It means, be what you are. Don't try to be Sally or Johnny or Fred next door; be yourself. God doesn't want a tree to be a waterfall, or a flower to be a stone. God gives to each one of us a special talent." Janice and Rabbit become unnaturally still; both are Christians. God's name makes them feel guilty.

Now these are two people, young married people, in Pennsylvania. Here they are, looking at the Mickey Mouse Club on television, and hearing the words of Socrates accompanied by a Mouseguitar. The scene is funny and rueful and true; in fact, I saw a rerun of the very same program not two weeks ago, and a few days later, Updike came down to the Library of Congress to do a reading. I asked him about this part of the book, and he said he just sat down with his children and took notes on the program. I like thinking of that: the modern novelist submitting to his world, and getting it down as it is, even if that means having to watch the Mickey Mouse Club.

But Rabbit and Janice are not sitting there watching what they are watching because they are forced to. As far as they are concerned, and as far as many of us are concerned, television is merely what *is*. Now I don't mean that Rabbit would have been saved from his life of nervous inconsequentiality by living in a university-and-culture-dominated society in which loudspeakers bawl the odes of Keats at every corner. No, but Rabbit's spiritual and mental poverty might conceivably have been somewhat less if he had had a little of what the University might have given him, or what the new—or old—literature might have given him. Rabbit is not just the protagonist of a fine novel. Most of contemporary Western humanity is very much like him. He works at a job he doesn't much care for because he is caught, like the rest of us, in the economic trap. He is married to someone he has grown indifferent toward. He remembers a few years of his life—those when he was playing high-school basketball—as the only really good ones he has ever had. He is still a very young man, but he is already very far gone toward living by the assumption that most middle-aged men take for granted: that the only worthwhile things in life after the age of twenty-five are liquor and sex, and toward the attitude that underlies this: that anything, even pain, is better than the ordinary reality that one lives in.

There is no avoiding many of the conditions that cause us to feel this way. Life is as it is: it is as we have made it and are making it, and as economic conditions, greed and inventions have made it. And I am not one to seek the salvation of man's soul by poetry and literature, or to believe, as Matthew Arnold apparently did, that poetry is a kind of substitute for religion. But I do very much believe in the life-enhancing possibilities of literature, and particularly of poetry. I believe in the act of self-understanding and self-expansion that literature can be, if the right person reads the right work. Suppose, for example, that Rabbit had read Céline's *Voyage à la Bout de la Nuit*, and had been capable of responding to it, and the strange peregrinations of its bum-hero, Bardamu? It is not inconceivable that he might have seen himself in a more tolerant light, even if only to the extent of thinking, "Jesus, I may be a heartless son-of-a-bitch, but I'm not as bad as *that* guy." Whether or not Rabbit might have become less heartless—or less a son-of-a-bitch—by this revelation is of course, like the rest of this speculation, a speculation. But he would at least have had a look at the full horror and glory (and horrible humor) of bum-dom, and his experience would have been amplified thereby, in those mysterious ways by which real literature works.

Now the contemporary university student is not the clod that Rabbit is. And it can certainly be assumed that he is capable of much greater and more kinds of expansion than Rabbit could ever be. The French writer Henry de Montherlant says that the secret of human life lies in *alternance*: alternation, or succession. Of course one does not have to be a bull-fighter, an amateur sprinter, a semiprofessional libertine and a novelist to practice *alternance*: these are merely the forms of it that Montherlant practices. But in turning from one thing, one activity or pursuit to another—or from one literary work or one author to another—the human being can bring in upon himself some of the variety and richness of experience that each of us ought to demand from his world as a sovereign right. Now, despite its well-advertised tendency to produce specialists, the university rightly seen is the veritable quintessence of *alternance*. The variety of new kinds of experiences made possible by the modern university is, quite simply, staggering. All one has to do is to look through a college catalogue to see that. And the students, despite the all-but-invincible apathy of some of them, are now as never before looking for the answers, and the experiences, among the university's varieties of alternance. And this is surely where the new literature comes in, for if it has anything, it has lots of different writers and approaches and techniques: thousands of them.

I could cite any number of these, as you could. But I *will* cite a couple, by way of illustration. Contemporary American poetry is now about equally balanced between two kinds of attitudes toward life, and each of these attitudes has its champion. Up until very recently the principal American poets were all followers of Robert Lowell, whose work is characterized by a kind of fierce self-abasement. This has been called the "confessional" school, but I think a better name might be "the school of personal complaint." Rather than typifying it and explaining it, I'd rather read a little of Lowell's verse, so that you can get not only the attitude but the peculiar fierce

Lowell tone. This is the end of a poem called "Waking Early Sunday Morning."

> O to break loose. All life's grandeur
> is something with a girl in summer. . . .
> elated as the President
> girdled by his establishment
> this Sunday morning, free to chaff
> his own thoughts with his bear-cuffed staff,
> swimming nude, unbuttoned, sick
> of his ghost-written rhetoric!
>
> No weekends for the gods now. Wars
> flicker, earth licks its open sores,
> fresh breakage, fresh promotions, chance
> assassinations, no advance.
> Only man thinning out his kind
> sounds through the Sabbath noon, the blind
> swipe of the pruner and his knife
> busy about the tree of life . . .
>
> Pity the planet, all joy gone
> from this sweet volcanic cone;
> peace to our children when they fall
> in small war on the heels of small
> war—until the end of time
> to police the earth, a ghost
> orbiting forever lost
> in our monotonous sublime.

I won't comment on this, except to point out the angle from which Lowell looks at things, at our world, at *the* world. The confusion, ignorance and viciousness of modern man have taken from the world all possibilities of joy. Memory—"something with a girl in summer"—is only painful, and we are given over entirely to small wars, terrors, monotony and self-pity.

There is plenty of reason to take this attitude, God knows. And the attitude will never have a more powerful and persuasive spokesman than Robert Lowell. All you have to do is to read the work of his imitators—Sylvia Plath, W. D. Snodgrass, Anne Sexton and Frederick Siedel—to see that, for they are all ludicrously inferior to him. But one of the things that poetry demonstrates is that no one attitude, and no one poetry, is definitive.

The other side of the American poetic picture is dominated by the work of Theodore Roethke, as different a poet from Lowell as could possibly be imagined. He is not time-bound in the sense that Lowell is. It seems to matter very little to Roethke whether he lives in the time of small wars, or cities, or inventions. He does not live in the world of the twentieth century so much as just in the world, period. He is mainly fascinated with his own life-long effort to join, and in a bodily as well as a mental sense, the eternal processes of nature: the wind, the fish and the stream, the worm, the snake and the bird.

> —Or to lie naked in sand,
> In the silted shallows of a slow river,
> Fingering a shell,
> Thinking:
> Once I was something like this, mindless,
> Or perhaps with another mind, less peculiar;
> Or to sink down to the hips in a mossy quagmire;
> Or, with skinny knees, to sit astride a wet log,
> Believing:
> I'll return again,
> As a snake or a raucous bird,
> Or, with luck, as a lion.
>
> I learn not to fear infinity,
> The far field, the windy cliffs of forever,
> The dying of time in the white light of tomorrow,
> The wheel turning away from itself,
> The sprawl of the wave,
> The on-coming water.

These are two attitudes toward our condition, and these are two magnificent American poets. Each in his way is speaking about the things that concern us most, and speaking in the marvelous tongue of a great—or near-great, anyway—poet. Anyone of student age who is in the least sensitive to language and to existence could not help being moved by one or both of these writers, and will, depending in turn on who and what *he* is, have his own favorite. For the new literature is by definition the literature that is in the process of being made *now*. It is not yet ossified in anthologies and textbooks, nor overlaid with generations of commentary. And it is as exciting a sensation as one can have to be a part of this opinion-making: to be, as students traditionally are, collaborators in the making of the literature they read: the literature that comes from their world.

But perhaps it is time we looked at this student himself. Who is he? What is he like? How is he like students of other times, and how is he unlike? I can begin by asserting that the student of today is a great deal different from the student of my days at Vanderbilt. There is not just his political and otherwise public activism, his dallying with drugs, his tastes in music, but something else far deeper than any of these things. There is, more than at any time in my life, a sense of *searching* in the student. This search—or, to be high-falutin, this quest—goes on all the time, night and day, year in and year out, in all kinds of places: this looking and looking for "my thing." It goes on in many different ways in different students, and in many different ways, sometimes, in the same student. For some students, perhaps for most, some part of this quest is literary, and ranges all the way from Lawrence Ferlinghetti—not a search that yields much, that!—to Marshall McLuhan, who is, more than a philosopher or, as he would have it, "an explorer," a writer. The Student Search, maybe the most important one in the history of the earth, involves a great many different things. It involves both the traditional school subjects and the new ones. It involves languages and mathematics and archeology and the other curriculum subjects, but it also involves a lot of other, and more personal, things. The students want, more than anything else, to make these school subjects, and other, non-school subjects, into personal *possessions*, having something to do with "their thing": with their own quota of personal, life-giving light, their sense of *consequentiality* and value, their way of making the world a place worth being in, to *them*.

If you want to see what forms this search takes in any given student's case, go with him to where he lives. There may be, for example, a huge picture of Allen Ginsberg dressed up as Uncle Sam glowering down on the bed. Or the student may be interested in the twelve-string playing of Leadbelly or the sitar technique of Ravi Shankar, he may write songs himself and sing them, he may make mobiles of wire and other things (one of the best ones I ever saw was made with whiskey bottles), he may "be crazy about Buckminster Fuller," he may collect (and not for the obvious reasons, either, always) pornography. But whatever fascinates him, there is an air of great mental and physical activity, wherever the student lives: *lives*.

It is as though the student realizes that he is not going to be a student forever, or indeed, much longer: that the shades of the prison-house are going to fall, that the life of consequence, the life of learning and of caring for what he cares for has to be lived now: that there is a certain tolerance on the part of the workaday world about this, and that it will allow him these few years of student-dom to live, as much as his means allow, as he wants most passionately to do.

This is a fearful judgment on the student, a fearful kind of pressure to put on him. Never have so many been so passionate for so many things, so many kinds of experience: causes, philosophers, painting, music, social action, political debate, "the new literature," film, the whole bit. And what the university must do for and by this student is to find its own mode of giving him *enough*—that is, enough of his own potential and his own enthusiasm: enough of *himself*—to carry him through the rest of his life, against the organized indifference of the world.

I was fortunate enough to be asked to be the first writer-in-residence at Reed College, in Portland, Oregon, and that is where these considerations were brought home to me in a terrible and wonderful way. Most of the kids there were awfully poor. The girls all had long stringy black hair and burning eyes and ate nothing but yeast (*that* year), and the fellows all played the guitar and wore Mexican rope-soled sandals. But the sense of exploration, of *quest*: the sense of intellectual excitement was breathtaking! A lot of the students lived on horse-meat (which was delicious, the way they cooked it, though don't ask me how they cooked it). They talked all night every night, and to be with them would either make a teacher cut his throat at his own academic "invincible apathy" or make him resolve to raise himself to their level of passionate and intelligent involvement.

The new literature is the literature of this generation of students. There are some guides in the older generation: in France, Sartre, and (surprisingly) Montherlant, but above all, Camus. In Germany, the more abstruse philosophers like Heidegger are admired, and poets like Rilke and Trakl. In Italy the film-makers like Fellini and Antonioni are admired more than any of the Italian writers. In English, Lowell and Roethke in poetry and novelists like J. P. Donleavy, Thomas Pynchon and Terry Southern and songwriters like Bob Dylan, the Beatles, Buffy St. Marie, and others, are much in the minds and ears of students.

This is but a partial and no doubt misleading summary, for I am not really in touch with the young so much as I would like to be. But as to literature, one of the main things that strikes me about the kids, and rather saddens me, is that they seem to pay more attention to writers—particularly to poets—who theorize about their work than to the actual works of these poets or any others. Take a writer like Charles Olson, for example. The theories sound fine, and the young people like Olson for furnishing them; the poetry itself is beside the point. Students are also intimidated no less than the rest of us by programmatic announcements of policy—aesthetic and otherwise—and by explanations that make clear what has been wrong with poetry all along, and what is now to be corrected by the application of these particular doctrines. You see this attitude everywhere, from the cloudy pronouncements of Olson about poetry written by something called "breath-units" to the even more ludicrous notions of Minnesota's Robert Bly that "the iamb is dead" and that the only possible salvation of English-speaking poetry is to imitate modern Spanish poetry: that is, to write pleasant little surrealistic poems about Midwestern cornfields in the manner of—or, as nearly as one can tell, without knowing the other language—say, García Lorca, or to write "political poems" (for which read propaganda) in the mode of the French *Surréalistes* of the twenties, is to contribute something of value to humanity. All this is such a phony kind of "newness" that it is hardly worth talking about. It is a genuine shame that such jackleg "ideas" have engaged any of the student population at all, and it will surely be on the heads of these humorless, talentless and aggressive older men that they have kept a few of the younger generation preoccupied with their notions when the young people could have been making an acquaintance with real poetry. The only kind of artistic newness worth talking about is new because it is the product of original sensibilities operating on material that engages them in the ways most fruitful for their craft.

In dealing with this situation, in affording the student the chance to encounter "the new literature," the university has two choices—or maybe I should say the university teacher has two choices. He can trust to his own taste and to the tastes of others he believes in, and simply expose his students to those writers and works he has decided are worth the acquaintance. Or, he can throw wide the gates and expose the students to everything possible: to every movement, writer and work the time-span of the course can encompass. If the teacher takes the second of these choices, he also opens the students up to the productions of people who use the guise of artists for their own non-artistic ends, be they self-aggrandizement or political rhetoric. In these cases, the student has lost his time, and lost what should be his legitimate heritage as a human being: the encounter with the genuine illuminations of art: with what is enlightening and life-enhancing in "the New Literature."

The apprehension of a true art takes sensitivity. It also takes daring. It takes both a markedly acute sensibility and a very great degree of emotional openness. These are qualities which university professors can help develop in students. And nowhere in the university curriculum is this kind of development needed more than in dealing with literature that is as yet untried in the refinery of time: as yet uncommented-upon by generations of other professors and critics. I believe very much in the student's being allowed to make his own discoveries either through classroom assignments or out of them (but preferably through both), and I also believe in his wasting a certain amount of time in reading unprofitable poems, stories and novels, for that is one of the ways in which he finds out what "unprofitable" means. But when he never progresses beyond the point of thinking that Ferlinghetti is a good poet—or even a poet at all—or that Hubert Selby, Junior, is a good novelist, or when he accepts Ginsberg's "Reality Sandwiches" as palatable, then one wonders where the hell his university education is, when it could be doing something for him.

Let me end with a reference to W. H. Auden. He says somewhere that one is appalled when one reads the back pages of the *New York Times* Book Review Section, where people write in to ask readers to identify quotations which have meant much to them. It is dreadful, Auden says, to see the kind of tripe that has sustained people in their most awful and intense moments, while real poetry stood helplessly by. I hope very much that the university's part in serving as a connective between the new literature and the new student will not result in the same kind of falsity of emotion: that teachers of literature and writing will find their own ways of enabling the students to carry on a real rather than a token quest, insofar as literature is concerned, so that with luck he can truly *make* his world, not only in time, but in height, breadth and depth as well. What we all must do is to militate against the "invincible apathy" of the world. And if we must grieve, let us not do it with greeting-cards.

THREE GIRLS OUTGOING
Pitzer College Commencement, 1965

President Atherton, Dean Elmott, graduating class and students of Pitzer College, I am entirely delighted to be with you at just this time, on this one afternoon of all our human lives, under just these circumstances. Having said these things, even *I* find it strange that I should want to begin what I am going to say by making a few remarks about . . . horse-meat.

I have only eaten horse-meat once, but both the taste of it and the occasion on which I ate it have stayed with me, and I am sure will continue to do so. It was when I first went to teach at Reed College in Portland, Oregon, a school for devoted students, political activists and dedicated folk-singers: a school where, as someone remarked, everybody has a beard except one or two of the girls. The second night I was in Portland a solemn, bearded student called on me and asked if I would like to have dinner with him and several of his friends. I accepted, and went with him into one of the poorer sections of Portland, where we climbed some of the most rickety stairs I have ever trembled upon, and came into a room with six or seven young men and women who belonged together. We ate horse-meat, not usually recommended for human consumption but purchased because it was cheap and the students were poor. Before the evening was over I felt that it was a distinct privilege to be there. The talk was fluid, serious and utterly open to any and all new ideas. The minds of the people in the room seemed to be *tuned* to each other's wavelengths; the receptivity and creativity, the passionate interest as well as the reasonableness on all sides of me were remarkable, *felt* remarkable. It was a good place, good company, a good feeling. Since that time, I have often tried to isolate what it was in that room . . . in the lives of all those present . . . that made up the feeling I describe. But perhaps it is not capable of isolation, or even of explanation. But one thing is clear: the life that we lived—and lived well—for a few hours in that nondescript, vital room was a thing that emerged from the people in it; it came from their orientation toward existence; it came from certain attitudes implicit in the way they took themselves and others.

Like most Americans—a predictable, pragmatic breed—I am usually reluctant to believe in imponderables; some Europeans are less reluctant. This passage from Antoine de Saint-Exupéry's *Letter to a Hostage* is the best description I have found of the state of mind and community that, to me, will forever have the gamy, grainy, complicated taste of horse-meat:

> This happened one day before the war, on the banks of the Saône, to one side of Tournus. We had chosen for dinner a restaurant whose plank balcony overhung the river. Propped on our elbows on a very simple table, knife-hacked with the initials of customers, we asked for two Pernods. Your doctor had forbidden alcohol to you, but one fudges a little on big occasions, and this was one. We didn't know why, but it was one. The thing that caused us to rejoice was more impalpable than the quality of the light. And, as two sailors a few yards away were unloading a barge, we asked them to join us. We signalled them from the balcony, and they came: came very simply. I think we found it natural to do this because of the invisible festivity going on in us, and they responded.
>
> The sun was good. Its warm honey bathed the poplars on the far shore, and the fields all the way to the horizon. We were gayer and gayer, without knowing why. The sun reassured us that it would shine, the river that it would run, the meal that it would be a meal, the sailors that they surely *had* responded to our invitation, the waitress that she would serve us with a kind of happy gentleness, as though she were taking part in an eternal celebration. We were fully at peace, in our own haven from the disorder of civilization. We felt ourselves pure, upright, luminous and indulgent. We couldn't have said what truth appeared so plainly to us that it needed no examination or explanation. But the feeling that we had above all others was that of certitude: a certitude almost prideful. The main thing was that we agreed. But on what? On the Pernod? On the meaning of life? On the gentleness of the day? We couldn't

> have said. But that agreement was so full, so final, so solidly established in human depth, that we would have fortified that insignificant little balcony, would have undergone a siege there, would have died behind machine guns to preserve what we had together.

That is an extreme and beautiful statement, I think. Times such as Saint-Exupéry describes are infinitely fragile and infinitely enduring, but above all they are necessary: they explain us and *are* us as we wish to be, as we exist at those times when we seem to ourselves to be existing as we were meant to. Nothing in life is as important as these states of being, and they must be guarded at all costs, against whatever things threaten them. They must be individually maintained, and one must develop one's personal strategies for maintaining them.

About ten years ago I went into the advertising business, and worked in New York and Atlanta, first as a copy-writer, then as a copy chief, then as a creative director for a large southern agency. I hated office work, a kind of genteel hell of absolute inconsequence, and every day I used to take a book of poems with me just to touch, every now and then, or as a reminder of the world where I lived most as I wished to. And I remember also the very distinct sense of danger I felt when carrying the book through the acres of desks where typists typed five carbons of the Tony Bennett Record Promotion: the distinct and delicious sense of subversiveness and danger in carrying a book or the manuscript of a new poem as if it were a bomb, here in this place that had no need of it, that would be embarrassed and nonplussed by it, that would finally destroy it by its enormous weight of organized indifference. But for me the main thing was the sense of danger and the sense of pride, the delicious sense of secrecy. I was risking in a very strange way not only the good will of my superiors (one of whom once told me I should have been reading sales reports at lunch) but at the same time defended the thing in me which was most living; for when that dies, one is like, well, like the others.

This is not another diatribe against the supermarkets, against conformity, against the *status quo* and the split-level ranch house. No; I'm talking about the forces that threatened the individual sense of being quite as much in Periclean Athens and Renaissance Florence as in New York or Los Angeles. We know those forces too well for me to spend much time talking about them. What I would emphasize is rather the individual ways of defending against them, like the little intellectual boy in Robie Macauley's novel *The Disguises of Love* who reads Nietzsche behind a comic book, instead of the other way around. The heroes of this address are like that little boy buried deep in *Beyond Good and Evil*, consummately protected from the scorn of his schoolmates by Batman and Robin.

The heroes that I would praise are those delicate and diligent defenders of the essential self in ways that are quite as original, some of them, as the things they defend. These private brinksmen, these devious and unsung battlers for the fragile treasure of personal meaning, are the subject-heroes of this afternoon, as I would have you remember it. Diarists and journal-keepers, letter-writers to the self, are among the best brinksmen we have, and for this reason I am a great reader of diaries, journals, notebooks and such; most of them are better than novels, for one feels more often the genuine concern for the essentials of a life, and less the concern for artistic effect, for the conventions of a form. This is, for example, the man who wrote under the name of W. N. P. Barbellion, a young English zoologist dying of multiple sclerosis: the bravest man I have ever encountered, in print or out.

His defenses, his ruses, are not so much against the crassness of the world but against death itself, and his knowledge of its certain proximity. He says "I must have some music or I shall hear the paralysis creeping. That is why I lie in bed and whistle." The courage and originality of that takes the breath: the dying man, hardly more than a boy, lying there defending himself against death, the last, the only enemy worthy of the name, by whistling.

Again, Alun Lewis, one of the finest poets of our century, killed in Burma in 1944, writes from the sick green inferno of jungle warfare: "My life belongs to the world. I will do what I can." Just that; no more.

On this mortal afternoon, we are here, really, to honor the graduating class of Pitzer College. But more importantly, we are here to honor *these* graduates. We have an unusual chance to do this, for there are only three of them. The first thing to note about them is that these are girls who took it upon themselves to invite, as commencement speaker, not a retired bank president or an educator or J. Edgar Hoover, but an American poet.

There is first the girl who is gravitating, seriously and with great dignity, toward a quiet farm life. Poets like to describe things, and I could describe that kind of life for a long time, for I know it well. A farm is something like a kind of practical Eden, and though I may never see this girl again, it will do me good to imagine her very womanly hands doing farm things and woman things, and of her watching the different greens at the different parts of the day and of the seasons, and the intimate and infinitely rewarding work with animals, and the constellations arranging themselves, each night, in the patterns they have always had, as the great silent evening of farms comes over another warm and hard-working isolated human house.

Another of these girls wants to go to India and teach. She has been there before, and has connected in personal and creative ways with the land and its people. I see those enormous masses of people, and I see also this frail, snapping-eyed witty girl humorously and patiently doing whatever she can, wherever she is, and it is a good thing to see.

Then there is the girl who will be going into the creative world, the world of the architect, the musician, the intellectual, the life of the mind, the frustration and the soaring joy beside which the soaring of these mountains is nothing: of the three this one is the one most capable of the savage wildness of ecstasy and creation, the occasional certitude that she has made a thing that could not have existed if it had not first happened, tentatively and delicately, in one out of all those human minds: if it had not first secretly happened to her.

Here they are, then, the quiet young wife and mother dreaming of farms, the serious and witty traveler and teacher among far peoples, and the eager young artist and intellectual.

This is a lovely, frail moment, and if, in it, I could say one thing to them, it would be this: remember that the sense of imperilment, the sense of danger, the sense of your values and your best selves being threatened at every moment by indifference, by coarseness, by apathy and necessity, is in fact your greatest stimulant and your greatest ally. It is against these forces, the great multitudinous anonymous modern abyss, that your personal values are defined as what they are: it is at the edge, on the brink, that your essences show themselves as they must be. So I say, develop your private brinksmanship, your strategies, your ruses, your delightful and desperate games of inner survival, whether they take the form of Batman Comics or whistling Handel's Water Music. What I most hope for is that these strategies will *work* for you: that you will come up with some good ones, ones that will enable you to live perpetually at the edge, but there very much on your own ground, and to live there with personal *style*, with dash and verve and a distinct and exhilarating sense of existing on your own terms as they develop, or as they become, with time, more and more what they have always been. This is what is meant by "having something to give," by "having a self to give." It is exactly on these terms, and no others, that one can say, when the time comes to say it, "My life belongs to the world. I have done what I could."

This book was designed by Quentin Fiore;
production was supervised by Fred M. Kleeberg.
It was composed in Sabon type by BC Research
in Columbia, S.C.; and printed and bound by
R. R. Donnelley & Sons, Harrisonburg, Virginia.

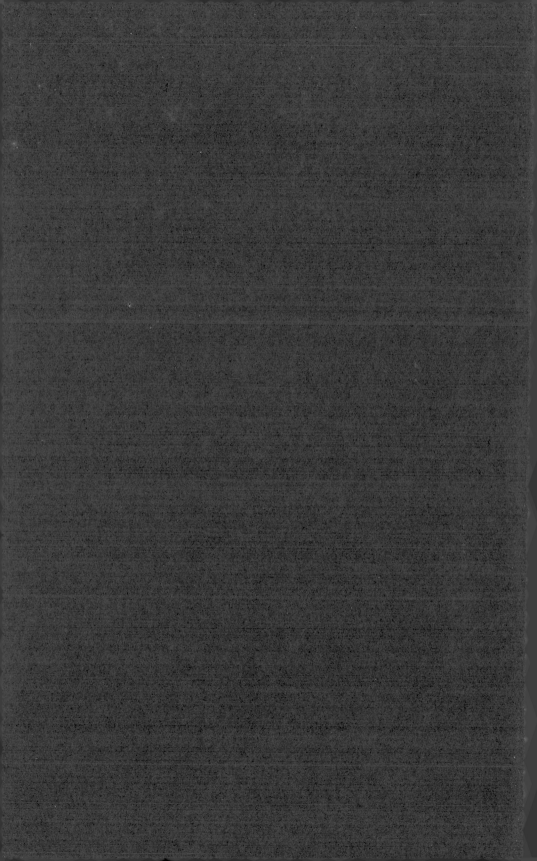